BREYER ANIMAL
COLLECTOR'S
GUIDE

IDENTIFICATION
AND VALUES

Felicia Browell

COLLECTOR BOOKS
A Division of Schroeder Publishing Co., Inc.

Cover Design: Beth Summers
Book Design: Benjamin R. Faust

Searching For A Publisher?

We are always looking for knowledgeable people considered to be experts within their fields. If you feel that there is a real need for a book on your collectible subject and have a large comprehensive collection, contact Collector Books.

Additional copies of this book may be ordered from:

COLLECTOR BOOKS
P.O. Box 3009
Paducah, KY 42002-3009

@ $19.95. Add $2.00 for postage and handling.

Printed in the U.S.A. by Image Graphics, Paducah, KY

❧ Contents ❧

Dedication 4

Acknowledgments 4

Preface 4

Introduction 5

Traditional Scale Horse Molds and Models 11

Classic Scale Horse Molds and Models 98

Little Bits Scale Horse Molds and Models 114

Stablemates Scale Horse Molds and Models 118

Other Animal Molds and Models 128

Clocks and More 139

Repaints, Remakes, and Test Colors 143

Appendix A — Cross Reference Tables 147

Appendix B — Suggested Reading 172

Glossary 173

Bibliography 173

Index 174

◈ Dedication ◈

This book is dedicated to everyone who contributed information, advice, suggestions for improvement, and their time for photo sessions: most notably Kelly Engelseipen, Jane and Rebecca Wagner, Lucy Kusluch, Pat Henry, Shirley Ketchuck, Penny Lehew, and Bonnie Valentine.

To my parents, Edward and Sandra Chmelovsky, for always being there, and my brother Phil for always making me laugh.

To my husband, Ray, for believing in me, despite myself.

And to all the Breyer model collectors out there who wanted this book for as long as I did.

◈ Acknowledgments ◈

This book would not have been possible without the unfailing support of many people:

First, all the collectors who have models pictured in this book — Kelly Engelsiepen, Pat Henry, Shirley Ketchuck, Lucy Kusluch, Penny Lehew, Bonnie Valentine, and Jane and Rebecca Wagner.

The folks at Collector Books — Lisa Stroup, editor; Gina Lage, assistant editor; and the layout experts who managed to decrypt my text.

And last but not least, the staff at Breyer Animal Creations, especially Stephanie Macejko, Renee Bordonara, and Kerstin Chalupa, thanks for your help, encouragement, and support.

◈ Preface ◈

1995: The idea for this book was born when I was in my teens and I started scanning the collectibles sections in book stores for something — anything — about Breyer models. However, I didn't do anything about writing it until December of 1993, when after much cajoling and pleading, I conned my husband into buying a Friesian (#485) for me when we went Christmas shopping at Toys "R" Us. I loved the model and convinced him that it was the perfect "toy" gift for our traditional exchange each Christmas. So I unwrapped it gleefully (he insisted on wrapping it), and sat by the Christmas tree examining it, studying it . . . well, you get the picture. Then I opened the 1993 catalog that came with it and started oohhing and ahhing over the other models I saw, and mentally started making my list. I was hooked — again. The compulsion to own these often beautiful and dynamic models that had begun when I was nine was apparently only dormant, not dead, even after a 13-year hiatus.

Shortly after that I spotted an ad for discount Breyer models in a national horse magazine. The address was less than 10 miles from my home! So I raided my parent's attic for the boxes of models I had put away before college. As I took them out, wiping off the accumulated dust, I was surprised to discover that I had accumulated 35 models in the seven years I had collected them. The ones I liked the most had the most rubs and scratches; they were battered (I had played with them for several years) but none were broken. Most had been gifts, some had come from the local flea markets, some were bought with babysitting or birthday money. It wasn't much of a start, but then, at that time I really didn't know what I was missing either. Then I went to see the local discount Breyer dealer. As she will attest, I rejoined the hobby with a vengeance.

"Where are the reference books?" I asked Bonnie, eager and enthusiastic for reference materials.

"There are insurance guides . . ." she replied.

"Insurance guides? These plastic toys are obviously very collectible now, so there ought to be, you know, a color guide I can buy at, say, the mall bookstore." Or somewhere.

"No. No color books. Collectors want one, but no one has done one yet," Bonnie went on. I felt disappointment — then the spark of inspiration.

Hmmm.

Why not? I had over nine year's experience as a technical writer and editor, and I had written, rewritten, or edited dozens of other people's books and documents. Maybe I could do this one for myself.

So I did.

Because I did not collect for so many years, I have no problem acknowledging that many of you have probably forgotten more than I currently know about the models. So I openly invite you to correct any mistakes you find and make suggestions for ways I can improve this book for future editions.

Enjoy the book and use it. I truly hope it inspires you to greater understanding and obsession, as it has me.

1997: In the two years since the first book appeared, my enthusiasm for the hobby hasn't waned. I took note of the flaws and problems with the first book and began updating. This edition, published with aid and much patience from Collector Books, is much more complete and better organized than the first edition, and of a higher quality. Still, because of the often conflicting information available, there will always be inadvertent omissions or errors; the invitation still stands to send me comments or input for later editions. Send them to me at 123 Hooks Lane, Canonsburg, PA 15317-1835. Thank you!

Felicia Browell

❧ Introduction ❧

Collecting Breyer Models

Breyer models have a relatively long and colorful history, and their popularity with collectors continues to grow. The following information covers the basics of collecting these models.

A (Very) Brief History of Breyer Animal Creations

Breyer Animal Creations started in 1950 with the Western Horse made for the Mastercrafter Clock Company. Breyer retained the mold in lieu of payment for making the mold, and soon after started making the horses for the C.W. Woolworth Co. (that Western Horse became #57). The models began selling, Woolworth's asked for more, and Breyer Animal Creations was born.

In 1984, Reeves International, Inc. bought Breyer, and the factory was moved to New Jersey, where it resides today.

Model Production

Reduced to its most basic components, the creation of a new mold sounds relatively simple; however, it can be a complicated and time-consuming iterative process. The life cycle starts with clay models, sculpted carefully by talented artists. Those clay models are used to make steel molds. These steel molds are very expensive to produce and are surprisingly fragile; they can be broken, as happened to the Sherman Morgan mold. Several months can elapse between approval of the sculpture and the start of model production.

The molds are used in an injection molding machine where cellulose acetate pellets are melted and injected into the mold under tremendous pressure. The plastic pieces are cooled on wooden cooling boards, then assembled, deburred, polished, and painted. Airbrushes are used for most of the painting; the painters use angles of the airbrush nozzle and model to get shadings for muscles, faces, and other parts. The eyes are airbrushed too, usually with a single tiny burst. Then the final details are added (e.g., eye whites or eye color, eye gloss, brands, or other details) by paintbrush.

The Traditional series model scale is approximately 1:9 to 1:8. The other scales are about 1:12 for Classics, 1:20 for Little Bits, and 1:32 for Stablemates.

Different sizes (scales) of Breyer Models

Molds and Models

A *mold*, for the purposes of this guide, is simply the body of a Breyer horse or animal. A *model* then, is the color, name, number, etc. that Breyer assigns to the current animal produced. For example, "Adios," "Yellow Mount," and "Rough n' Ready" are all *models* made from the Adios *mold* — in silhouette they look the same, but the names, colors (bay, chestnut pinto, dun), and numbers (50, 51, and 885) vary. In this guide, the name of the first model made from a mold is the name used for that mold.

Regular Runs versus Special Runs

Regular runs are simply those models that are shown in the annual dealer and consumer catalogs. Some people call these *catalog runs*.

All models not shown in the catalogs, which are made for special events or for retailers, are called *special runs*. Special run models can come from a variety of Breyer-sponsored events, toy store chains, tack or department store catalogs, etc. Other special runs come from Breyer as mid-season releases, which are available through their normal retail and dealer sources.

Special runs made from popular molds are in high demand; if you want to be assured of getting one, you should reserve one from your local or mail-order dealer as soon as you know you want it. Even then you are not guaranteed to get one, because the number of models produced is often limited.

About the Catalogs

Two catalogs are available for most years: the dealer catalog and the consumer catalog. (There are some gaps where neither catalog seems to have been available, or they are just extremely rare.) Recent dealer catalogs (1990 and after) are about 8¼ by 11½ inches; prior catalogs are slightly smaller. Over the years consumer catalogs were made in many sizes and forms, the most current being a multi-fold credit card-sized version. Earlier consumer catalogs were brochure style, or half-sheet sized pages stapled in the middle. Whatever form they come in, these items are just as collectible as the models.

Collectors and dealers should note that the catalogs often show models in mirror-image; that is, the pictures are accurate except that they are the mirror image of the actual model. Whatever the reason for this, it is surprisingly common, even in recent catalogs.

Mold Variations

Variations in the molds sometimes come from intentional adjustments, such as removing a brand (as on the Trakehner and Hanoverian), adding or modifying parts (adding a different mane and tail to Halla, or a horn to the Running Stallion), and correcting original mold problems like instability (Stock Horse Mare and Smoky).

Height variations can also occur. While the models themselves shrink over time (probably due to the gradual evaporation of the solvents in the plastic), different batches of plastic can also produce models that are noticeably smaller than others.

Also, you will find that a catalog might show a mold (e.g., Stock Horse Mare) in different colors, with significant variations in listed heights and lengths. These variations do not mean there is more than one steel mold used to produce the plastic animal; rather they probably reflect different methods of measuring or different batches of plastics used at the time the model was measured.

Colors

Breyer's names for model colors are often imprecise. One coloration (reddish brown body, black mane and tail, stockings, no black on legs, and black hooves) might be called bay on one model, and chestnut on another. Also, keep in mind that the color name used can cover a wide variety colors in a range from light to dark, yellowish to reddish, brownish to grayish, etc. The color on the model you have can be significantly different from the color shown in the catalog, this guide, or the model that another collector or dealer has on his or her shelf.

Color and Marking Variations

Almost every Breyer regular and special run has some variations in paint color and markings. Many variations in markings are quite common (two socks or three, stenciled bald face or bald because it just lacks paint). Some variations are shown in this guide, either in separate photos or with the variations shown next to each other in the regular picture.

Another common variation is a lack of a specific detail, or lack of some part of the model's normal color. Models without black eyes, or without some part of their mane painted are often considered novelty items rather than mistakes.

Decorator Colors

There are currently six decorator colors, four older ones and two recent additions. Decorator models, whether the older ones from the early '60s or the recent special runs, are highly prized by collectors. All of these decorators have pink hooves, ears, and pink shaded muzzles (although the pink details can be faint).

Please note that not all decorators were made in the 1960s; some were made after 1990 as special runs for various events.

Gold Charm is a solid, metallic gold. These models have white manes, tails, socks or stockings, and usually a bald face; some have very distinct white facial markings.

Wedgewood approximates the color of good Wedgwood china (a pure cornflower blue), and a well-kept, well-painted model looks very much like porcelain. These models have white manes, tails, socks, and a bald face. (The generally accepted spelling for the model horse color is different than the trademarked name of the china.)

Copenhagen is the dappled version of Wedgewood. These models have medium to heavy dappling (giving a pale or medium blue tone), white manes, tails, socks, and some white markings on the face (bald or a blaze).

Florentine is the dappled version of Gold Charm. Like the other old decorators, Florentine models usually have white manes, tails, socks or stockings, and are bald-faced (recent ones can be slightly different — see the listings for details).

Silver Filigree and *Ageless Bronze* are two new colors introduced in the '90s. Silver Filigree is a sparsely dappled metallic silver, to date used on only one model (see Proud Arabian Mare). Ageless Bronze is a dark, semi-metallic bronze color, again, to date used on only one model (see the traditional Black Stallion).

Woodgrain

In the late 50s and early 60s Breyer produced some models to appear as if they were carved from wood — a brown with light and dark streaks like the grain in wood. Skillfully painted models are so realistic that they really can fool you from a distance.

Light and dark variations of woodgrain exist; the lighter version is more common, and the darker versions tended to be used on models found on lamps.

Other Unusual Colors

Two other colors are an old "antique bronze" (seen on a Buffalo), and an "antique gold" (seen on an Elephant). The Buffalo's color strongly resembled a well-aged, cast bronze piece with copper highlights. It was apparently the original finish, and a former Breyer division employee confirmed that some models were finished this way in the company's early years. It was not clear on which other molds this color was used. The Elephant's origin is less certain; rumors of elusive gold Elephants have been circulating for so long that it is hard to tell how much is true. The gold Elephant I examined appeared to be an original finish Breyer animal; however, I have seen no documentation and have had no confirmation from Breyer or Reeves that such a creature was (to their knowledge) ever produced. It could be that such pieces were produced by employees for guests at the factory, or were produced as test colors, but never used in regular production.

Also, several special run models have been produced in pink, purple, and blue. Some of these were flocked and had fake hair manes and tails as well, and some were done using colored plastic.

Markings

Actual markings often vary from those pictured in catalogs. There might be three socks on a model shown in the catalog, and the actual model could have four. Also, markings often varied from the beginning of a model's production to its end, especially for those models in production for an extended period of time — for example, for Misty there are three known variations in the pinto pattern. Other variations can be as simple as the skill level of the person or persons who painted the model, the paint color, and how carefully the model was handled during painting and drying. Poorly defined pinto markings (blurred edges, smears), overspraying of a second color, too many or too few spots or dapples, etc. are examples of variations. Most of these are considered flaws by those who live- or photo-show their models.

Socks and stockings, or hoof color can also vary from year to year on models with the same name and/or number. Likewise, bald faces, body shading, the painter's skill, and the color itself can vary because of the different painters and different years the model was produced. This gives us, for example, the notorious pumpkin orange "palomino" Family Arabians, and blurry pinto marking on many models.

Eye Whites and Other Painted Details

On some models there are additional details that are added by hand. These markings can include:

— white markings at the edge of the eyes called *eye whites*

— eye (iris) colors (brown or blue), or tri-color eyes

— a pink, red, or black line for the mouth

— pink, black, or other color(s) for the hoofs
— ribbon, braid, and bow details on manes and tails
— brands or symbols (e.g., Native American symbols) on hips, necks, etc.
On some models, the presence or absence of these details can help determine the model's age and value.

Dappling and Roaning

There are several types of dappling and roaning you can find on Breyer models. *Overdappling* is a method where multiple applications of a paint color are spattered onto the model until it is completely covered. *Resist dappling* is a method where a resistant substance (like grease) is spattered onto the model either before any other paint is applied or after the first one or two coats of color; then painting is finished and the resist substance removed. This leaves lighter or white spots where the resist was (in this book, white spots are usually called *bubble dappling* because of their appearance). The resist method is newer than overdappling.

Another painting technique results in a roaned appearance. Fine speckles of paint are sprayed onto a prepared model to get tiny, pinpoint size spots. In this book, this color is either called roan or flea-bit gray, depending on the other markings and colors on the model.

Model Finish

The usual finish for the vast majority of Breyer models is a matte (dull) paint finish. Unfinished plastic areas can appear slightly glossed because of the translucency of the cellulose acetate used. Sometimes a model is profoundly matte (as in the first Friesian model #485) due to the paints and painting techniques used. Other models have a semi-gloss finish, which again is usually the result of the particular paints used. Glossy models, on the other hand, are usually profoundly glossy (when in good condition). Most of these were produced in Breyer Animal Creations' early days; however, they still occasionally produce glossy models in regular and special runs.

Another "finish" is called *chalky* by collectors. Chalkies are found in two forms: as the plastic itself or as a white base coat. The plastic chalkies probably resulted from experiments with different plastics or different processing techniques during the oil crisis years in the early and mid-'70s. The bare plastic on this type of chalky appears denser and more solidly white (rather than translucent). The white painted chalkies probably used different colored plastics — the white base coat was used to cover the plastic's original color so the model color would show accurately and consistently.

The pearly finish is yet another anomaly in model appearance. These literally appear to have pearlescent qualities, and this effect usually appears to be within the plastic instead of just in the paints used.

Flocked models have a fuzzy coating, often have glass eyes, and usually have smooth hooves. Sometimes these were produced in bizarre colors (e.g., purple).

Examples of different finishes.

Stickers, Numberings, and Mold Marks

In addition to all the different colors and markings on Breyer animals, the presence of stickers, numbers written on the model, or variations in mold marks can help pinpoint a model's age and value.

Stickers

Stickers were used on some of Breyer's early models, and were first rectangular gold foil then blue ribbon shaped (made from paper). The blue ribbon stickers are much more common than the gold foil, although both are rare and very difficult to find intact. Generally, collectors agree that stickers weren't used after about 1970, so if you find a model with a sticker, you know it is an older one.

Signed and Numbered Models

Some special run models are signed and/or numbered. The information written on models from the factory can include any or all of the following: the year produced, the model number and the run quantity, and the special run source (for example, JAH). This information is usually located on the model's belly.

Sometimes collectors ask someone to sign their models, usually a Breyer/Reeves "celebrity" or the owner or trainer of the horse the model represents. For example, John Lyons (a famous horse trainer) was asked to sign hundreds of Bright Zip models (see San Domingo) at BreyerFest '94. Such signatures may or may not increase the value of a model — it depends entirely on whether the collector interested in purchasing it cares whether the model is signed. Signatures of this type are usually done on a model's belly, although they can appear anywhere. Recently, collectors have begun asking for signatures on the boxes, too.

Mold Marks

Various mold marks have been used over the decades. You can see them on most models on the inside hind leg or on the belly. Some early versions of some models have no marks and such models are sometimes considered more collectible. However, you should be careful when assuming that a model without a mold mark is automatically more valuable — some molds do not have the mold marks at all, and never did.

Most marks include the following information:
— USA or China, or, more rarely, Mexico as the country of manufacture
— BMC, B, Breyer, Breyer Molding Company, Reeves, or some combination of these
— A date (year)
— A copyright (C)
— Sometimes you will also find the sculptor's name (for example, "C.Hess"), and other trademark owners of the model name (20th Century Fox, etc.).

Again, be careful about reading too much into mold mark information; dates used on a *mold* rarely indicate the date the *model* was made — they are usually just the date the mold was created. This is especially noticeable on the Stablemate molds where virtually every one has a "1975" or "1976" on it — even the models made this year!

Model Condition

Model condition is of overriding importance when determining value. Not even the rarest model is worth more than a small fraction of its "normal" value if it is broken, badly yellowed, stained, scratched, or has large areas of paint rubbed off or otherwise removed.

How Condition Affects Value

Any damage to a model or its finish can greatly affect its value. Some models with only slight damage are worth little to collectors, or have value only as bodies for remaking and repainting. The degree to which a model is devalued depends on the extent of damage and the base value of the same model in good condition. Many collectors have their own way of determining value based on condition, but in general, five to ten percent (of the value determined for a mint model) is subtracted for each degree of damage. Some of the common levels are the very common ear and tail tip rubs (which might lower the value by ten percent or so from mint), extensive rubs (fifty percent of the value of good condition model), all the way to breaks (which can lower a model's value to ten percent or less of a good condition model).

Yellowing is a common problem, and is most noticeable on models with some unfinished plastic showing (e.g., stockings and bald faces). Models can yellow quickly, slowly, or not at all. The degree of discoloration might be linked to the different batches of the cellulose acetate used to make the models. Storage conditions also appear to affect the degree and speed that models yellow, and if you or a family member smokes tobacco, this also appears to contribute to the problem. Sunlight is the most widely recommended method for whitening yellowed models. Care should be taken that the model doesn't get too hot (which can cause bloating or leg bowing) and that the model is turned to keep the bleaching effect even. Also, too much time in the sun might make the plastic brittle. Not all yellowed models will whiten. Badly yellowed models are usually worth only 40 to 50 percent of a good condition model.

Rubs and scratches are also common. These can happen during production, shipping, or handling after purchase, but are most common in models that children (or pets) play with. Older models that have been played with or carelessly stored will usually have rubs or scratches and finding an old model in perfect condition is relatively rare.

Breaks are bad; these permanently decrease the model's value (to 10 to 20 percent of a good condition model), its desirability for collectors, and its potential for showing. Sometimes breaks can be repaired so the damage is hardly visible. However, repair is difficult and the model will always be weaker in that area. To strengthen a broken leg, for example, a small hole can be drilled in the center of both pieces and a small pin inserted (this is difficult to do well). For plastic models, an acetone based epoxy is recommended. Pure acetone can also be used but is extremely hazardous — it should be used only by an adult who has the proper facilities to ensure safety. Unless the model is extremely rare, often the best use for broken ones is remaking. See the *Repaints, Remakes, and Test Colors* chapter for some ideas on this. Broken models are usually worth only $2 to $12 dollars each.

Keep in mind that some models are so common that even those in excellent condition are worth little (the palomino Family Arabians, for example).

But also remember that if a model is very rare, even one in poor condition can sometimes be restored, or might have some value simply as is. Always check insurance guides or ask a knowledgeable collector before remaking a model about which you are uncertain.

Model Showing

Model showing is a lot like showing real horses — the competition can be tough and the classes can be crowded. Horses are groomed and tacked up, just like for a real horse show. The differences come in how the horses are transported (wrapped carefully in towels, bags, and bubble pack), and in the space required to show 20 of your herd. Pick up almost any of the model horse newsletters and you will see many ads for live and photo shows.

Shows are worth seeing and participating in, and can teach future horse owners not only proper tack fitting and class standards, but good sportsmanship as well. Aside from the opportunities for learning, they are often simply a lot of fun.

Live Shows

Live shows parallel real horse shows as much as possible. They offer divisions for novice and experienced showers, halter and performance classes, open classes and classes for specific breeds or types, and more. In addition, the classes are often broken down into model-specific subclasses; for example, original finish or repaint/remake classes.

Models must be in excellent condition to live show. Scratches and rubs are only marginally acceptable and only then on the rarest models (decorators and woodgrains). Variations and test colors often show very well (again, when the model is in perfect condition).

Photo Shows

Photo showing is like live showing, except that you send your photos to the judges. This allows you to spend as much time as needed setting up a shot to show a model at its best. Good photos often look so real that people need to look twice to realize that they are seeing a model horse and not a live one (this is the goal). Classes are usually similar to live show classes.

Where to Learn More

A few insurance and informational references are available, and there are several well-established, high-quality newsletters available. I highly recommend some of the newsletters for their informative articles on the models, remaking, and events. See Appendix B for a list of some of these publications.

Breyer's model horse magazine, *Just About Horses*, is another source of good information. With a current circulation of over 17,000, it provides articles, news, model history, event information, and (once or twice a year) offers a special run Breyer animal that is available only to its subscribers. The information given in articles is fairly accurate, although some collectors dispute some of it because of the often conflicting information available (for example, how many, or in what years a model was produced).

Other information about special run models can come from catalog pages from retail outlets (such as JC Penney, Sears, Spiegel, and Montgomery Wards), and brochures or catalogs from mail order sources (such as State Line Tack, Bentley Sales, and Black Horse Ranch).

How to Use this Guide

The model descriptions given are as concise as possible, while allowing for enough detail to distinguish between similar models. The models are divided into several major sections (Traditional Horses, Classic Horses, Little Bits, Stablemates, and Other Animals), then are alphabetically listed by the common mold name (as for the horse sections) or by general subject (animals). An "S" at the beginning of a model's description designates a special run.

The following is the general format used to describe regular run models.

Model number, years produced. *Model or set name*. Finish, color; markings. Other details (if any). Value.

The following is the general format used to describe special run models (the "S" stands for Special Run).

S year(s) produced, source. *Model or set name*. Finish, color; markings. Other details (if any). Value.

The descriptions are very concise, but the terms used are broad, such as "bald face," "socks," "stockings," etc. What one collector might call an unstenciled blaze might be termed a bald face in the descriptions. Likewise, what are called socks can mean any white leg markings below mid-cannon, and stockings can be from mid-cannon to the knees or hocks.

Descriptions that begin with "also" indicate that that description is different than the previous, while the model is identical (i.e., the release date or source differ, but the model is the same).

If you know the current model (name or number) made from a specific mold, but do not know the mold, you can use the cross references in Appendix A to find the mold name.

About the Values

The values given in this guide are *average* prices for *average* condition models. In this case, average condition means with ear tip, tail, and hoof rubs, but no significant damage. Yellowed models or those with slight to significant scratches or rubs are worth 10 to 70 percent less, broken models are worth $2 to $12 (depending on the scale and specific mold), while models in perfect condition are generally worth about 10 to 15 percent more than the listed value.

An Important Note to Antique Dealers

Recently, the prices seen by collectors at antique stores and secondhand Breyer model dealerships have been rising. Unfortunately, this appears to be more often due to misinformation acquired from uninformed sources than an actual increase in value for the models generally found in such places. Be very careful that you correctly identify both the model you are selling and the condition it is in before setting a price on a Breyer model if you really want to sell it. Fair prices and reasonable condition ratings will bring you not only a good reputation among the always-growing collector community, but more business as well when word gets around that you know the true worth of what you are selling.

Also keep in mind that sometimes molds have dates inscribed in them — these dates are generally the year the mold was created, not the year the model was made. Again, be sure you correctly identify the model you have before you put a value on it.

☙ Traditional Scale Horse Molds and Models ❧

The Traditional scale horses are by far the most numerous of Breyer's models. This section describes the horse molds and models in this scale. The two donkey and two mule molds are also included here because of their scale and their species. In recent years, Breyer Animal Creations has begun introducing two to four new molds each year; in 1997 Breyer introduced five new Traditional Series molds (including the Porcelain Great Horse).

Action Stock Horse Foal

Mold #236; introduced in 1984.

Action Stock Horse Foals
top row
1.) 236: 1984 – 86. *Chestnut Stock Horse Foal*. Matte, chestnut; flaxen mane and tail, gray hooves, left hind stocking. $15.40.

2.) 237: 1984 – 88. *Bay Pinto Stock Horse Foal*. Matte, bay pinto; black points, socks, gray hooves. In the 1987 catalog, it was called Action American Paint Horse Foal. $14.70.

3, 4.) 238: 1984 – 88. *Appaloosa Stock Horse Foal*. Matte, gray appaloosa; black points, hooves, blanket over hindquarters. In the 1987 and 1988 catalogs, it was called Action American Appaloosa Stock Horse Foal. $14.70.

bottom row
1.) 225: 1987 – 88. *Action American Buckskin Stock Horse Foal*. Matte, buckskin; black points, no dorsal stripe. Generally, this was a darker, oranger buckskin than the later #891, and had solid points. $14.70.

also S 1984: Sears. *Collectible Stock Horse Family*. Matte, buckskin; black points, lighter than #225, otherwise the same. Set included matching Stock Horse Mare and Stock Horse Stallion S 1984 (buckskin). $19.60.

2.) 810: 1989 – 93. *Action Appaloosa Foal*. Matte, chestnut leopard appaloosa; chestnut mane and tail, grayish-red muzzle, knees, and hocks, socks, gray hooves, black and brown spatters all over. $14.70.

3.) 891: 1994 – 95. *Sunny Action Foal*. Matte, light dun; dark gray points, faint dorsal stripe, dun ankles. These are lighter and yellower than #225. $13.30.

Action Stock Horse Foals
top row
1.) 934: 1995 – 96. *Cricket Quarter Horse Foal.* Matte, brown bay; black points, right socks, blaze. $14.00.
2.) S 1984: JC Penney. *Stallion Mare and Foal Set.* Matte, red bay; black points, left hind sock. Some models have variations in stockings (e.g., none); JC Penney catalog misleading in naming this one; included Stock Horse Stallion S 1984 (light gray). $19.60.
3.) S 1984 – 85: JC Penney. *Pinto Mare and Foal Set.* Matte, black pinto; white mane, black tail, socks. Set included Stock Horse Mare S 1984 (pinto). $19.60.

bottom row
1.) S 1992: JC Penney. *Frisky Foals Set.* Matte, yellow dun; gray shading. Set included Nursing Foal, Proud Arabian Foal, and Running Foal S 1992. $16.80.
2.) S 1986: JC Penney. *Breyer Traditional Collector's Family Set.* Matte, bay roan peppercorn appaloosa; darker chestnut splash spots, gray mane and tail, three socks (not right hind). Set included matching Stock Horse Mare and Stallion S 1986. $18.90.

Adios

Mold #50; introduced in 1969.

Adios
top row
1.) 50: 1969 – 80. *Adios Famous Standardbred.* Matte, bay; black points, hind socks. Was also called Adios Standardbred; in 1972 – 73 was also in Presentation collection, mounted on wooden base (shown). $35.70 ($135.10 Presentation).
2.) 51: 1970 – 87. *Yellow Mount Famous Paint.* Matte, chestnut pinto; "solar eclipse" marking on left side, left hind stocking and bald face (both stenciled) hooves are brown or black except on left hind where it is pink. In 1972-73 this model was also in the Presentation collection, mounted on wooden base. Some later models had no spot on forearm. $36.40 ($131.60 Presentation).

bottom row
1.) 705: 1988 – 89. *Standing Quarter Horse Stallion.* Matte, apricot dun; darker/reddish mane, tail, knees, and hocks, dorsal stripe, socks, gray or natural hooves. $26.60.
2.) 830: 1990. *Quarter Horse Stallion.* Matte, black roan; black points (no shaded muzzle), gray speckles. $32.90.

Adios
top row
1.) 853: 1991 – 92. *Mesa.* Matte-semi-gloss, bay; very dark bay, no markings. $27.30.
2.) 885: 1993 – 95. *Rough n' Ready — Quarter Horse.* Matte, red dun; darker reddish points, star and blaze, hind stockings/socks. $24.50.

bottom
1.) 911: 1995 – 96. *Clayton Quarter Horse.* Matte, dapple palomino; white mane and tail, stockings, gray/darker knees and hocks, resist dappling. $19.80.

Adios
top row
1.) S 1980: Just About Horses subscriber special. *Adios.* Unpainted. $42.00.
2.) S 1978: Vales of Phoenix (200). Matte, buckskin; black points. $262.50.

bottom
S 1987: Black Horse Ranch and other mail order companies (1000). Matte, dapple gray; darker mane and tail, socks, lighter face. $42.00.

Adios
top row
1.) S 1987: JC Penney. *Traditional Western Horse Collector Set.* Matte, leopard appaloosa; light chestnut specks, strong shading on shoulders and hind legs. It is hard to see the spots on the model shown, but they are there. Set included Foundation Stallion and San Domingo S 1987. $38.50.
2.) S 1987: Black Horse Ranch and other mail order companies (1000). Matte, palomino; same color or slightly lighter mane and tail, hind stockings. $39.90.

bottom
S 1993: JC Penney. *Breyer Three Generations Appaloosa Set.* Matte, bay appaloosa; blanket pattern, black points, socks, blaze. Set included Quarter Horse Yearling and Rough Coat Stock Horse Foal S 1993. $30.10.

Adios
S 1995: BreyerFest '95 Dinner Model. *Mego.* Matte, palomino pinto; white mane and tail, stockings, pink/natural hooves, shaded muzzle, hand painted eyes. Represents the real paint horse, Amigo. $76.30.

Adios models not shown:
S 1980s: Model Horse Congress? *Adios.* Matte/semi-gloss, black. $267.00.
3095: 1976. *Breyer Rider Gift Set.* Matte, palomino; stockings, gray hooves, white or lighter mane and tail. Set included Brenda doll, saddle and bridle; very few actually made it to sales points (5 made). $287.00 ($353.50 complete).
S 1986: Longhorn-Potts. Matte, shaded chestnut. $293.00.

New for 1997:
981: 1997 – current. *Best Tango, Quarter Horse.* Matte, light bay; black points, hind socks, striped hooves (might also have low front socks). $15.00.

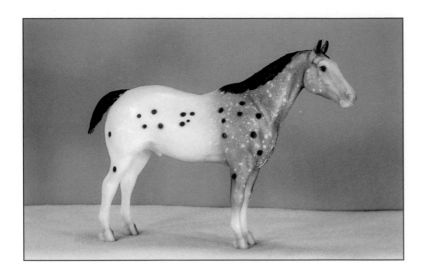

Amber (not shown)

Mold #488. New mold for 1997.

3197: 1997 – current. *Amber and Ashley, Twin Morgan Foals.* Matte, chestnut; right socks, star. Set included Ashley #3197. $8.00.

Appaloosa Performance Horse

Mold #99; introduced in 1974.

Appaloosa Performance Horse

99: 1974 – 80. *Appaloosa Performance Horse.* Matte, chestnut roan appaloosa; dark brown/black mane and tail, blanket pattern from shoulders to tail with brown spots, forequarters brown with white/lighter resist spots on head, neck, and shoulders, stockings, bald face, striped hooves. $31.50.

Appaloosa Performance Horse
top row
1.) 3095: 1980 – 85. *Brenda Breyer Gift Set.* Matte, chestnut appaloosa; flaxen mane and tail, blanket on hindquarters, dark brown/black hooves. Set included Brenda doll, bareback pad and bridle. $32.90 ($44.80 complete).
2.) 946: 1996 – current. *Diamondot Buccaneer, Appaloosa.* Matte, gray roan appaloosa (varnish roan); darker gray mane and tail, shaded face, hocks, knees, and striped hooves. $20.70.

bottom row
1.) S 1984: JC Penney. *Appaloosa Stallion.* Matte, gray appaloosa; blanket pattern, black points. $55.30.
2.) S 1989: Horses International (500). Matte, alabaster; light gray mane, tail, knees, and hooves. $49.00.

Appaloosa Performance Horse
top row
1.) S 1989: Horses International (500). Matte, sorrel; rich chestnut color with darker knees and hocks, flaxen mane and tail, socks. $49.00.
2.) S 1989: Horses International (500). Matte, black leopard appaloosa; small spots, light gray mane, tail, and hooves. $49.00.

bottom row
1.) S 1989: Horses International (500). Matte, red roan; chestnut mane and tail. $49.00.
2.) S 1990: Sears. *Appaloosa American Classic Set.* Matte, black appaloosa; blanket pattern, white face, and hind socks (all stenciled). Included Running Stallion and Stud Spider S 1990. $37.80.

Aristocrat

Mold # 496; introduced in 1995.

Aristocrat
top
496: 1995 – 96. *Aristocrat, Champion Hackney.* Matte, bay; black points, four socks. $17.60.

bottom
S 1996: BreyerFest '96 Raffle model (26). *Malibu.* Matte, Wedgewood; four socks, pink hooves and muzzle. $750.00.

Aristocrat models not shown:
S 1996: Just About Horses special offer (4500). *Horsepower Set, Giltedge.* Glossy, Florentine; four socks, natural hooves, and shaded muzzle. Set included yellow die-cast "Breyer Molding Company" truck, or a 1997 Misty of Chincoteague calendar. $37.00 ($43.00 complete).

New for 1997:
978: 1997-current. *Sweet Confession, Hackney Pony.* Matte, dark bay; sparsely resist dappled, black points, rounded star, hind socks. $14.00.

Ashley (not shown)

Mold #489; new mold for 1997.

3197: 1997 – current. *Amber and Ashley, Twin Morgan Foals.* Matte, chestnut; three socks (not left fore), star. $8.00.

Balking Mule

Mold #207; introduced in 1968.

Balking Mule
top row
1.) 208: 1968 – 71. *Balking Mule.* Matte/semi-gloss, liver chestnut/seal brown; same color or darker legs, brown or dark red bridle. $119.00.
2.) 207: 1968 – 73. *Balking Mule.* Matte, bay/chestnut; darker mane and tail, gray hooves, brown or dark red bridle. $119.00.

bottom row
1.) S 1993: Black Horse Ranch (400). Matte, alabaster; light gray points, hooves, black bridle. $67.90.
2.) S 1993: Black Horse Ranch (400). Matte, buckskin; gray points (lower legs are body color), black bridle. $72.10.

Balking Mule
top row
1.) S 1993: Black Horse Ranch (400). Matte, chestnut; stockings, slightly darker mane and tail, dark brown or black bridle. $67.90.
2.) S 1993: Black Horse Ranch (400). Matte, black appaloosa; blanket pattern with black spots, socks/stockings, dark brown bridle. $67.90.

bottom row
1.) S 1993: Black Horse Ranch (400). Matte, leopard appaloosa; black points, speckles, and bridle. $67.90.
2.) S 1993: Black Horse Ranch (400). Matte, dun; slightly darker points, black bridle, gray shaded muzzle. $67.90.

New for 1997:
S 1997: BreyerFest Raffle Model (26). *Cactus.* Matte, red roan; overdappled red roan, chestnut points, gray hooves, black or dark gray halter. $850.00.

Belgian
Mold #92; introduced in 1964.

Belgian
1.) 992: 1964 – 65. *Belgian.* Matte, woodgrain; no markings. $670.00.
2.) and bottom — 93: 1964 – 67. *Belgian.* Glossy, dapple gray or dapple black; socks, bald face. Color varied from gray to black (shown). $406.00 ($544.00 dapple black).

Belgian
top row
94: 1965 – 80. *Belgian.* Matte, chestnut/sorrel; flaxen mane and tail, stockings, bald face, gray hooves, red on yellow ribbon. Light variation also shown. $39.20.

bottom row
92: 1965 – 71. *Belgian.* Matte, smoke; white mane and tail, bald face, stockings, gray hooves, red on yellow ribbon. Light variation also shown. $77.00.

Belgian
top row
1.) 906: 1995. *Goliath the American Cream Draft Horse.* Matte, light palomino; white mane and tail, blaze, socks, gray hooves, blue on red ribbon. Commemorative Edition (10,000). $44.10.
2, 3.) S 1979, 1984: Model Congress, Riegseckers and others (about 200). Semi-gloss, dapple gray; lighter dapple gray. Both years with yellow on red tail ribbon. $147.00.

bottom row
1.) S 1982 – 83: Montgomery Ward. Semi-gloss, black; yellow on red ribbons. Some called Percherons; came in set with Shire S 1982. $53.20.
2.) S 1984: Riegseckers. Matte, palomino; white mane and tail, blaze, stockings, gray hooves, red on yellow ribbons. $98.70.

Belgian

top row

1.) S 1984: Horses International. Matte, red roan; overdappled, chestnut points, gray hooves, red on white ribbon. $224.00.
2.) S 1984: Riegseckers. Matte, sorrel; lighter ones look palomino; white mane and tail, stockings, gray hooves, red on yellow ribbon. $87.50.

bottom row

1.) S 1984 – 85: Disney World. Semi-gloss, black; white on light blue ribbon. $94.50.
2.) S 1984 – 86: Dick Eighmey's Wagon Shop. Matte, dapple gray; dark gray or black mane and tail, bald face, stockings, gray hooves; gold tail ribbon. $50.40.

Belgian

top row

1.) S 1987: mail order companies. Matte, bay; black mane and tail, bald face, red on yellow tail ribbon. $51.10.
2.) S 1987: mail order companies (1200). Matte, blue roan appaloosa; body color blue-gray, black points, blanket pattern over hindquarters and most of barrel, light gray specks, yellow on red tail ribbon. $49.70.

bottom row

1.) S 1987: mail order companies. Semi-gloss, black; red on white ribbons. $49.70.
2.) S 1986 – 87, 1988: Your Horse Source and other mail order companies. Matte, dapple gray; dark gray or black mane and tail, bald face, stockings, gray hooves; red on yellow tail ribbon. $50.40.

Belgian

1.) S 1987: mail order companies. Matte, sorrel; same as #94; mane and tail can be cream. Reissue. $46.90.
2.) S 1992: Sears. *Drafters Set.* Matte, alabaster; light gray mane, tail, knees, hocks, and hooves, light blue on white tail ribbon. Set included palomino Shire and liver chestnut Roy S 1992. $36.40.

Big Ben

Mold #483; introduced in 1996. This mold was introduced as a portrait of the champion Canadian show jumper, Big Ben.

Big Ben
483: 1996 – current. *Big Ben.* Matte, chestnut; hind socks, star and stripe. $17.50.

Black Beauty

Mold #89; introduced in 1979.

Black Beauty (Traditional)
top row
1.) 89: 1979 – 88. *Black Beauty.* Matte, black; various stockings, diamond-shaped star. $25.90.
2.) 802: 1989 – 90. *Fade to Grey.* Matte, dark dappled gray; black points, bald face or narrow blaze, socks/stockings, dark gray hooves. $28.70.

bottom
833: 1991. *Dream Weaver.* Matte, sorrel; flaxen mane and tail, right stockings, broad blaze and white muzzle. Limited Edition. $32.20.

Black Beauty Variations (Traditional)
89: *Black Beauty* variations

Black Beauty 2 (Traditional)
top row
1.) 919: 1995 – 96. *Donovan Running Appaloosa Stallion.* Matte, gray appaloosa; blanket pattern with chestnut spots, black points, resist dappled in gray areas, three socks (not right fore), some have striped hooves. $22.90.
2.) S 1980: Just About Horses subscriber special. *Black Beauty.* Unpainted. $48.30.

bottom
S 1984: Sears. *Running Horse Family Set.* Matte, red bay; black points, gray hooves. Included Running Mare and Foal S 1984 (bay). $46.90.

The Black Stallion
Mold #401; introduced in 1981.

The Black Stallion (Traditional)
top row
1.) 401: 1981 – 88. *The Black Stallion.* Semi-gloss, black; natural/gray hooves. In 1987, was called Walter Farley's Black Stallion® United Artists, 1981. $29.40.
also 2095: 1981 – 83. *The Black Stallion, Book and Poster Set.* Semi-gloss, black; same as #401. Set included paperback book and color poster. $47.60 complete.
also 3000: 1982 – 85. *The Black Stallion and Alec Set.* Semi-gloss, black; same as #401. Set included Alec doll, racing silks/saddle /bridle. $58.80 complete.
2.) 811: 1989 – 90. *Majestic Arabian Stallion.* Matte, leopard appaloosa; black points, gray hooves, brown and black splash spots. Some have only black or only brown spots. $28.70.

bottom row
1.) 832: 1991. *Hyksos the Egyptian Arabian.* Semi-gloss, Ageless Bronze; darker points, painted eyes (brown and black). This color is considered a new decorator color. Commemorative Edition; numbered (7500 made). $57.40.
2.) 899: 1994 – 95. *Greystreak Action Arabian.* Matte, gray; black points, left fore and right hind socks. $24.50.

The Black Stallion (Traditional)
top row
1.) 905: 1995. *Princess of Arabia.* Matte, light dapple gray; white mane and tail, pink shaded nose, resist dappling. Limited Edition; included costumed rider. $55.30.
2.) 905: 1995. *Princess of Arabia.* Matte, red roan; chestnut points, chestnut speckles. Limited Edition; included costumed rider (this color was an unannounced color change around mid-year). $55.30.
3.) S 1988: JC Penney. *English Horse Collector's Set.* Matte, sandy bay; black points. Set included Justin Morgan and Indian Pony S 1988. $37.10.

bottom row
1.) S 1994: Breyer Tour/Signing Party model. *Ofir.* Matte, dark bay; black points, socks, star and snip, natural hooves. Some models do not have the snip. $57.40.
2.) S 1996: Toys "R" Us. *Sapphire.* Matte, buckskin; black points, three socks (not right fore). Given SR model number 705196, Medallion series (came with gold tone medallion on blue ribbon). $22.60.

New for 1997:
983: 1997 – current. *Equus, Arabian, Racehorse and Equus Magazine Namesake.* Matte, alabaster/gray; mostly white with shaded knees, face, snip (might have striped or natural hooves). $15.00.

Brighty

Mold #375; introduced in 1974.

Brighty
top
2075: 1974 – 81. *Brighty Gift Set.* Matte, gray; darker points, stockings on forelegs. Set included Marguerite Henry's "Brighty of the Grand Canyon" paperback (shown) and carrying case. $36.40 complete.
also 375: 1982 – 87. *Marguerite Henry's Brighty.* Matte, gray; same model as in set #2075. $26.60.

bottom
376: 1991 – current. *Brighty 1991, or Marguerite Henry's Brighty.* Matte, brownish-gray; white muzzle, lighter lower legs, shoulder stripe. $14.30.

Brown Sunshine

Mold #484; introduced in 1996.

Brown Sunshine
484: 1996 – current. *Brown Sunshine.* Matte, sorrel; white mane and tail, lighter lower legs, gray hooves. $16.30.

Bucking Bronco (shown in Classic chapter)

This mold, although always listed by Breyer Animal Creations with the Traditional scale models, is in the Classic scale. See the Classic Mold Chapter for mold and model descriptions.

Buckshot

Mold #415; introduced in 1985. Sculpted by Bob Scriver.

Buckshot
top row
1.) 415: 1985 – 88. *Buckshot Famous Spanish Barb.* Matte, grulla; leg striping, black points, looks like a blanket appaloosa with its white hindquarters, gray speckling in blanket area or no spots at all. Artist Series; some models are very blue. $32.20.
2.) 416: 1988 – 89. *Spanish Barb.* Matte, chestnut pinto; darker mane, tail, lower front legs, hind legs are white, face is paler with shaded muzzle. $30.80.

bottom row
1.) 922: 1995. *Cody.* Matte, dark bay pinto; same pattern as #416, darker color, black points. Production from 1/95 to end of 6/95. $27.30.
2.) 923: 1995. *Hickock.* Matte, blue roan pinto; same pattern as #416 and #922, gray-blue color, with darker speckles. Production from 7/95 to end of 12/95. $27.30.

Buckshot 2
S 1994: BreyerFest '94 Raffle Model (21). *Winchester.* Glossy, charcoal; socks, white mane and tail. $798.00.

Cantering Welsh Pony
Mold #104; introduced in 1971.

Cantering Welsh Pony
top row
1.) 104: 1971 – 73. *Cantering Welsh Pony.* Matte, bay; black points, yellow ribbons. $84.00.
2.) 106: 1971 – 74. *Cantering Welsh Pony.* Matte, seal brown; black mane and tail, bald or solid face, blue ribbons. $94.50.

bottom row
1.) 105: 1971 – 76. *Cantering Welsh Pony.* Matte, chestnut; flaxen mane and tail, bald face, stockings, red ribbons. The bay (#104) was mistakenly pictured in the 1974 and 1975 catalogs, although it wasn't available. $42.00.
2.) 105: 1979 – 81. *Cantering Welsh Pony.* Matte, chestnut; flaxen mane and tail, solid face, stockings, no ribbons. $39.20.

Cantering Welsh Pony
top row
1.) 866: 1992 – 93. *Plain Pixie.* Matte, red roan; no ribbons, cream base color with red speckles, chestnut points. $24.50.
2.) 892: 1994 – 95. *Tara.* Matte, bay; resist dappled, black points, right hind sock, star, no ribbons. $22.80.

bottom row
1.) S 1980: Just About Horses subscriber special. *Cantering Welsh Pony.* Unpainted. $58.10.
2.) S 1986: Just About Horses subscriber special (about 2000). Matte, dapple gray; darker gray or black points, shaded face, dorsal stripe, red ribbons. $126.00.

Cantering Welsh Pony
top row
1.) S 1988: Small World (500). Matte, red roan; grayish red points, stockings, pink hooves, yellow ribbons. $93.10.
2.) S 1988: Small World (500). Matte, red dun; darker mane and tail, stockings, bald face, pink hooves, metallic blue ribbons. $93.10.

bottom row
1.) S 1988: Small World (500). Matte, liver chestnut; flaxen mane and tail, darker knees and hocks, bald face, socks, natural hooves, green ribbons. $93.10.
2.) S 1988: Small World (500). Matte, flea-bit gray; gray mane, tail, knees, hocks, and speckles, pink hooves, red ribbons. $93.10.

Cantering Welsh Pony
top
S 1987: horse show (about 20). Matte, red bay; black points, stockings, alternating red and yellow ribbons. Officially unreleased; were made for horse shows (real) but never made it to show ring. $350.00.

bottom
S 1987: Small World (less than 100). Matte, dapple gray; darker gray or black points, gold ribbons. $115.50.

Cantering Welsh Pony
top row
1.) S 1990 – 91: Country Store. *Three Piece Horse Set.* Semi-gloss, rose gray; dappled, grayish points, socks, gray hooves and shaded muzzle, no ribbons. Set included Pony of the Americas and Haflinger S 1990. $35.70.
2.) S 1992: Sears. *Horses Great and Small Set.* Matte/semi-gloss, black; narrow blaze, socks, natural hooves, no ribbons. Set included Clydesdale Stallion and Merrylegs S 1992. $27.30.

bottom
S 1995: QVC. *Parade of Breeds.* Matte, bay roan; light gray body with chestnut speckles, dark chestnut face with dark shaded muzzle, black points that turn chestnut where the black meets the gray body. Set included Proud Arabian Mare and Saddlebred Weanling S 1995. $28.70.

Cantering Welsh Pony
S 1996: Just About Horses subscriber special (3500). *Sassafras.* Matte, palomino pinto; white mane and tail, snip. $35.00.

Cantering Welsh Pony model not shown:
S late 1980's?: Model Horse Congress? Matte, dun; barred legs, no ribbons. $210.00.

Clydesdale Foal

Mold #84; introduced in 1969.

Clydesdale Foal
top row
1.) 84: 1969 – 89. *Clydesdale Foal.* Matte, chestnut; darker or grayish mane and tail, bald face, stockings, gray hooves. Also used in #8384 (included green felt stable blanket and Clydesdale Mare); 1987 – 89 dealer catalogs showed lighter bay. $12.60.
2.) 826: 1990 – 91. *Clydesdale Foal.* Matte, light bay; yellowish bay, black mane, tail, and knees, stockings, gray hooves. $19.60.

bottom row
1.) 894: 1994 – 95. *Satin Star.* Matte, dark chestnut; white mane and tail, stockings, blaze, gray hooves. $14.70.
2.) S 1979: mail order companies (200). Matte, dapple gray; darker mane and tail, bald face, stockings. This is called "wild dapple" by collectors. $80.50.

Clydesdale Foal
top row
1.) S 1982 – 84: JC Penney. *Clydesdale Family Set.* Matte, bay; "True Bay"; black mane and tail, stenciled white legs and belly, bald face. $46.90.
2.) S 1988: Horses International (500). Matte, black; stockings, star, gray hooves. $49.70.

bottom row
1.) S 1988: Horses International (500). Matte, dapple gray; small dapples, gray mane and tail, shaded body, stockings. $49.70.
2.) S 1988: Horses International (500). Matte, gray; medium slate gray, darker mane and tail, stockings. $49.70.

New for 1997:
988: 1997 – current. *Quincy, Clydesdale Foal.* Matte, chestnut pinto; darker mane and tail, front socks, rear legs have high white stockings that connect to white belly, bald face. $10.00.

Clydesdale Mare

Mold #83; introduced in 1969.

Clydesdale Mare
top row

1.) 83: 1969 – 89. *Clydesdale Mare.* Matte, chestnut; darker mane and tail, bald face, stockings, gray hooves. Also used in set #8384 with Clydesdale Foal (set included green felt blankets). $18.90.
2.) 825: 1990 – 91. *Clydesdale Mare.* Matte, light bay; stockings, black mane, tail, and shaded knees and face, broad blaze to chin, gray hooves. $27.30.

bottom row

1.) 826: 1992 – 93. *Shire Mare.* Matte, dark chestnut/bay; stockings, darker points, broad blaze covering muzzle, pink shaded muzzle. $23.80.
2.) S 1979: mail order companies (200). Matte, dapple gray; darker points, bald face; stockings. This is called "wild dapple" by collectors. $122.50.

Clydesdale Mare
top row

1.) S 1980: Just About Horses subscriber special. *Clydesdale Mare.* Unpainted. $45.50.
2.) S 1982 – 84: JC Penney. *Clydesdale Family Set.* Matte, red bay; black mane and tail, stenciled white legs and belly, bald face. Called "True Bay." $71.40.

bottom row

1.) S 1983 – 84: Sears. *Clydesdale.* Flocked, bay; stockings, blaze, red ribbons. Set included leather and chain halter and lead, model had gelding parts added. $91.00.
2.) S 1987: mail order companies (1100). Matte, light dapple gray; gray mane and tail, bald face, stockings. $49.00.

New for 1997:

987: 1997 – current. *Dempsey, Clydesdale Mare.* Matte, chestnut pinto; darker points, front socks, rear legs have high white stockings that connect to white belly, broad blaze over much of face. $15.00.

Clydesdale Stallion

Mold #80; introduced in 1958.

Clydesdale Stallion
top row

1.) 80: ca. 1958 – 63. *Clydesdale.* Glossy, bay; black mane and tail, bald face, stockings, gray hooves, gold ribbons. In the 1987 – 89 catalogs, markings are stenciled (blaze, stockings). Early models have gold bobs; available in no-muscle (shown) and muscled versions, with muscled versions probably made during the last one or two years. $118.30 ($126.70 no muscle).
2.) 82: 1961 – 65. *Clydesdale.* Glossy, dapple gray; dark gray mane and tail, bald face, stockings, gold bobs. Available in no-muscle and muscled versions; color variations shown on next page. $108.50 ($122.50 no muscle).

bottom row

1.) 980: ca. 1960 – 65. *Clydesdale.* Matte, woodgrain; no markings. Available in no-muscle and muscled versions. $203.00 ($217.00 no muscle).
2.) 80: ca. 1972 – 89. *Clydesdale Stallion.* Matte, bay; black mane and tail, bald face, stockings, alternating white and red bobs, red tail ribbon, natural hooves. In 1987 – 89, the markings were stenciled (blaze, stockings). $22.40.

Clydesdale Stallion
top row
1.) 80: ca. 1964 – 72. *Clydesdale.* Matte, bay; black mane and tail, bald face, stockings, gold bobs and tail ribbon, natural hooves. $45.50.
2.) 824: 1990 – 91. *Clydesdale Stallion.* Matte, light bay; light yellowish bay, bald face, gold and white bobs, gold tail ribbon. $27.30.

bottom row
1.) 868: 1992 – 95. *Highland Clydesdale.* Matte, bay; high stenciled white hind leg markings that continue to belly, front stenciled stockings over knees, broad blaze, blue and white bobs, blue tail ribbon. $23.80.
2.) 3170: 1994 – 95. *Circus Extravaganza Set.* Matte, roan/flea-bit gray; red, white, and blue bobs. Set included Little Bits Clydesdale #3170. $23.80.

Clydesdale Stallion
top row
1, 2.) S 1979, 1984/85: mail order companies (100 – 200). Matte or semi-gloss, light dapple gray; bald face, stockings, gray mane and tail, gold bobs and tail ribbon. The first model shown is from 1979, the second from 1984. $106.40.

bottom row
1.) 962: 1996 – current. *Laddie II, Shire.* Matte, black pinto; stenciled white overo pinto markings onto belly, front stenciled stockings over knees, broad blaze, red and white bobs and tail ribbon. $21.40.
2.) S 1982 – 84: JC Penney. *Clydesdale Family Set.* Matte, bay; "True Bay" (very similar to #80 from 80s) with all red bobs, bald face, black mane and tail, stenciled stockings. $61.60.

Clydesdale Stallion
top row
1.) S 1987: mail order companies (1200). Matte, dapple gray; sparsely dappled, gray mane and tail, bald face, red and white bobs, red tail ribbon. $49.00.
2.) S 1992: Sears. *Horses Great and Small Set.* Matte, grulla; shaded body, yellow and blue bobs, yellow tail ribbon, right stockings. Set included Cantering Welsh Pony and Merrylegs S 1992. $33.60.

bottom
S 1993: BreyerFest '93 Dinner Model (less than 1500). *Grayingham Lucky Lad.* Semi-gloss, black; stenciled stockings and bald face, red mane with red and white bobs and tail ribbon. Represented the real horse, who was present (special guest) at BreyerFest '93. $84.00.

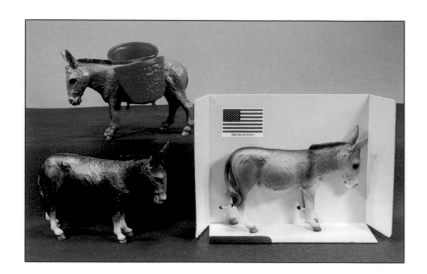

Donkey

Mold #81; introduced in 1957 or 1958.

Donkey

top

1.) 82: 1958 – 60. *Donkey.* Matte, gray; same as #81 but with baskets. Variation shown that is battleship gray with black mane. $175.00 with baskets.

bottom row

1.) 81: 1957/8 – 74. *Donkey.* Matte, gray; stockings, dark mane and tail, pale muzzle. Some were battleship gray; these were probably produced during oil crisis years. $25.90.

2.) 390: 1992. *Donkey.* Matte, gray; stockings, darker mane and tail, dorsal stripe and shoulder stripe. $20.30.

El Pastor

Mold #61; introduced in 1974.

El Pastor

top row

1.) 61: 1974 – 81. *El Pastor, Paso Fino.* Matte, bay; black points, left socks, most have a star. $39.20.

2.) 116: 1987. *Precipitado Sin Par (Cips Champion Paso Fino).* Matte, bay pinto; stockings, black points, broken stripe (star and lower stripe with snip), matte pink hooves, eyewhites, bi-color eyes, red in nostrils. Limited Edition. $46.90.

bottom

867: 1992 – 95. *Tesoro.* Matte, palomino; stockings, white mane, tail, and narrow blaze, gray shaded muzzle, gray hooves. $23.80.

El Pastor

top

914: 1995 – 96. *Tobe, Rocky Mountain Horse.* Matte, chocolate sorrel; flaxen mane and tail, star, socks, striped hooves, resist dappled. $20.20.

bottom

S 1987: horse owner (100). Matte, bay; black points, left socks (solid face). $112.00.

New for 1997:

S 1997. Breyer Fall Show Horse. *Desperado.* Semi-gloss, black pinto; high white stockings, broken blaze, small patches of white on body. Made for dealers who host a Breyer show day (in production 8/97 through 11/97 only); given SR number 700297. $15.00.

Family Arabian Foal

Mold #9; introduced in 1961.

Family Arabian Foal
top row
1.) 9: 1961 – 66. *Arabian Foal.* Glossy, alabaster; gray hooves, mane, and tail. $15.40.
2.) 9: 1967 – 73. *Arabian Foal.* Matte, alabaster; gray hooves, mane, and tail. $12.60.
3.) 15: 1961 – 66. *Arabian Foal.* Glossy, bay; stockings, narrow blaze, black hooves, black mane and tail. $16.10.

bottom row
1.) 15: 1967 – 74. *Arabian Foal.* Matte, bay; stockings, narrow blaze, black hooves, black mane and tail. Also used for night lights. $13.30.
2.) 6: 1961 – 66. *Family Foal.* Glossy, palomino; stockings, bald face, gray hooves, white mane and tail. Also used for night lights. $15.40.

Family Arabian Foal
top row
1, 2.) 6: 1967 – 87. *Family Foal.* Matte, palomino; stockings, bald face, gray hooves, white mane and tail. In 1977 – 81 catalogs, this was called Family Foal; in 1987 it was called Palomino Family Foal. $12.60.
3.) S 1983: JC Penney. Matte, light chestnut; flaxen mane and tail, narrow blaze. Set included Family Arabian Mare and Stallion S 1983. $24.50.

bottom row
1, 2.) 203: 1968 – 74. *Arabian Foal.* Matte, charcoal; stockings, bald face, gray hooves, white mane and tail. The first model is a brownish charcoal color and the second is blacker. $14.70.

Family Arabian Foal
top row
1.) 39: 1963 – 67. *Arabian Foal.* Glossy, gray appaloosa; black points, bald face, gray or black hooves, splash spots on hindquarters. $17.50.
2.) 39: 1968 – 71. *Arabian Foal.* Matte, gray appaloosa; black points, bald face, gray or black hooves, splash spots on hindquarters. $14.70.
3.) 203: 1961 – 67. *Arabian Foal.* Glossy, charcoal; stockings, bald face, white mane and tail, pink/natural hooves. $16.80.

bottom row
1.) 909: 1963 – 67. *Arabian Foal.* Matte, woodgrain; no markings. $32.90.
2.) 708: 1988. *Family Arabian Foal.* Matte, liver chestnut; white mane and tail, bald face, stockings, pink/natural hooves. $18.20.
3.) 816: 1989 – 90. *Family Arabian Foal.* Matte, bay; black points, hind socks, gray or black hooves. $15.40.

Family Arabian Foal
top row
1.) 841: 1991 – 93. *Family Arabian Foal.* Matte, red chestnut; darker mane and tail. $14.00.
2.) 874: 1993 – 94. *Ara-Appaloosa Foal.* Matte, leopard appaloosa; gray points, brown spots. $14.00.
3.) S 1978: Model Congress (200). Matte, black; no markings. $57.40.

bottom row
1.) S 1982: JC Penney. Matte, dark chestnut; darker mane and tail, narrow blaze. Set included Family Arabian Mare and Stallion S 1982. $24.50.
2.) S 1988: Enchanted Doll House. Glossy, alabaster; gray mane, tail, hooves. $21.00.
3.) S 1991: Sears. *Spirit of the Wind Set.* Matte, dapple gray; black points, bald face. Set included Family Arabian Mare S 1991. $19.60.

New for 1997:
995: 1997 – current. *Julian, Family Arabian Foal.* Matte to semigloss, dark chestnut; darker points, lighter muzzle, hind socks. $8.00.

Family Arabian Mare
Mold #8; introduced in 1961.

Family Arabian Mare
top row
1.) 38: 1961 – 67. *Arabian Mare.* Glossy, gray appaloosa; black points, bald face, splash spots on hindquarters. $28.70.
2.) 8: 1961 – 66. *Arabian Mare.* Glossy, alabaster; gray mane, tail, and hooves, pink shaded muzzle. $25.20.

bottom row
1.) 14: 1961 – 66. *Arabian Mare.* Glossy, bay; black mane, tail, and hooves, stockings, blaze. Also used for night lights, one version had a wood base. $27.30.
2.) 14: 1967 – 74. *Arabian Mare.* Matte, bay; black mane, tail, and hooves, stockings, blaze. $23.80.

Family Arabian Mare
top row
1.) 38: 1968 – 71. *Arabian Mare.* Matte, gray appaloosa; black points, bald face, splash spots on hindquarters. $24.50.
2.) 8: 1967 – 73. *Arabian Mare.* Matte, alabaster; gray mane, tail, and hooves, pink shaded muzzle. $21.70.

bottom row
1, 2.) 202: 1961 – 67. *Arabian Mare.* Glossy, charcoal; stockings, bald face, white mane and tail, gray hooves. Variation shown (first model has eyewhites). $27.30.

Family Arabian Mare
top row
1.) 202: 1967 – 73. *Arabian Mare.* Matte, charcoal; stockings, bald face, white mane and tail, gray hooves. $24.50.
2.) 5: 1961 – 66. *Family Mare.* Glossy, palomino; white mane and tail, stockings, bald face, gray hooves. $21.70.

bottom row
1.) 5: 1967 – 87. *Family Mare.* Matte, palomino; white mane and tail, stockings, bald face, gray hooves. Catalog names varied: in 1977 – 81 it was called Family Mare, and in 1987 it was called Palomino Family Mare. $14.00.
2.) 908: 1963 – 67. *Family Arabian Mare.* Matte, woodgrain; no markings. $55.30.

Family Arabian Mare
top row
1.) 707: 1988. *Family Arabian Mare.* Matte, liver chestnut; flaxen mane and tail, socks, star, pink/natural hooves. $31.50.
2.) 815: 1989 – 90. *Family Arabian Mare.* Matte, bay; black points, hind socks, black hooves. $26.60.

bottom row
1.) 873: 1993 – 94. *Ara-Appaloosa Mare.* Matte, leopard appaloosa; gray points, chestnut splash spots. $23.10.
2.) S 1978: Model Congress (200). Matte, black; no markings. $98.70.

Family Arabian Mare
top row
1.) S 1982: JC Penney. Matte, dark chestnut; darker mane and tail, blaze, stockings. $41.30.
2.) S 1983: JC Penney. Matte, chestnut/sorrel; flaxen mane and tail, blaze, stockings. $41.30.

bottom row
1.) S 1988: Enchanted Doll House (100). Glossy, alabaster; light gray mane, tail, hooves. $29.40.
2.) S 1991: Sears. *Spirit of the Wind Set.* Matte, dapple gray; black points, bald face, right hind sock. $29.40.

New for 1997:
996: 1997 – current. *Galena, Family Arabian Mare.* Matte, shaded chestnut; darker points, lighter face, left hind sock. $13.00.

Family Arabian Stallion
Mold #7; introduced in 1959.

Family Arabian Stallion
top row
1.) 7: 1959 – 66. *Arabian Stallion.* Glossy, alabaster; gray mane, tail, and hooves. $20.80.
2.) 7: 1967 – 73. *Arabian Stallion.* Matte, alabaster; gray mane, tail, and hooves. $18.00.

bottom row
1.) 13: 1959 – 66. *Arabian Stallion.* Glossy, bay; black mane, tail, and hooves, star and snip, stockings. Model shown has eyewhites and blue ribbon sticker. $25.20.
2.) 13: 1966 – 73? *Arabian Stallion.* Matte, bay; black mane, tail, and hooves, star and snip, stockings. $23.10.

Family Arabian Stallion
top row
1, 2.) 37: 1963 – 67. *Arabian Stallion.* Glossy, gray appaloosa; black points, bald face, splash spots on hindquarters. $29.40.
3.) 37: 1968 – 71. *Arabian Stallion.* Matte, gray appaloosa; black points, bald face, splash spots on hindquarters. $25.20.

bottom row
1.) 4: 1961 – 66. *Family Stallion.* Glossy, palomino; white mane and tail, stockings, bald face, gray hooves. Model shown has eyewhites. $21.70.
2.) 4: 1967 – 87. *Family Stallion.* Matte, palomino; white mane and tail, stockings, bald face, gray hooves. Catalog names varied: in 1977 – 81 it was called Family Stallion, and in 1987 it was called Palomino Family Stallion. $15.40.

Family Arabian Stallion
top row
1.) 201: 1963 – 67. *Arabian Stallion.* Glossy, charcoal; white mane and tail, stockings, bald face, pink/natural hooves. Model shown has eyewhites. $25.90.
2.) 201: 1968 – 73. *Arabian Stallion.* Matte, charcoal; white mane and tail, stockings, bald face, pink/natural hooves. $26.60.

bottom row
1.) 907: 1963 – 67. *Family Stallion.* Matte, woodgrain; no markings. $55.30.
2.) 706: 1988. *Family Arabian Stallion.* Matte, liver chestnut; flaxen mane and tail, darker knees and hocks, stockings, blaze, pink/natural hooves. $30.10.

Family Arabian Stallion
top row
1.) 814: 1989 – 90. *Family Arabian Stallion*. Matte, bay; black points, hind socks, black hooves. $25.20.
2.) 872: 1993 – 94. *Ara-Appaloosa Stallion*. Matte, leopard appaloosa; black or dark gray points, brown and black splash spots. $23.80.

bottom row
1.) 964: 1996. *Realto, Arabian*. Matte, light gray; yellowish mane and tail, gray hooves, gray shaded face with stripe down to white muzzle. In production 1/96 through 6/96. $19.40.
2.) 965: 1996. *Calife, Arabian*. Matte, shaded gray; gray mane, tail, knees and hocks, socks, lightly resist dappled, natural hooves. In production 7/96 through 12/96. $19.40.

Family Arabian Stallion
S 1978: Model Congress (200). Matte/semi-gloss, black; no markings. $91.70.

Family Arabian Stallion
top row
1.) S 1983: JC Penney. Matte, chestnut/sorrel; flaxen mane and tail, star, socks. $41.30.
2.) S 1982: JC Penney. Matte, liver chestnut; darker brown mane and tail, blaze. $39.90.

bottom row
1.) S 1988: Enchanted Doll House (100). Glossy, alabaster; gray hooves, mane, and tail. $34.30.
2.) S 1991 – 92: Sears. *Arabian Horses of the World Set*. Matte, black point alabaster; black legs, mane, and tail, shaded muzzle. Included Proud Arabian Mare and Proud Arabian Stallion S 1991. $28.70.

New for 1997:
997: 1997 – current. *Devil Wind, Family Arabian Stallion*. Matte, dark bay; black points, three socks (not left hind), natural hooves. $13.00.
S 1997: Toys "R" Us. *No Doubt*. Matte, red roan; speckle roaning, chestnut points, gray muzzle, left socks. Medallion Series; given SR number 702797. $15.50.

31

Fighting Stallion

Mold #31; introduced in 1961.

Fighting Stallion
top row
1.) 34: 1961 – 71. *Fighting Stallion.* Glossy, charcoal; white mane and tail, stockings, pink/natural hooves. Model shown has eyewhites. $119.00.
2, 3.) 32: 1961 – 67. *Fighting Stallion.* Glossy, gray appaloosa; gray points, gray hooves, pink and gray shaded muzzle. Color variation shown (darker legs, different spotting). $122.50.

bottom row
1.) 33: 1961 – 67. *Fighting Stallion.* Glossy, palomino; white mane and tail, stockings, bald face. $91.00.
2.) 33: 1968 – 73. *Fighting Stallion.* Matte, palomino; white mane and tail, stockings, bald face. $65.10.

Fighting Stallion
top row
1.) 30: 1961 – 64. *Fighting Stallion.* Glossy, alabaster; gray hooves, pink and gray shaded muzzle. $91.00.
2.) 30: 1965 – 85. *Fighting Stallion.* Matte, alabaster; gray hooves, pink and gray shaded muzzle. $26.60.

bottom row
1.) 35: 1961 – 87. *Fighting Stallion.* Matte, bay; black mane, tail, and hooves, stockings, bald face. $25.90.
2.) 931: 1963 – 73. *Fighting Horse.* Matte, woodgrain; socks, narrow blaze, black hooves. $106.40.

Fighting Stallion
top row
1.) 1031: 1963 – 65. *Fighting Stallion.* Glossy, Copenhagen; white points, bald face, shaded pink muzzle, ears, and hooves. $1,050.00.
2.) 2031: 1963 – 65. *Fighting Stallion.* Glossy, Florentine; white points, bald face, shaded pink muzzle, ears, and hooves. $1,050.00.

bottom row
1.) 3031: 1963 – 65. *Fighting Stallion.* Glossy, Gold Charm; white points, bald face, shaded pink muzzle, ears, and hooves. $1,050.00.
2.) 4031: 1963 – 65. *Fighting Stallion.* Matte, Wedgewood; white points, bald face, shaded pink muzzle, ears, and hooves. $1,050.00.

Fighting Stallion
top row
1.) 709: 1988 – 90. *Fighting Stallion.* Matte, black leopard appaloosa; gray points, socks, gray hooves, small splash spots all over body and neck. $35.70.
2.) 855: 1992. *Chaparral.* Matte, buckskin pinto; black tail, knees, and half of mane, blaze, front stockings, natural hooves. Limited Edition. $37.80.

bottom row
1.) S 1985: JC Penney. *Circus Set with Ringmaster.* Flocked, white; white hair mane and tail, black hooves. Included Alec doll in Ringmaster's costume, bridle, red plum, and red and white surcingle. $87.50 ($108.50 complete).
2.) S 1993: JC Penney. *Wild Horses of America Set.* Matte, sorrel; white mane and tail, bald face, stockings. Set included Mustang and Foundation Stallion S 1993. $29.40.

Fighting Stallion
897: 1994 – 95. *Ponokah-Eemetah.* Matte, dark bay appaloosa; black points, blanket pattern, assorted painted on Native American symbols (eight) varied by production date. Six designs shown. $28.00.

Fighting Stallion
top row
1.) 949: 1996 – current. *Clue II, American Quarter Horse.* Matte, palomino; white mane and tail, hind stockings, narrow blaze, shaded muzzle. $20.30.
2.) S 1993: Toys "R" Us. *Bay Fighting Stallion.* Matte, bay; stockings, bald face, black mane and tail. Basically a reissue of #35. $28.70.

bottom
S 1996: Just About Horses subscriber special. *Sierra.* Matte, red dun; chestnut points, lighter body. Included certificate. $45.50.

Five Gaiter

Mold #52; introduced in 1962.

Five Gaiter
top row
1.) 51: 1962 – 66. *Five Gaiter*. Glossy, alabaster; pink muzzle, gray hooves, turquoise on yellow ribbons. Shown with red eyes (which were earlier models) later models have black eyes. $114.10 ($122.50 red eyes).
2, 3.) 53: 1962 – 71. *Five Gaiter*. Glossy, palomino; white mane and tail, bald face, stockings, pink hooves, red on yellow ribbons. Color variations shown. $114.10.

bottom row
1.) 951: 1963 – 65. *Five Gaiter*. Matte, woodgrain; star, socks, black hooves, blue on white ribbons. $147.00.
2.) 52: 1963 – 86. *Five Gaiter*. Matte, sorrel; charcoal brown mane and tail, bald face, stockings, red on white braids. Model shown has eyewhites. $29.40.

Five Gaiter
top row
1.) 1051: 1964 – 65. *Five Gaiter*. Glossy, Copenhagen; white points, bald face, shaded pink muzzle, ears, and hooves, black on blue ribbons. $1,050.00.
2.) 2051: 1964 – 65. *Five Gaiter*. Glossy, Florentine; white points, bald face, shaded pink muzzle, ears, and hooves, black on gold ribbons. $1,050.00.

bottom row
1.) 3051: 1964 – 65. *Five Gaiter*. Glossy, Gold Charm; white points, bald face, shaded pink muzzle, ears, and hooves, black on gold ribbons. $1,050.00.
2.) 4051: 1964 – 65. *Five Gaiter*. Matte, Wedgewood; white points, bald face, shaded pink muzzle, ears, and hooves, black on blue ribbons. $1,050.00.

Five Gaiter
top row
1.) 109: 1987 – 88. *American Saddlebred*. Matte, dapple gray; white mane and tail, dark gray knees and hocks, bald face, socks, pink hooves, black on red ribbons. $46.20.
2.) 117: 1987 – 89. *Project Universe*. Matte, chestnut pinto; white tail, brown and white mane, narrow blaze, black on gold ribbons. $32.20.

bottom row
1.) 140: 1988 – 90. *Wing Commander*. Matte, brown/bay; black mane and tail, socks, narrow blaze, red ribbons. This model represented the actual horse, and the catalog noted "American Saddlebred — Five-Gaited World Champion 1948 – 1953." $30.80.
2.) 827: 1990 – 91. *Pinto American Saddlebred*. Matte, black pinto; white tail, black and white mane, narrow blaze, red on white ribbons. $35.70.

Five Gaiter

top row

1.) 862: 1992 – 93. *Kentucky Saddlebred.* Matte, chestnut; darker mane and tail, narrow blaze, socks. $25.90.

2.) 904: 1994 – 95. *CH Imperator.* Glossy, dark chestnut; star and snip, right hind socks, blue on red ribbons. $27.30.

bottom row

1.) S 1980: Just About Horses subscriber special. *Five Gaiter.* Unpainted. $49.00.

2.) S 1994: Just About Horses subscriber special (2000). *Moonshadows.* Matte, blue roan; black points, hind socks, snip, silver on blue ribbons. $76.30.

Five Gaiter

S 1996: JC Penney. *Gaited Breeds of America.* Matte, bay pinto; black legs, black and white mane, white tail, three socks (not right fore), gold on white ribbons. Set included Midnight Sun and Saddlebred Weanling S 1996. $18.00.

Foundation Stallion

Mold #64; introduced in 1977.

Foundation Stallion

top row

1.) 64: 1977 – 87. *Black Foundation Stallion.* Matte, black; no markings. $28.00.

2.) 85: 1980 – 87. *Azteca.* Matte, dapple gray; darker points, mane, and tail. In 1987 had socks, white tail, gray hooves. Variations are known. $31.50.

bottom

710: 1988 – 91. *American Indian Pony.* Matte, red roan/flea-bit gray; reddish-gray points, socks, natural hooves. $28.00.

Foundation Stallion

869: 1992. *Lakota Pony*. Matte, alabaster with blue markings; blue chest and rump with Native American markings. Four different markings available (all shown). Collectors report that there is a variation that has all four markings on one horse. $36.40.

Foundation Stallion
top row

1.) 870: 1993. *Fugir Cacador Lusitano Stallion*. Matte, buckskin; black points, dorsal stripe, shaded muzzle. Limited Edition. $28.70.
2.) S 1980: Just About Horses subscriber special. *Foundation Stallion*. Unpainted. $49.00.

bottom

S 1983: Montgomery Wards. *Palomino Horse and Foal Set*. Matte, palomino; white mane and tail, stockings, gray hooves. Set included Stock Horse Foal S 1983. $98.00.

Foundation Stallion
top row

1.) S 1984: mail order companies (about 500). Matte, alabaster; gray mane and tail, pink/natural hooves. $60.90.
2.) S 1987: JC Penney. *Traditional Western Horse Collector Set*. Semi-gloss, charcoal/chocolate chestnut; white/flaxen mane and tail, stockings, pink/natural hooves. "Mustang"; Included San Domingo and Adios S 1987 (red dun). $39.90.

bottom

S 1993: JC Penney. *Wild Horses of America Set*. Matte, bay appaloosa; black points, right hind sock, blanket pattern with splash spots. Set included Fighting Stallion and Mustang S 1993. $30.80.

Foundation Stallion
top row
1.) 967: 1996 – current. *Appaloosa Champion.* Matte, red roan appaloosa; chestnut mane and tail, white half-apron face marking, shadings on neck, legs, and chest, chestnut spots on body. $20.20.
2.) S 1996: Toys "R" Us. *Titan Glory.* Matte, bay; black points, three socks (not right fore), broad strip and white muzzle. Given SR model number 705096; Medallion Series. $19.50.

bottom
S 1996: Mid-States Distributing. *Rusty Diamond.* Matte, chestnut; shaded, dorsal stripe, no white. $23.00.

Friesian
Mold #485; introduced in 1992.

Friesian
top row
1.) 485: 1992 – 95. *Friesian.* Matte, black; no markings, natural hooves; the profoundly matte color was created using layers of flat blue and gray. $22.40.
2.) 3175: 1994 – 95. *Action Drafters, Big and Small.* Matte, dark bay; black points, left hind sock; sparsely resist dappled. Set included Little Bits Clydesdale #3175. $23.80.

bottom
943: 1996 – current. *JB Andrew, Adopt-a-Horse Drafter Type.* Semi-gloss, black; "freeze brand" on neck. Portrait model of the real horse, a 16+ hand Mustang who competes in dressage. $21.10.

New for 1997:
S 1997: West Coast Model Horse Collector's Jamboree (1000). *Kris Kringle.* Matte, light dapple gray; dapples mainly on lower body, black base of tail and stripes in mane, gray knees and hocks, shaded muzzle. $45.00.

Fury Prancer
Mold #P40; introduced in 1954.

Fury Prancer
top row
1, 2.) P40: 1954 – 58. *Fury Prancer.* Glossy, dark plum brown; broad blaze, stockings, black hooves, gold tack, hard plastic English saddle. came with Mountie (P440), Davy Crockett (P540), or Kit Carson (P540); all with snap-girth saddles. $66.50 ($129.50 complete).
3.) P40: 1954 – 64. *Black Beauty.* Glossy, black; bald face, stockings, gray hooves, most with silver tack, models labeled Black Beauty came with silver tack and silver trimmed saddle; this model also came with Mountie (P440). $78.40 ($124.30 with rider).

bottom row
1.) P45: 1954 – 63. *Fury Prancer.* Glossy, alabaster; gray mane, tail, and hooves, gold tack, brown rubbery plastic saddle with pull through girth. with Robin Hood (P145), William Tell (P145), or Canadian Mountie (P445). Robin Hood and William Tell came with red plastic sword and bow. This model, when sold without the rider, had a reddish-brown snap-girth saddle. $60.90 ($142.50 with rider).
2.) P41: 1954 – 63. *Fury Prancer.* Glossy, black pinto; bald face, white mane, black tail with white tip, socks, gray hooves; black saddle, gold tack. also came with Indian Brave or Chief (P241) and accessories. $73.50 ($122.00 with rider).

Fury Prancer
top row
1, 2.) 27: 1956 – 63. *Fury.* Glossy, black; diamond star, low socks, gray hooves, gold or black tack, chain reins. Variations shown with paper "TV's Fury" saddle, and one with hard plastic saddle with gold trim. $52.50 ($87.50 with Fury saddle).

3.) P43: 1956 – 63. *Fury Prancer.* Glossy, palomino; white mane and tail, bald face, stockings; came with red saddle, shown with Lucky Ranger (P343), also with Cowboy (P343). Color variations known. $60.90 ($157.50 with rider).

bottom
P42: 1956 – 67. *Fury Prancer.* Glossy, chestnut pinto; bald face, socks, gray hooves, reddish plastic snap girth saddle. Came with Lucky Ranger or Cowboy (P342), or Indian Brave or Indian Chief (P242). $67.90 ($158.20 with rider).

Fury Prancer
P945: 1958 – 62. *Fury Prancer.* Matte, woodgrain; no markings. $476.00.

Galiceno

Mold #100; introduced in 1978.

Galiceno
top
100: 1978 – 82. *Galiceno.* Matte, bay; black points. $34.30.

bottom
888: 1994 – 95. *Freckle Doll.* Matte, bay pinto; black points, blaze, white patch on left side. $21.00.

Gem Twist

Mold #495; introduced in 1993.

Gem Twist
top row
1.) 495: 1993 – 95. *Gem Twist Champion Show Jumper.* Matte, alabaster; gray shaded tail, knees, and hocks, natural hooves, red ribbons (patterns vary). First models produced with red ribbon variation (different than shown in catalog). $21.00.
2.) 959: 1996 – current. *Monte, Thoroughbred.* Matte, chestnut; shaded, white fetlocks, striped hooves, alternating green and orange braids, blaze. $22.70.

bottom
S 1996: Mid-season release. *First Competitor.* Matte, buckskin; black points, socks, reverse 'C' star, and red, white, and blue braids. Came with English saddle and bridle, and blue and white saddle pad (with red USA on it). Given SR number 701196. $29.30.

Grazing Foal

Mold #151; introduced in 1964.

Grazing Foal
top row
1.) 152: 1964 – 70. *Grazing Foal.* Matte, black; bald face, stockings. $39.20.
2.) 153: 1964 – 81. *Grazing Foal.* Matte, palomino; stockings, bald face, white mane and tail, gray hooves. $20.30.
3.) 151: 1964 – 76, 1978 – 81. *Grazing Foal.* Matte, bay; black points, front socks, bald face. $20.30.

bottom row
1.) 3165: 1993 – 95. *Buttons and Bows Gift Set.* Matte, chestnut/red dun; darker mane and tail, hind stockings. Set included Grazing Mare #3165. $15.40.
2.) S 1991: JC Penney. *Grazing Foal.* Matte, bay appaloosa; black points, blanket pattern with splash spots. $19.60.

Grazing Mare

Mold #141; introduced in 1961.

Grazing Mare
top row
1.) 142: 1961 – 71. *Grazing Mare.* Matte, black; bald face, stockings. $66.50.
2.) 141: 1961 – 80. *Grazing Mare.* Matte, bay; black points, front socks/stockings, bald/blaze face. $33.60.

bottom row
1, 2.) 143: 1961 – 80. *Grazing Mare.* Matte, palomino; stockings, bald face, white mane and tail, gray hooves. $33.60.

Grazing Mare
top row
1.) 3165: 1993 – 95. *Buttons and Bows Gift Set.* Matte, chestnut/red dun; darker mane, tail, knees, and hocks, dorsal stripe, narrow blaze. Set included Grazing Foal #3165. $25.90.
2.) S 1989 – 90: Sears. *Mare and Foal Set.* Matte, bay appaloosa; blanket pattern, black points. Set included Nursing Foal S 1989. $35.70.

bottom
S 1995: JC Penney. *Serenity Set.* Matte, buckskin; black points, small star. Set included Lying Down Foal S 1995 (buckskin). $32.20.

Haflinger

Mold #156; introduced in 1979.

Haflinger
top row
1.) 156: 1979 – 84. *Haflinger.* Matte, sorrel; flaxen mane and tail, darker lower legs, gray hooves. Color variations exist. $26.60.
2.) 850: 1991 – 92. *Mountain Pony.* Matte, sorrel; same as #156 but with gray knees and hocks, model shown is lighter, and has socks. $23.80.

bottom row
1.) 883: 1993 – 94. *Scat Cat — Children's Pony.* Matte, bay roan leopard appaloosa; cream body, black points, chestnut shaded head, blaze, chestnut splash spots. $18.90.
2.) 926: 1995 – 96. *Sargent Pepper Appaloosa Pony.* Matte, gray leopard appaloosa; gray points, black stenciled spots. $18.40.

Haflinger 2
top row
1, 2.) S 1984 – 85: Horses International. Matte, sorrel; gray mane and tail. Variations known with brown-gray mane and tail and with socks. $37.80.

bottom row
1.) S 1990 – 91: Country Store (900). *Three Piece Horse Set.* Matte, chestnut pinto; white hind legs, grayish mane and tail, stripe on lower nose, gray shaded muzzle. Set included Cantering Welsh Pony and Pony of the Americas S 1990. $32.20.
2.) S 1996: Sears Wish Book. *Appaloosa Performance Champion.* Matte, chestnut blanket appaloosa; white mane and tail. $19.70.

Halla

Mold #63; introduced in 1977.

Halla
top row
1, 2.) 63: 1977 – 85. *Halla, Famous Jumper.* Matte, bay; black points, small star. Variations known with no star (shown). $32.20.
3.) 820: 1990 – 91. *Noble Jumper.* Matte, dapple gray; black points, hind socks. $31.50.

bottom row
1.) 490: 1992 – 94. *Bolya the Freedom Horse.* Matte, buckskin; black points, front socks, star. Retooled mane and tail (more of each). $25.90.
2.) S 1989: JC Penney. *International Equestrian Collector's Set.* Matte, flea-bit gray; gray points, tiny gray speckles. $33.60.

Hanoverian

Mold #58; introduced in 1980.

Hanoverian
top row
1.) 58: 1980 – 84. *Hanoverian.* Matte, bay; dark bay, black points. $35.00.
2.) 887: 1994. *Gifted.* Matte, bay; black points, stockings, blaze. Limited Edition. $51.10.

bottom row
1.) S 1980: Just About Horses subscriber special. *Hanoverian.* Unpainted. $47.60.
2.) S 1986: Horses International. Matte, dapple gray; white base coat, socks, white spatter spots. $199.50.

Hanoverian
top row
1.) S 1987: Your Horse Source. Matte, alabaster; light gray mane and tail. $84.00.
2.) S 1987: Your Horse Source. Matte, medium bay; black points, stockings, broad blaze. $84.00.

bottom row
1.) S 1987: Your Horse Source. Matte, red chestnut; slightly darker mane and tail. $84.00.
2.) S 1987: Your Horse Source. Matte, black; no markings. $84.00.

Hanoverian
top row
1.) S 1989: JC Penney. *International Equestrian Collector Set.* Matte, dark dapple gray; black points. Included Halla and Morganglanz S 1989. $54.60.
2.) S 1990 – 91: German Export (about 250). *Vaulting Horse.* Matte, black; stockings, blaze. $119.00.

bottom
S 1993: Spiegel. *Dressage Set of Two Horses.* Matte, mahogany bay; black points, left socks. Included Misty's Twilight S 1993. $42.70.

Hanoverian
top
S 1995: JC Penney. *Art Deco, Dressage Horse.* Semi-gloss, black pinto; black head, chest and parts of barrel, white legs, natural hooves, half of tail is black. $31.50.

bottom
951: 1996 – current. *Borodino II, Hanoverian.* Matte, bay; black points, three socks (not left hind), blaze. $21.20.

Henry, Norwegian Fjord

Mold #482; introduced in 1996.

Henry, Norwegian Fjord
482: 1996 – current. *Henry, Norwegian Fjord.* Matte, buckskin/dun; black or grayish points, shaded muzzle, black dorsal stripe, black and white mane and tail. $18.00.

Hobo (shown in Classic chapter)

This mold, although sometimes listed by collectors with the Traditional scale models, is in the Classic scale. See the Classic Mold Chapter for mold and model descriptions.

Ideal American Quarter Horse

Mold #497; introduced in 1995.

Ideal American Quarter Horse
top row
1.) 497: 1995. *AQHA Ideal American Quarter Horse.* Matte, chestnut; darker muzzle and hooves. Number 1 in 4-year Limited Edition series; collectors can register models with AQHA. The model shown first on the bottom row was packaged as #498 in early 1996 (those models were recalled); it might be worth about 10 percent more but only if it is still in its box and can be shown to be the accidental release. The version shown second on the bottom row is popularly called the Q2 version for the home shopping channel where it was sold; it was produced in an incorrect color. $32.90 ($53.00 Q2 version).
2.) 498: 1996. *1996 — Progeny of Leo, AQHA American Quarter Horse.* Matte, chestnut; darker points, blaze, socks. Number 2 in 4-year Limited Edition series; collectors can register models with AQHA. Models released early in 1996 were very similar to #497. $18.70.

bottom row
1, 2.) same as top row, 1 (variations of #497).

New for 1997:
499: 1997. *AQHA Offspring of King P-234.* Matte, bay; black points, diamond-shaped star, left hind sock. Number 3 in 4-year Limited Edition series; collectors can register models with AQHA. $14.00.

Indian Pony

Mold #175; introduced in 1970.

Indian Pony
top row
1.) 177: 1970 – 71. *Indian Pony.* Matte, alabaster; light gray mane and tail, red hand print on left haunch, blue square on left neck. In 1972 – 73, this model was also in the Presentation collection, mounted on wooden base. $176.00 ($241.50 Presentation).
2.) 176: 1970 – 72. *Indian Pony.* Matte, buckskin; (dun) brown mane and tail, lower legs, red sun mark on left haunch, blue dots on left side of neck. $162.00.

bottom row
1.) 175: 1970 – 76. *Indian Pony.* Matte, brown pinto; brown mane and tail, gray hooves, spots have soft edges. In 1972 – 73, this model was also in the Presentation collection, mounted on wooden base. $63.00 ($101.50 Presentation).
2.) 174: 1973 – 85. *Indian Pony.* Matte, dark bay appaloosa; very dark bay, black points, blanket pattern over hindquarters. $37.10.

Indian Pony
882: 1993. *Ichilay.* Matte, light gray; darker gray points, red speckle roaning, and Native American symbols. Four designs (all shown). $32.90.

Indian Pony
top row
1.) 929: 1995 – 96. *Cheyenne American Mustang.* Matte, roan; black points, left fore sock, stripe and snip, chestnut shaded head. $20.20.
2.) S 1980: Just About Horses subscriber special. *Indian Pony.* Unpainted. $49.70.

bottom row
1.) S 1994: Export (about 500). *Chinook.* Matte, dark dapple gray; black/dark gray points. $77.00.
2.) S 1988: JC Penney. *English Horse Collector's Set.* Matte, red dun; darker mane and tail, gray knees and hocks, bald face. Included Black Stallion and Justin Morgan S 1988. $39.90.

Indian Pony
top row
1.) S 1987: Black Horse Ranch (333). Matte, bay; black points, hind stockings, bald face. $75.60.
2.) S 1987: Black Horse Ranch (333). Matte, leopard appaloosa; gray points, black spots, stockings. $75.60.

bottom row
1.) S 1987: Black Horse Ranch (250). Matte, gray leopard appaloosa; black/dark gray points, sparsely spotted over most of body. $75.60.
2.) S 1987: Black Horse Ranch (333). Matte, dapple gray; black points, medium to dark gray, large dapples, right hind sock. $79.10.

Indian Pony
top
S 1991: BreyerFest '91 Dinner Model (about 2500). *Mustang Lady, Endurance Champion.* Matte, gray; shaded body, red and white number "brand" along neck, right hind sock, darker points. $95.20.

bottom
S 1994: BreyerFest '94 Judges/Host Model (about 30). Matte, red roan; chestnut points, cream base coat, then chestnut over-dappling. $462.00.

Indian Pony model not shown:
S 1996: PetSmart. *Halayi.* Matte, golden palomino snowflake appaloosa; resist spots on hindquarters only, white mane and tail, stockings, blaze, gray shaded knees, hocks, and muzzle. $38.00.

New for 1997:
986: 1997 – current. *Full Speed, Appaloosa.* Matte, shaded palomino appaloosa; snowflake appaloosa, white mane, tail, socks, and resist type spots on haunches, barrel, shoulders, and face, gray shaded knees, hocks, muzzle, and ears, natural hooves. $15.00.
S 1997: Breyer Breakfast Model. *Sirocco, Breyer Breakfast Tour Horse.* Matte, chestnut pinto. Made for and available at Breyer Tour Stops only; given SR number 700397. $17.00.

Iron Metal Chief, Missouri Fox Trotter

Mold #486; introduced in 1997.

Iron Metal Chief, Missouri Fox Trotter

971:1997 – current. *Iron Metal Chief, Missouri Fox Trotter.* Matte, black; star and stripe, snip, hind socks, blue and yellow ribbons. $17.00.

John Henry

Mold #445; introduced in 1988. Sculpted by Jeanne Mellin Herrick.

John Henry
top row
1.) 445: 1988 – 90. *John Henry.* Matte, dark bay; no markings, gray hooves. $29.40.
2.) 836: 1991 – 93. *Joe Patchen Sire of Dan Patch.* Matte, black; star and stripe, pink shaded muzzle, stockings, pink/natural hooves. $28.00.

bottom row
1.) 961: 1996. *The Cree Indian Horse, Naytukskie-Kukatos.* Matte, bay pinto; extensive white markings, eye spot and "moustache" marking on right side of face, black mane and tail, right foreleg with black hoof and lower leg, other hoofs natural; red cords from feather on right neck and blue zigzag on inner left foreleg. In production 1/96 through 6/96. $22.70.
2.) 961: 1996. *The Cree Indian Horse, Naytukskie-Kukatos.* Matte, bay pinto; extensive white markings, eye spot and "moustache" marking on right side of face, black mane and tail, right foreleg with black hoof and lower leg, other hoofs natural; blue cords from feather on right neck and yellow zigzag on inner left foreleg. In production 7/96 through 12/96. $22.70.

John Henry
top

S 1994: JC Penney. *Western Horse.* Matte, dark bay; black points, socks, natural hooves. $31.50.

bottom

S 1992: Sears. *Quiet Foxhunters Set.* Matte, dark chestnut; darker mane and tail, socks, star and stripe. Set included Roemer and Rugged Lark S 1992. $31.50.

Jumping Horse

Mold #300; introduced in 1965.

Jumping Horse

300: 1965 – 88. *Jumping Horse.* Matte, bay; black mane and tail, bald face, socks, black hooves, later models have solid face and legs, sepia shaded wall with green base. Three variations shown. $34.30.

Jumping Horse
top row

1.) 886: 1994. *Starlight.* Matte, very dark bay; black points, three socks (not right fore), five-point star, brown wall and base. Limited Edition. $36.40.

2.) S 1982 – 83: Sears. Matte, seal brown; black points, diamond star, sepia wall with green base. $74.90.

bottom

S 1991: Just About Horses subscriber special (1000). *Jumping Horse.* Matte, black; socks/stockings, bald/blaze, reddish wall with gray base. $94.50.

Jumping Horse
top

S 1995: QVC (1000). *Jumping Gem Twist.* Matte, alabaster; gray knees, hocks, shaded hooves and tail, slate gray wall and base. $84.00.

bottom

S 1995: BreyerFest '95 Raffle Model (26). *Mystique.* Glossy, gray appaloosa; blanket pattern over hindquarters, small spots, darker points, bald face. $805.00.

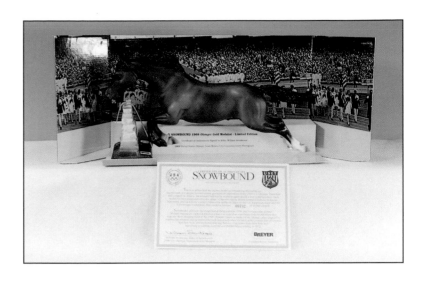

Jumping Horse

S 1996: USET/USOC/Miller's Harness Company (about 5,000). *Snowbound*. Matte, bay; black points, shaded body, triangle star and broad snip, three socks (not left fore), body has some resist dappling; jump base is painted grass green. Made to commemmorate the Olympics (this horse was a 1968 Gold medalist in Mexico City under William Steinkraus). $43.80.

Justin Morgan

Mold #65; introduced in 1973.

Justin Morgan
top row

1.) 65: 1977 – 89. *Justin Morgan*. Matte, red bay; black points. In 1987 catalogs, this was called "Marguerite Henry's Justin Morgan." $28.50.

also 2065: 1973 – 81. *Justin Morgan Gift Set*. Matte, red bay; black points (same as #65). Included paperback copy of Marguerite Henry's "Justin Morgan Had a Horse" and carrying case. $34.00 complete.

2.) 822: 1990 – 92. *Morgan*. Matte, dark bay; black points. $25.90.

bottom row

1.) 878: 1993 – 94. *Double Take*. Matte, dark chestnut; right fore and left hind socks, darker mane and tail, stripe below forelock. $23.10.

2.) 945: 1996 – current. *Tri-Mi Boot Scootin' Boogie*. Matte, black; natural hooves, four high stockings, broad blaze with spots in it. $18.50.

Justin Morgan

S 1988: JC Penney. *English Horse Collector's Set*. Matte, light chestnut; darker mane and tail, shaded knees and hocks, left hind sock. Included Black Stallion (Traditional) and Indian Pony S 1988. $32.90.

Khemosabi

Mold #460; introduced in 1990.

Khemosabi
460: 1990 – 95. *Khemosabi* +++. Matte, red bay; black points, broken blaze, socks, natural hooves. $18.20.

Kipper

Mold #9960; introduced in 1986. Problems with the mold and plastic used mean this mold will likely never be produced in another model.

Kipper
9960: 1986. *Kipper.* Matte, chocolate brown; black hair mane and tail, some may have dapples on hindquarters. This model was derived from Norman Thelwell's cartoon character and made from a softer, rubbery plastic. Pumpkin and Midget were also supposed to be made, but these models were never released. $54.60.

Lady Phase

Mold #40; introduced in 1976.

Lady Phase
top
1.) 3075: 1976 – 85. *Lynn Anderson's Lady Phase Gift Set.* Matte, chestnut; flaxen mane and tail, three socks (not right fore). Set included book about Lynn Anderson and Lady Phase, a blue ribbon, and carrying case. $49.70 complete.
also 40: 1976 – 85. *Lynn Anderson's Lady Phase.* Matte, chestnut; flaxen mane and tail, three socks (not right fore). Same as #3075. $37.80.

bottom row
1.) 860: 1992 – 94. *Family Appaloosa Mare.* Matte, black leopard appaloosa; gray points, stenciled spots. $31.50.
2.) 711: 1988. *Breezing Dixie Famous Appaloosa Mare.* Matte, dark bay appaloosa; black points, star, stenciled white blanket over hips (not touching tail), hand painted eyes, nostrils, and (sometimes) hooves. Limited Edition. $56.70.

Lady Phase
top row
1.) S 1980: Just About Horses subscriber special. *Lady Phase.* Unpainted. $49.70.
2.) S 1980: Model Congress/VaLes (about 400). *Lady Phase.* Matte, buckskin; black points, bald face (200 with pink, 200 with black nose). $91.70.

bottom row
1.) S 1983 – 84: JC Penney (80 – 200). *Buckskin Mare and Foal.* Matte, buckskin; black points, solid face in 1983 then bald face in 84. 1983 Penney catalog shows (incorrectly) a buckskin Running Foal with the Lady Phase, the 1984 catalog shows her with the correct Stock Horse Foal. $77.00.
2.) S 1989: Breyer Signing Party model. Matte, red roan/flea-bit gray; reddish mane, tail, knees, and hocks. $54.60.

Lady Phase
top row
1.) S 1990: JC Penney. *Breyer Traditional Horse Set.* Matte, dapple gray; black points, bald face, dorsal stripe. "Middle Style Quarter Horse"; included Quarter Horse Gelding (palomino) and Rugged Lark (chestnut) S 1990. $46.90.
2.) S 1992: Sears. *Spirit of the West Gift Set.* Matte, dark bay pinto; black points, stenciled blaze, three socks (not left fore). Included Stock Horse Foal S 1992 (pinto). $37.80.

bottom row
1.) S 1992: Black Horse Ranch (1500). *Night Deck.* Matte, black; left hind sock. $37.10.
2.) S 1993: Equitana 93, German Export. *Prairie Flower — Equitana 93.* Matte, bay appaloosa; blanket pattern from mid-barrel back, small spatter spots, four socks, narrow blaze. $74.90.

Lady Phase
top row
1.) S 1993: Toys "R" Us. *Watchful Mare and Foal.* Matte, light shaded gray; light gray points. Given SR number 700593; included Stock Horse Foal S 1993. $33.60.
2.) S 1994: JC Penney. *Horse Salute Gift Set.* Matte, chestnut leopard appaloosa; reddish mane, tail, knees, and hocks, stenciled chestnut spots (same pattern as #860). Included Morganglanz and Phar Lap S 1994. $34.30.

bottom
S 1995: BreyerFest '95 Judges/Host model (about 30). Matte, palomino; shaded muzzle, white mane and tail, hind socks. $581.00.

Lady Roxana

Mold #425; introduced in 1986. Sculpted by Rich Rudish.

Lady Roxana
top row
1.) 425: 1986 – 88. *Lady Roxana.* Matte, alabaster; gray points, hooves; Artist Series. $27.30.
2.) 426: 1988 – 89. *Prancing Arabian Mare.* Matte, chestnut; flaxen mane and tail, three socks (not left fore), gray hooves. $27.30.

bottom row
1.) 3160: 1993. *Proud Mother and Newborn Foal.* Matte, dark chestnut; lighter mane and tail, stockings, natural hooves. Set included Classic Andalusian Foal #3160. $24.50.
2.) 3161: 1993. *Proud Mother and Newborn Foal.* Matte, apricot dun; darker points, left fore sock, gray hooves. Set included Classic Andalusian Foal #3161. $24.50.

Lady Roxana
939: 1996. *Cinnamon, Appaloosa.* Matte, bay appaloosa; blanket pattern (jagged edges), dark spots in blanket, white spots outside of blanket, black points, socks, star. Limited Edition; bottom model is the 1996 Sears version (note the ribbon, and darker body color). $20.30.

Legionario

Mold #68; introduced in 1979.

Legionario
top row
1.) 68: 1979 – 90. *Legionario III.* Matte, alabaster; shaded gray tail, muzzle, hocks and knees, gray and natural hooves. Note brand on left hip. $27.30.
also 3070: 1979 – 81. *Legionario III Gift Set.* Matte, alabaster; same as #68. Set included book "The Andalusian a Rare Breed" and carrying case. $39.90 complete.
2.) 851: 1991 – 92. *Spanish Pride.* Matte, bay; black points, left fore stocking. $29.40.

bottom row
1.) 880: 1993 – 94. *Medieval Knight.* Matte, gray/roan; shaded body, grayish-red points. $25.20.
2.) 918: 1995 – 96. *Promenade Andalusian.* Matte, bay; socks, stripe and white muzzle, brown base of mane and tail with the rest of each white. The 1996 catalog called this "Promenade, Lusitano." $20.20.

Legionario
top row
1.) S 1980: Just About Horses subscriber special. *Legionario*. Unpainted. $49.00.
2.) S 1984: Model Congress, and mail order companies. Matte, chestnut; flaxen mane and tail, stockings. $108.50.

bottom
S 1991: BreyerFest '91 (21). Glossy, Florentine; hind stockings. $931.00.

Legionario
top
S 1985: JC Penney. Flocked, white; white hair mane and tail, black hooves, blue glass eyes. Included Brenda doll in circus costume, white leather bridle, red and white surcingle and crupper, and a red plume that hooked to the bridle. $89.60 ($107.10 complete).

bottom
S 1995: West Coast Model Horse Collector's Jamboree (875). *El Campeador*. Matte, dark dapple gray; black points. came with maroon hang tag with gold foil lettering "JAMBOREE 1995 AD." $79.80.

New for 1997:
977: 1997 – current. *Galant, Lusitano*. Matte, shaded chestnut; darker points, blaze, left front sock. $15.00.
S 1997: Toys "R" Us. *Stardust*. Matte, dapple gray; "polka dot" dapples, white mane and tail, socks, natural hooves, pink muzzle. Medallion Series; given SR number 702597. $16.70.

Llanarth True Briton

Mold #494; introduced in 1994.

Llanarth True Briton
494: 1994 – 96. *Llanarth True Briton, Champion Welsh Cob*. Matte, dark chestnut; darker mane and tail, "C" shaped star, three socks (not right fore), striped hooves. $21.40.

New for 1997:
979: 1997. *Sunny Boy, Welsh Cob*. Matte, shaded palomino; white mane and tail, socks, wide blaze, gray shaded knees, hocks, hooves, and chin. In production 1/97 through 6/97. $15.00.
980: 1997. *Silverton, Welsh Cob*. Matte, shaded steel gray; black points, wide blaze, three socks (not left fore). In production 7/97 through 12/97. $15.00.

Lying Down Foal

Mold #245; introduced in 1969.

Lying Down Foal
top row
1.) 167: 1969 – 73. *Lying Down Foal.* Matte, red roan; over-dapple roaning, solid mane and tail. $56.00.
2.) 166: 1969 – 73, 1975 – 76. *Lying Down Foal.* Matte, buckskin; black lower legs, mane and tail, shaded muzzle. $28.70.
3.) 165: 1969 – 84. *Lying Down Foal.* Matte, black appaloosa; bald face, blanket pattern over hindquarters. $19.60.

bottom row
1.) 245: 1985 – 88. *Lying Down Unicorn.* Matte, alabaster; gray mane, tail, hooves, and beard, gold twisted horn. $23.80.
2.) S 1991: JC Penney. *Adorable Horse Foal Set.* Matte, sorrel; flaxen mane and tail. Included Grazing Foal, Running Foal, and Scratching Foal S 1991. $21.00.

Lying Down Foal
top row
1.) 941: 1996. *Robin & Hot Tamale "H.T."* Matte, chestnut leopard appaloosa; chestnut mane, tail, knees, hocks, and shaded face, chestnut spots on body. Set included Quarter Horse Yearling #941; in production 1/96 through 6/96. $11.70.
2.) 942: 1996. *Bosley Blue & Trusty.* Matte, gray leopard appaloosa; gray mane, tail, knees, hocks, hooves, and shaded face, gray spots on body. Set included Quarter Horse Yearling #942; in production 7/96 through 12/96. $11.70.

bottom row
1.) S 1995: Just About Horses subscriber special (2000). *Buster and Brandi Twin Appaloosa Foal Set.* Matte, bay appaloosa; black points, right hind sock, blaze, blanket over hindquarters. Set included Scratching Foal S 1995. $41.30.
2.) S 1995: JC Penney. *Serenity Set.* Matte, buckskin; dark gray or black points, bald face. Included Grazing Mare S 1995. $19.60.

New for 1997:
1997: Toys "R" Us. *Unicorn IV Black Pearl.* Glossy, white pearl; added horn. Given SR number 702197. $13.70.
1997: Toys "R" Us. *Unicorn IV White Pearl.* Glossy, black; added horn. Given SR number 702297. $13.70.

Man O'War

Mold #47; introduced in 1969.

Man O'War (Traditional)
top row
1, 2.) 47: 1969 – 95. *Man O'War.* Matte, red chestnut; darker mane and tail, diamond on forehead, black halter with gold trim. Some had slate gray hand painted hooves, but usually the hooves were just black or dark gray. In 1972 – 73, this model was also in the Presentation collection, mounted on wooden base. $19.60 ($94.50 Presentation).
3.) 966: 1996 – current. *My Prince, Thoroughbred.* Matte, medium brown chestnut; shaded, darker mane and tail, dark brown halter with gold trim. $20.00.

bottom row
1.) S 1990: Sears. *Race Horse Set.* Glossy, red chestnut; darker mane and tail, diamond on forehead, black halter with gold trim. Included Sham and Secretariat S 1990. $32.90.
2.) S 1991: BreyerFest '91 Raffle Model (21). Glossy, Gold Charm, white diamond star, gray hooves. $784.00.

Marabella, Morgan Broodmare (not shown)

Mold #487; new mold for 1997.

973: 1997 – current. *Marabella, Morgan Broodmare*. Matte, bay; black points, four socks, snip. $15.00.

Midnight Sun, Tennessee Walker

Mold #60; introduced in 1972.

Midnight Sun
top row
1.) 60: 1972 – 87. *Midnight Sun, Tennessee Walker*. Matte, black; natural or gray hooves, red on white braids. $28.70.
2.) 704: 1988 – 89. *Tennessee Walking Horse*. Matte, red bay; black points, red on white braids, gray hooves. $31.50.

bottom
854: 1992. *Memphis Storm*. Glossy, charcoal; white mane and tail, painted eyes with eyewhites, stockings, pink hooves, red on white braids. $39.20.

Midnight Sun
top row
1.) 913: 1995 – 1996. *High Flyer Tennessee Walker*. Matte, chestnut pinto; stockings, blaze, white on blue braids. $21.40.
2.) S 1984: Model Horse Congress (240). Matte, sorrel; flaxen mane and tail, black on red braids. $98.60.

bottom row
1.) S 1996: World Champion Horse Equipment. *Tennesee Walking Horse*. Matte, black; white on red ribbons. $38.20.
2.) S 1996: JC Penney. *Gaited Breeds of America*. Matte, liver chestnut; blaze, lighter belly, red and white ribbons. Set included Five Gaiter and Saddlebred Weanling S 1996. $19.60.

New for 1997:
S 1997: World Champion Horse Equipment (6000). Matte, dark palomino; white mane and tail, hind socks, bi-color eyes, pink on muzzle between nostrils, dark brown on white ribbons. The retailer split this into 1500 numbered, and 4500 plain; given SR number 70109. $31.00.

Misty

Mold #20; introduced in 1972.

Misty
top row
1.) 20: 1972 – current. *Marguerite Henry's Misty*. Matte, palomino pinto; palomino circle around right eye, natural hooves. Variations include double eye circle and glossy finish. Also sold in set #2169 with Stormy. $13.30 ($89.60 glossy, $80.50 double eye circle)
also 2055: 1972 – 81. *Misty Gift Set*. Matte, palomino pinto; same as #20. Set included paperback copy of Marguerite Henry's "Misty of Chincoteague" and carrying case. $35.70 complete.
2.) S 1984: Sears. Flocked, palomino pinto; white hair mane and tail, brown glass eyes. Included flocked Stormy S 1984. $49.00.

bottom row
1.) S 1992: JC Penney (1500). Matte, palomino pinto; cold cast porcelain. $93.10.
2.) 79293: 1993. *Performing Misty*. Glossy, palomino pinto; porcelain Hagen-Renaker, made for and sold through Breyer and other sources. Included 3-legged stool that Misty stood on. $42.00.

Misty Variations
20: *Misty.* Variations in the pinto pattern.

Misty
S 1990: BreyerFest '90 Raffle Model (21). Glossy, Florentine; white mane and tail, bald face, stockings, pink hooves, muzzle, and ears. $910.00.

Misty's Twilight

Mold #470; introduced in 1991.

Misty's Twilight
top row
1.) 470: 1991 – 95. *Misty's Twilight.* Matte, chestnut pinto; white legs, blaze, darker lower half of tail. $21.70.
2, 3.) 950: 1996 – current. *Dover, Trakehner.* Matte, bay; black points, three socks (not left fore), blaze. Color variation shown. $21.10.

bottom row
1.) S 1993: Spiegel. *Dressage Set of Two Horses.* Matte, black; three socks (not right fore), green braids. Included Hanoverian S 1993. $34.30.
2.) S 1996: West Coast Model Horse Collectors Jamboree (1000). *Flabbehoppen, Knabstrupper.* Matte, bay/roan leopard appaloosa; gray knees and hocks, pink hooves, socks, lower half of tail is gray, striped gray mane with red, white, and blue braids, chestnut neck and head, non-stenciled blaze, dark brown spots on body and neck, pink shadings behind elbows and on flank (some models are distinctly lighter or darker than others). Came with white hang tag with gold foil picture of the horse and "JAMBOREE 1996" on it. $55.00.

New for 1997:
S 1997: State Line Tack. *1997 Breyer Horse* (temporary name). Matte, palomino; white mane and tail, blaze, gray shaded muzzle, left socks, SLT brand on right hip. $23.90.

Morgan

Mold #49; introduced in 1965.

Morgan
top row
1, 2.) 49: 1965 – 71. *Morgan.* Matte, bay; most models had bald face, stockings/socks. In the last year of production, some models had star or no markings on face; some of these were apparently made for Morgan Horse shows (solid face variety). $56.00 ($91.00 star version, $157.50 solid face).
3, 4.) 48: 1965 – 87. *Morgan.* Matte, black; stockings/socks, bald face/diamond star, gray hooves. In dealer catalogs, the 1965 – 75 photos showed the bald face version and the 1976 – 87 catalogs showed the diamond star version. $37.10 ($29.40 star version, $70.00 solid face).

bottom row
1.) 948: 1963 – 65. *Morgan.* Matte, woodgrain; no markings. $482.00.
2.) 702: 1988 – 89. *Morgan.* Matte, light bay; black points, gray hooves, star and narrow stripe. $30.10.

Morgan
top row
1.) 831: 1990 – 91. *Show Stance Morgan.* Matte, dark red chestnut; star, right fore sock. $27.30.
2.) 858: 1992 – 93. *Vermont Morgan.* Matte, chocolate sorrel; flaxen mane and tail, stockings, gray hooves. $27.30.

bottom row
1.) 901: 1994 – 95. *Lippitt Pegasus.* Matte, red bay; black points, left hind sock, star. $24.50.
2.) S 1980: Just About Horses subscriber special. *Morgan.* Unpainted. $44.80.

Morganglanz

Mold #59; introduced in 1980.

Morganglanz
top row
1.) 59: 1980 – 87. *Morganglanz.* Matte, chestnut; flaxen mane and tail, stockings, stripe, gray hooves. Note brand on left thigh. $29.40.
2.) 847: 1991 – 95. *Black Beauty 1991.* Matte, black; star or stripe, right front sock; most models had the Trakehner brand removed, on some it remained. $23.80.

bottom
S 1980: Just About Horses subscriber special. *Morganglanz.* Unpainted. $49.00.

Morganglanz
top row
1.) S 1989: JC Penney. *International Equestrian Collector's Set.* Matte, bay; black points, stockings, black hooves. Included Halla and Hanoverian S 1989. $36.40.
2.) S 1993: mid-season release. *Appaloosa Sport Horse.* Matte, leopard appaloosa; gray points, splash spots, shaded face, natural hooves. Included English Saddle; given SR number 700893. $44.80 ($52.50 with saddle).

bottom
S 1994: JC Penney. *Horse Salute Gift Set.* Matte, bay; black points, socks, blaze, pink hooves. Set included Lady Phase and Phar Lap S 1994. $32.20.

Morganglanz
top row
1.) 955: 1996 – current. *Samsung Woodstock, Westphalian.* Matte, chestnut; slightly darker mane and tail, star and blaze, three socks (not right fore), no brand, light gray hooves. $19.80.
2.) S 1995: USET Festival of Champions (1000). *Pieraz (Cash).* Matte, flea-bit gray; white mane and tail, gray shaded muzzle, hooves, and ears. $54.60.

bottom
S 1996: JC Penney. *Swedish Warmblood.* Matte, palomino; white mane and tail, stockings, gray shaded knees, hocks, and hooves. $28.60.

Mustang

Mold #87; introduced in 1961.

Mustang
top row
1.) 85: 1961 – 66. *Mustang.* Glossy, alabaster; light gray mane, tail, and hooves. Photo shows red eye version (earlier models), black-eyed version was produced later. $111.30 ($116.20 red eyes).
2.) 86: 1961 – 66. *Mustang.* Glossy, gray appaloosa; white mane and tail, stockings, bald face, black splash spots. $115.50.

bottom row
1.) 88: 1961 – 70. *Mustang.* Glossy, charcoal; white mane and tail, stockings, bald face. $110.60.
2.) 87: 1961 – 86. *Mustang.* Matte, buckskin; black points, bald face, dorsal stripe on some. $29.40.

Mustang
top
3085: 1963 – 65. *Mustang.* Glossy, Gold Charm; white mane and tail, stockings, bald face, pink muzzle, ears, and hooves. $1,050.00.

bottom
4085: 1963 – 65. *Mustang.* Matte, Wedgewood; white mane and tail, stockings, bald face, pink muzzle, ears, and hooves. Also shown below. $1,050.00.

Mustang
top
2085: 1963 – 65. *Mustang.* Glossy, Florentine; white mane and tail, stockings, bald face, pink muzzle, ears, and hooves. $1,050.00.

bottom
1.) 1085: 1963 – 65. *Mustang.* Glossy, Copenhagen; white mane and tail, stockings, bald face, pink muzzle, ears, and hooves. $1,050.00.
2.) 4085, as described above.

Mustang
top row
1.) 985: 1963 – 66. *Mustang.* Matte, woodgrain; socks, black hooves. $322.00.
2.) 118: 1987 – 89. *American Mustang.* Matte, sorrel; flaxen mane and tail, stockings, gray hooves, darker muzzle. $30.80.

bottom row
1.) 828: 1990 – 91. *Paint American Mustang.* Matte, bay pinto; black points, apron face. $35.70.
2.) 896: 1994 – 95. *Mustang.* Matte, roan; very dark chestnut points, chestnut shading on face and back, blaze. $25.90.

Mustang
top
S 1988: Black Horse Ranch (333). Matte, alabaster; gray mane and tail, very light gray hooves. $77.00.

bottom row
1.) S 1988: Black Horse Ranch (333). Matte, bay appaloosa; black points, blanket pattern over hindquarters, bald/blaze face, chestnut splash spots. $77.00.
2.) S 1988: Black Horse Ranch (333). Matte, leopard appaloosa; black spots, light gray points. $77.00.

Mustang
top
S 1988: Black Horse Ranch (333). Matte, palomino; bald face, stockings, white mane and tail. $77.00.

bottom row
1.) S 1988: Black Horse Ranch (333). Matte, flea-bit gray; medium gray mane and tail, light gray knees and hocks, gray speckles over body. $77.00.
2.) S 1988: Black Horse Ranch (333). Matte, red dun; red mane and tail, bald face, stockings, dorsal stripe. $77.00.

Mustang
top row
1.) 963: 1996 – current. *Baron, Mustang.* Glossy, mahogany bay; black points, right hind sock, natural hooves, blaze. $21.40.
2.) S 1978: Model Congress (200). Semi-gloss, black; no markings. $182.00.

bottom
S 1988: Model Horse Collector's Supply Co. (1000). *Ruby.* Matte, dappled chestnut/red roan; solid chestnut mane and tail, resist dappling, three socks (not right fore), blaze, shaded muzzle. $47.10.

Mustang
top row
1.) S 1992: BreyerFest '92 Dinner Model (about 1700). *Turbo The Wonder Horse.* Matte, palomino; white mane and tail, gray shaded nose, gray hooves, right socks, slightly metallic body color. $77.00.
2.) S 1993: JC Penney. *Wild Horses of America Set.* Semi-gloss, black; left fore sock. Included Foundation Stallion and Fighting Stallion S 1993. $31.50.

bottom row
1, 2.) S 1995: Breyer Tour Model. *Rawhide the Wild Appaloosa Mustang.* Matte, dun roan appaloosa; left hind sock, slightly reddish dark brown points. Color variation shown. $44.10.
3.) S 1996: Equitana USA. *Amerigo.* Matte, palomino pinto; blue eyes, natural hooves, shaded muzzle. $36.40.

Mustang
S 1996: BreyerFest '96 Judges/Host Model (about 30). Glossy, dark dapple gray; black or dark gray mane and tail, socks, bald face/blaze, eyewhites. $475.00.

Nursing Foal

Mold #3155FO; introduced in 1973.

Nursing Foal
top row
1.) 3155: 1973 – 84. *Thoroughbred Mare and Foal Gift Set.* Matte, light chestnut; darker mane and tail. Set included Thoroughbred Mare #3155, and carrying case. $22.40.
2.) 3180: 1994 – current. *Medicine Hat Mare and Foal Gift Set.* Matte, chestnut pinto; darker mane and tail. Set included Thoroughbred Mare #3180. $10.80.
3.) S 1982 – 83: Sears. *Pinto Mare and Suckling Foal.* Matte, bay pinto. Set included Thoroughbred Mare S 1989. $30.10.

bottom row
1.) S 1989 – 90: Sears. *Mare and Foal Set.* Matte, leopard appaloosa; chestnut mane, tail, knees, and hocks. Set included Grazing Mare S 1989. $22.40.
2.) S 1992: JC Penney. *Frisky Foals Set.* Matte, palomino pinto; white mane and tail, blaze. Set included Action Stock Horse Foal, Proud Arabian Foal, and Running Foal S 1992. $19.60.
3.) S 1996: JC Penney. *Pride and Joy.* Matte, light chestnut; socks. Set included Thoroughbred Mare S 1996. $12.00.

Old Timer

Mold #200; introduced in 1966.

Old Timer
top row

1.) 200: 1966 – 76. *Old Timer.* Matte, alabaster; light gray mane and tail, yellow hat with darker band, dark brown/black harness. $37.10.
2.) 205: 1966 – 87. *Old Timer.* Glossy, dapple gray; darker gray mane and tail, matte black/dark brown harness with gold buckles and chain, yellow hat. $39.90.

bottom row

1.) 206: 1988 – 90. *Old Timer.* Matte, bay; black points, right hind sock, blaze, tan hat with red band, brown harness with gold chain and buckles. $30.10.
2.) 834: 1991 – 93. *Old Timer.* Matte, red roan; darker mane and tail, dark hooves, blue hat with a red band. $30.10.

Old Timer
top row

1.) 205: 1966 – 87. *Old Timer.* Glossy, dapple gray; darker gray mane and tail, glossy black/dark brown harness with gold buckles and chain, yellow hat. $38.50.
2.) 935: 1995 – current. *McDuff Old Timer.* Matte, gray appaloosa; blanket pattern with few spots, darker points, white hat with red band. $22.90.

bottom

S 1983: Montgomery Wards. Matte, alabaster; less gray than #200, yellow hat with yellow band. $53.20.

Old Timer

S 1984: liquor company. Matte/semi-gloss, dapple gray; dark brown or black harness, yellow hat with yellow band; model had holes drilled in shoulders for pins from wagon shafts. Included wooden A & P wagon painted red and yellow containing a decanter of bourbon. $70.00 ($136.50 complete).

Pacer

Mold #46; introduced in 1967.

Pacer
top row
1.) 46: 1967 – 87. *Pacer*. Matte/semi-gloss, dark bay; mane and tail are same color or slightly darker, three or four socks, black halter with gold trim, gray hooves. Earlier models had a red-brown halter. $30.80.
2.) 2446: 1982 – 87. *Brenda Breyer and Harness Racing Set*. Matte, alabaster; light gray points. Included Brenda doll in racing silks, plastic sulky, leather harness and bridle; set shown below. $56.00 ($72.10 complete).

bottom row
1.) 819: 1990. *Dan Patch*. Matte/semi-gloss, red bay; black points, star, right hind coronet, natural hooves. Limited Edition. $39.20.
2.) 940: 1996. *Laag, Standardbred*. Matte, light dapple gray; shaded gray, resist dapples, darker knees, hocks, hooves, and muzzle. Commemorative Edition (10,000). $27.20.

Pacer
2446: the complete *Brenda Breyer and Harness Racing Set*.

Pacer
top row
1.) S 1982: Aldens (200). Matte, black; natural hooves. $85.40.
2.) S 1984: Reigseckers (100). Matte, sorrel; flaxen mane and tail, right hind sock. Included Brenda doll in racing silks, plastic sulky, leather harness and bridle. $66.50 ($86.80 complete).

bottom row
1, 2.) S 1981 – 85: Sears. Matte, bay; black points, socks/stockings. Included Brenda doll in racing silks, plastic sulky, leather harness and bridle; color variation shown. $63.00 ($85.40 complete).

Pacer
top row
1.) S 1982 – 83: JC Penney. Matte, light chestnut/sorrel; lighter/flaxen mane and tail, socks/stockings. $91.00.
2.) S 1984: Reigseckers (100). Matte or semi-gloss, dapple gray; darker gray points, stockings. $91.00.

bottom row
1.) S 1984: Reigseckers (100). Matte, palomino; white mane and tail, socks/stockings. $91.00.
2.) S 1995: JC Penney. *Race Horses of America.* Matte, bay; black points, hind socks. Set included Phar Lap and Stock Horse Stallion S 1995. $27.30.

New for 1997:
S 1997: Toys "R" Us and other retailers (7500). *Beat the Wind.* Matte, shaded light gray; gray shaded shoulders, face, hindquarters, legs are gray at joints, mane and tail are gray at ends, dorsal stripe, white snip on face, blue halter. Represents the ideal pacing horse. $27.00.

Phar Lap

Mold #90; introduced in 1985.

Phar Lap
top row
1.) 90: 1985 – 88. *Phar Lap Famous Race Horse.* Matte, red chestnut; reverse "C" shaped star (and other irregular shapes), left hind sock. $30.10.
2.) 803: 1989 – 90. *Galloping Thoroughbred.* Matte, dark bay; black points, faint left hind sock. $27.30.

bottom row
1.) 838: 1991 – 92. *Hobo.* Matte, buckskin; black points, natural hooves, shaded muzzle. $25.90.
2.) 881: 1993 – 94. *Wild American Horse.* Matte, gray dun/grulla; darker mane, tail, and dorsal stripe, star and narrow blaze, socks/stockings, primitive stripes on legs, pink hooves. $23.80.

Phar Lap
top row
1.) 921: 1995 – 96. *Native Diver Champion Thoroughbred.* Matte, black; arrow-shaped star and narrow blaze, right hind coronet band. $17.80.
2.) S 1990: BreyerFest '90 Dinner Model (first BreyerFest). *Dr. Peaches, Three-Day Event Champion.* Matte, bay; star, snip, black points. $102.90.

bottom row
1.) S 1994: JC Penney. *Horse Salute Gift Set.* Matte, dark bay; right fore and left hind socks, black points. Included Lady Phase and Morganglanz S 1994. $28.00.
2.) S 1995: Toys "R" Us. *Dustin.* Matte, buckskin; peachy color, gray-brown points with tri-color mane and tail, large star, socks/stockings, no dorsal stripe. $30.10.

Phar Lap
top row
1.) S 1988: Your Horse Source (500). Matte, red bay; black points, hind socks. $81.90.
2.) S 1988: Your Horse Source (500). Matte, dark chestnut; darker mane and tail. $82.60.

bottom row
1.) S 1988: Your Horse Source (500). Matte, dark dapple gray; darker points, right fore sock, blaze, very small dapples. $92.40.
2.) S 1988: Your Horse Source (500). Matte, sorrel; flaxen mane and tail, socks. $82.60.

Phar Lap
S 1995: JC Penney. *Race Horses of America.* Matte, dapple gray; darker points, hind socks, lighter face with pink on muzzle, hind hooves are natural, front hooves are gray. Set included Pacer and Stock Horse Stallion S 1995. $29.40.

Pluto

Mold #475; introduced in 1991.

Pluto
top row
1.) 475: 1991 – 95. *Pluto the Lipizzaner.* Matte, light gray; shaded mane, tail, muzzle, knees, hocks, and hooves. $22.40.
2.) 956: 1996 – current. *Embajador XI, Andalusian.* Matte, medium dapple gray; lighter face, flank, and tail, darker legs. $20.20.

bottom row
1.) S 1993: Spiegel. Matte, very light dapple gray; darker mane, tail, knees, and hocks, natural hooves. apparently this model is light enough that from a distance it does not appear different than #475. $78.40.
2.) S 1995: Export. *Favory.* Matte, red roan; grayish-chestnut mane and tail, gray knees, hocks, ankles, and hooves, gray shaded muzzle. $72.80.

Polo Pony (shown in Classic Chapter)

This mold, although sometimes listed by collectors with the Traditional scale models, is in the Classic scale. See the Classic Mold Chapter for mold and model descriptions.

Pony of the Americas

Mold #155; introduced in 1976.

Pony of the Americas
top row
1, 2.) 155: 1976 – 80. *Pony of the Americas.* Matte, leopard appaloosa; gray hooves, stenciled chestnut spots; added shoes. The "Six Spot" variation has spots clustered near tail (shown). $32.20 ($48.30 six-spot version).

bottom row
1.) 154: 1979 – 84. *Pony of the Americas.* Matte, bay/chestnut appaloosa; black mane and tail, blanket pattern over hindquarters. $28.70.
2.) 821: 1990 – 92. *Rocky, Champion Connemara Stallion.* Matte, dapple dun; yellowish, with brown shaded body, darker points. $25.20.

Pony of the Americas
top row
1.) 884: 1993 – 94. *Pantomime.* Matte, black appaloosa; blanket over hindquarters and barrel, socks, star and stripe. $18.90.
2.) 876: 1993 – 95. *Just Justin Quarter Pony.* Matte, coffee dun; black points, blaze. $20.30.

bottom row
1.) S 1990 – 91: Country Store. *Three Piece Horse Set.* Matte, black leopard appaloosa; black points, black splash spots. Set included Cantering Welsh Pony and Haflinger S 1990. $30.80.
2.) S 1996: Breyer Show hosts/dealers. *Show Horse, Cream of Tartar.* Matte, palomino blanket appaloosa; white mane and tail, three stockings (not left fore), blaze, gray shaded muzzle, ears, and left front hoof (other hooves natural). Given SR number 700196; came with Certificate of Authenticity. $20.20.

Proud Arabian Foal

Mold #218; introduced in 1956.

Proud Arabian Foal
top row
1.) 9: 1956 – 60. *Arabian Foal.* Glossy, alabaster; black/dark gray points, black/dark gray hooves. $25.20.
2.) 15: 1956 – 60. *Arabian Foal.* Glossy, bay; black mane and tail, blaze. $41.30.
3.) 39: 1956 – 60. *Arabian Foal.* Glossy, gray appaloosa; black/dark gray points, black/dark gray hooves. $94.50.
4.) 218: 1973 – 76, 1978 – 81. *Proud Arabian Foal.* Matte, alabaster; gray mane, tail, and hooves. $15.40.

bottom row
1, 2.) 219: 1973 – 80. *Proud Arabian Foal.* Matte, mahogany bay; black/dark gray points, black/dark gray hooves, various socks (variation shown). $15.40.
3, 4, 5.) 220: 1973 – 88. *Proud Arabian Foal.* Matte, dapple gray; black/dark gray points, black/dark gray hooves, various socks. The 1982 and 1985 – 88 catalogs showed this model with socks and gray points, and in 1983 – 84 showed black points with no socks (variations shown). Apparently the black point version was produced in 1983 only. $15.10.

Proud Arabian Foal

top row

1.) 806: 1989 – 90. *Proud Arabian Foal.* Matte, rose gray; gray points and hooves, stockings. $51.10.
2.) S 1983: JC Penney. *Assorted Mare and Foals Stable Set.* Matte, red bay; black points, narrow blaze. Set included Proud Arabian Mare and Stock Horse Foal S 1983, and Stock Horse Foal (Rough Coat) #29 (Phantom Wings). $19.60.
3.) S 1988: Sears. *Arabian Mare and Foal Set.* Matte, red bay pinto; black points, hind socks. Included Proud Arabian Mare S 1988. $28.70.

bottom row

1.) S 1992: JC Penney. *Frisky Foals Set.* Matte, chestnut/bay; black mane and tail, blaze, one or both hind socks. Set included Action Stock Horse Foal, Running Foal, and Nursing Foal S 1992. $26.60.
2.) S 1996: Sears Wish Book. *Spotted Legacy Gift Set.* Matte, chestnut pinto. Set included Proud Arabian Mare S 1996. $20.30.

New for 1997:

974: 1997 – current. *SS Morning Star, Pinto Half-Arabian.* Matte, bay pinto; darker points, high white stockings, thin star, natural hooves. Represented the daughter of Karma Gypsy (Proud Arabian Mare #948). $8.00.

Proud Arabian Mare

Mold #215; introduced in 1956 (old mold), revised between 1960 and 1971 to new (current) version.

Proud Arabian Mare

top row

1.) 14: 1956 – 60. *Arabian Mare.* Glossy, alabaster; medium gray mane, tail, and hooves; model shown has dark line on lips (commonly called lip liner). Old mold. Also used in night lights (see the Lamps section for an example). $53.20.
2.) 8: 1956 – 60. *Arabian Mare.* Glossy, bay; black mane and tail. Old mold. $80.50.

bottom row

1.) 908: 1956 – 60. *Arabian Mare.* Matte, woodgrain; no markings (markings on model shown were added by previous owner). Old mold. $637.00.
2.) 38: 1959 – 60. *Arabian Mare.* Glossy, gray appaloosa; blanket pattern with splash spots, black points, bald face. Old mold. $252.00.

Proud Arabian Mare

top row

1.) 2155: 1972 – 73. *Proud Arabian Mare Gift Set.* Matte, dapple gray; black/dark gray points, black/dark gray hooves, various socks/stockings. Included blue and white braided halter and carrying case. Early models (1971 – 81) were semi-gloss, and 1982 – 83 catalogs showed black points (although apparently only the 1983 models were produced with them), later models had smaller dapples and dark gray points. $45.50 complete ($84.30 complete with black point version).
also 215: 1971 – 88. *Proud Arabian Mare.* Matte, dapple gray; same as #2155. $25.20 ($72.80 black point version).
2.) 217: 1972 – 76, 1978 – 81. *Proud Arabian Mare.* Matte, alabaster; light gray mane and tail. $25.20.
also 2175: 1972 – 73. *Proud Arabian Mare Gift Set.* Matte, alabaster; same as #217. Included green and white braided halter and carrying case. $44.80.

bottom row

1.) 216: 1972 – 80. *Proud Arabian Mare.* Matte or semi-gloss, mahogany bay; black points, front socks. $30.80.
also 2165: 1972 – 73. *Proud Arabian Mare Gift Set.* Matte, mahogany bay; same as #216. Included red and white braided halter and carrying case. $46.20.
2.) 805: 1989 – 90. *Proud Arabian Mare.* Matte, dappled rose gray; gray muzzle, knees, hocks, and hooves, rose-gray mane and tail, socks. $27.30.

Proud Arabian Mare
top row
1.) 840: 1991 – 92. *Proud Arabian Mare.* Matte, red sorrel; flaxen/lighter mane and tail, stockings, gray hooves. $25.90.
2.) S 1980: Just About Horses subscriber special. *Proud Arabian Mare.* Unpainted. $46.90.

bottom row
1.) S 1983: JC Penney. *Assorted Mare and Foals Stable Set.* Matte, red bay; black points, blaze, gray hooves. Set included Proud Arabian Foal, Stock Horse Foal S 1983, and Stock Horse Foal (Rough Coat) #29 (Phantom Wings). $58.10.
2.) S 1985: Model Horse Congress (about 250). Matte, light chestnut; same color or slightly lighter mane and tail, stockings, gray hooves. $123.00.

Proud Arabian Mare
top row
1.) S 1986: horse shows (about 50). Matte, black; markings varied (number of socks, star, blaze, or bald face). $175.00.
2.) S 1988: Sears. *Arabian Mare and Foal Set.* Matte, red bay pinto; black points, "jigsaw" pinto, left hind sock. Included matching Proud Arabian Foal S 1988. $42.00.

bottom row
1.) S 1991 – 92: Sears. *Arabian Horses of the World Set.* Matte, flea-bit gray; gray points, light chestnut speckles over body, pink hooves. Set included Proud Arabian Stallion and Family Arabian Stallion S 1991. $30.10.
2.) S 1994: Just About Horses subscriber special (1500). *Steel Dust.* Matte, gray; shaded gray, darker points, right hind sock. $78.40.

Proud Arabian Mare
top row
1.) 948: 1996 – current. *Karma Gypsy, Pinto Half-Arab.* Matte, bay pinto; white mane, black tail and hocks, hind socks, black muzzle with white snip, natural hooves (some are striped). $19.40.
2.) S 1995: QVC. *Parade of Breeds.* Matte, bay; black points, right hind sock. Set included Cantering Welsh Pony and Saddlebred Weanling S 1995. $26.60.

bottom
S 1996: Sears Wish Book. *Spotted Legacy Gift Set.* Matte, chestnut pinto. Included Proud Arabian Foal S 1996. $21.30.

Proud Arabian Mare
top
S 1986: Model Horse Congress/Breyer Sponsored Shows (5 – 11). Matte, dark rose gray; darker gray points. $175.00.

bottom
S 1993: BreyerFest '93 Judges/Host Model (about 30). Glossy, Silver Filigree; white mane and tail, socks, bald face, pink shaded muzzle, ears, and hooves. $630.00.

Proud Arabian Stallion
Mold #212; introduced in 1971.

Proud Arabian Stallion
top row
1.) 212: 1971 – 80. *Proud Arabian Stallion.* Matte or semi-gloss, mahogany bay; black points, blaze, two to four socks/stockings, and some models had slightly textured coats. Some variations are shown below. In 1972 – 73, this model was also in the Presentation collection as "Witez II" mounted on wooden base. $30.10 ($95.00 Presentation).
2.) 213: 1972 – 88. *Proud Arabian Stallion.* Matte or semi-gloss, dapple gray; black/dark gray points and hooves, socks. The 1983 – 84 catalogs showed black points (these were actually produced for only about six months in 1983); other catalogs showed dark or medium gray points, and various socks. $105.00 ($227.50 black point version).

bottom row
1.) 211: 1971 – 76, 1978 – 81. *Proud Arabian Stallion.* Matte, alabaster; light gray mane, tail, hooves. $28.00.
2.) 804: 1989 – 90. *Proud Arabian Stallion.* Matte, dapple rose gray; rose-gray mane and tail, gray muzzle, knees, hocks, and hooves. $28.70.

Proud Arabian Stallion Variations
212: *Proud Arabian Stallion* marking variations.

Proud Arabian Stallion
top row
1.) 839: 1991 – 94. *Proud Arabian Stallion*. Matte, light dapple gray; gray mane and tail, socks, shaded muzzle. $25.20.
2.) 933: 1995 – 96. *Sundown Proud Arabian Stallion*. Matte, sorrel; flaxen mane and tail, socks, shaded muzzle, snip. $20.00.

bottom row
1.) S 1980: Just About Horses subscriber special. *Proud Arabian Stallion*. Unpainted. $49.70.
2.) S 1983 – 84: JC Penney. *Arabian Stallion with English Tack Set*. Matte, bay; black points, various socks/stockings, bald or blaze, or more rarely a star. Included leather bridle and English saddle. $58.80 ($73.50 complete).

Proud Arabian Stallion
top
S 1991 – 92: Sears. *Arabian Horses of the World*. Matte, bay; black points, three socks (not right fore), blaze. Set included Family Arabian Stallion and Proud Arabian Mare S 1991. $42.00.

bottom
S 1984: Montgomery Ward. Flocked, bay; three socks (not left hind), blaze, black points, glass eyes. Came with halter and lead. $65.10 ($76.30 complete).

Proud Arabian Stallion
top row
1.) S 1987: Black Horse Ranch (333). Matte, red bay; black points, pink nose, or snip. $70.70.
2.) S 1987: Black Horse Ranch (333). Matte, black; stockings. $70.70.

bottom
S 1987: Black Horse Ranch (333). Matte, sorrel; orangish body color with lighter mane and tail, gray hooves. $70.70.

Proud Arabian Stallion model not shown:
19841: 1984. *Open Top Buggy*. Flocked, chestnut; three socks (not left hind), chestnut hair mane and tail, black hooves. Part of the Miniature Collection. Came with Riegseckers cart; also sold through Montgomery Ward. $227.50.

New for 1997:
972: 1997. *Freedom, the Legend of the Bloody Shoulder Arabian*. Matte, flea-bit gray; chestnut speckles with chestnut blotch on shoulder, gray shaded face and hooves. Commemorative Edition (10,000). $16.00.

Quarter Horse Gelding

Mold #98; introduced in 1959.

Quarter Horse Gelding
top row

1.) 99: 1959 – 66. *Quarter Horse.* Glossy, bay; black points, black/dark brown halter, broken blaze, most have eyewhites. Also used in night lights. $104.30.
2.) 98: 1961 – 80. *Quarter Horse.* Matte, buckskin; black points, black/dark brown halter, most without dorsal stripe. $30.80.

bottom row

1.) 999: 1963 – 65. *Quarter Horse.* Matte, woodgrain; broken blaze, stockings, black halter and hooves. $168.00.
2.) 97: 1971 – 80. *Appaloosa Gelding.* Matte, chestnut appaloosa; black/dark brown halter, broken blaze, front stockings/socks, blanket pattern over hindquarters with splash spots. Some variations have no socks. $30.10.

Quarter Horse Gelding

S 1984: mail order companies (less than 30?). *Quarter Horse Gelding.* Matte, bay (chestnut); Some might have been flocked, *very* few actually made it into the hands of collectors. $150.50.

Quarter Horse Gelding
top row

1.) 924: 1995 – 96. *Majesty Quarter Horse.* Matte, light dapple gray; sparsely dappled using resist method, socks, black halter, white mane and tail, darker knees and hocks. $20.30.
2.) S 1987: mail order companies (1400). Matte, chestnut; darker mane and tail, black halter, white legs. $32.90.

bottom row

1.) S 1989. *Silver.* Matte, gray; slate gray, black points, black halter, painted eyes, nostrils, gray or black hooves. This was the first Commemorative Edition (numbered), but was not shown in catalogs (5000). $48.30.
2.) S 1990: JC Penney. *Breyer Traditional Horse Set.* Matte, palomino; white mane and tail, bald face, stockings, brown halter. "Early Style Quarter Horse"; set included Lady Phase (dapple) and Rugged Lark S 1990. $31.50.

Quarter Horse Yearling
Mold #101; introduced in 1970.

Quarter Horse Yearling
top row
1.) 101: 1970 – 80. *Quarter Horse Yearling.* Matte, liver chestnut; crooked blaze, hind socks or all stockings, gray hooves. Some chalkies made. $28.70.
2, 3.) 102: 1970 – 80. *Quarter Horse Yearling.* Matte, palomino; crooked blaze, lighter mane and tail, stockings, gray hooves. Color variation shown. In 1972 – 73 was also in Presentation collection, mounted on wooden base. $28.70 ($103.60 Presentation).

bottom
103: 1971 – 88. *Appaloosa Yearling.* Matte, sandy bay appaloosa; darker or black mane and tail, crooked blaze, blanket pattern over hindquarters with splash spots. $28.00.

Quarter Horse Yearling
top row
1.) 927: 1995. *Thunder Bay Quarter Horse.* Matte, dark bay; socks, diamond star, black points, striped hooves. Some models do not have striped hooves. $21.00.
2.) 937: 1995 – 96. *Calypso Quarter Horse.* Matte, dun; darker red-brown mane and tail, red shaded knees, hocks and ankles, narrow blaze, left hind stocking. $18.40.

bottom row
1.) 941: 1996. *Robin & Hot Tamale "H.T."* Matte, chestnut semi-leopard appaloosa; darker mane and tail, three socks (not right fore), spots on body, blaze. Set included matching Lying Down Foal #941. $15.10.
2.) 942: 1996. *Bosley Blue & Trusty.* Matte, gray semi-leopard appaloosa; darker mane and tail, three socks (not right fore), spots on body, blaze. Set included matching Lying Down Foal #942. $15.10.

Quarter Hourse Yearling
top row
1.) S 1989: Just About Horses subscriber special (1500). *Quarter Horse Yearling.* Matte, black roan; black points, gray speckles over body. $60.20.
2.) S 1992: BreyerFest '92 Raffle Model (21). Matte, buckskin; black points, dorsal stripe, left hind sock. This model was made in honor of Marney J. Walerius, after her death. Marney worked with Breyer for many years to help them choose new colors, and this was one she wanted to see on her favorite mold. $672.00.

bottom
S 1993: JC Penney. *Breyer Three Generations Appaloosa Set.* Matte, bay appaloosa; black points, hind socks, blanket pattern with splash spots. Set included Adios and Stock Horse Foal (Rough Coat) S 1993. $28.00.

Race Horse

Mold #36; introduced in 1954. The two models made from this mold are made from a different, harder, more brittle plastic than the vast majority of Breyer models.

Race Horse
top
36: 1954 – 66/67. *Derby Winner Race Horse.* Glossy, chestnut; bald face and stockings, black halter and hooves; came with brown hard plastic saddle. $77.00.

bottom
936: 1959 – 65. *Race Horse.* Matte, woodgrain; socks, star, black hooves and, black halter. $147.00.

Rearing Stallion (shown in Classic Chapter)

This mold, although always listed by Breyer Animal Creations with the Traditional scale models, is in the Classic scale. See the Classic Chapter for mold and model descriptions.

Roemer

Mold #465; introduced in 1990.

Roemer
top row
1.) 465: 1990 – 93. *Roemer Dutch Warmblood.* Matte, dark chestnut; blaze and white chin, stockings, pink hooves. $25.90.
2.) 900: 1994 – 95. *Vandergelder, Dutch Warmblood.* Matte, bay; black points, gray hooves. $23.10.

bottom row
1.) S 1992: Sears. *Quiet Foxhunters Set.* Matte, seal bay/brown; black points, diamond star, three socks (not left fore). Set included John Henry and Rugged Lark S 1992. $29.40.
2.) S 1994: mid-season release. *Domino.* Matte, black pinto; high stenciled stockings, ½ white tail, broken stripe. Included black leather dressage saddle, and quilted saddle blanket. $48.30.

Roy the Belgian

Mold #455; introduced in 1989. Sculpted by Francis Eustis, a breeder of (and authority on) Belgians.

Roy the Belgian
top row
1.) 455: 1989 – 90. *Roy, Belgian Drafter.* Matte, sorrel/light chestnut; flaxen mane and tail, socks, gray hooves, shaded muzzle. $32.20.
2.) 837: 1991 – 93. *Belgian Brabant.* Matte, gray dun; base color gray with chestnut shading, darker points. $28.70.

bottom row
1.) 953: 1996 – current. *Sebastian, Percheron.* Matte, gray roan; gray mane and tail, chestnut shaded knees, hocks, and face, three socks (not right hind), speckles all over. $21.20.
2.) S 1992: Sears. *Drafters Set.* Matte, chocolate sorrel; flaxen mane and tail, socks, gray hooves, broad blaze. Set included Belgian and Shire S 1992. $30.80.

Rugged Lark

Mold #450; introduced in 1989. Sculpted by Pam Talley Stoneburner.

Rugged Lark
top row
1.) 450: 1989 – 95, 1997. *Rugged Lark Champion American Quarter Horse Stallion.* Matte, bay; black points. The 1997 re-release was to celebrate Rugged Lark receiving the 1996 Silver Spur Award. $19.60.
2.) 958: 1996. *Little Andy Wind "Bo Diddley" Quarter Horse.* Matte, chestnut; gray hooves and shaded muzzle, stripe. $18.40.

bottom row
1.) S 1990: JC Penney. *Breyer Traditional Horse Set.* Matte, red chestnut; darker mane and tail, left hind stocking, blaze, gray hooves. "Modern style" Quarter Horse. Set included Quarter Horse Gelding and Lady Phase S 1990. $27.30.
2.) S 1992: Sears. *Quiet Foxhunters Set.* Matte, dappled gray; shaded gray, small dapples, bald face, darker points. Included Roemer and John Henry S 1992. $30.10.

Running Foal

Mold #130; introduced in 1963.

Running Foal 1
top row
1.) 1130: 1963 – 65. *Running Foal.* Glossy, Copenhagen; white points, bald face, pink hooves, muzzle, and ears. $560.00.
2.) 2130: 1963 – 65. *Running Foal.* Glossy, Florentine; white points, bald face, pink hooves, muzzle, and ears. $560.00.

bottom row
1.) 3130: 1963 – 65. *Running Foal.* Glossy, Gold Charm; white points, bald face, pink hooves, muzzle, and ears. $560.00.
2.) 4130: 1963 – 65. *Running Foal.* Matte, Wedgewood; white points, bald face, pink hooves, muzzle, and ears. $560.00.

Running Foal 2
top row
1.) 131: 1963 – 70. *Running Foal.* Matte, smoke; white points, bald face. $30.10.
2.) 130: 1963 – 71. *Running Foal.* Matte, alabaster; gray mane, tail, and hooves. $29.40.
3.) 133: 1963 – 73. *Running Foal.* Glossy, dapple gray; bald face, right hind stocking, dapples mostly on hindquarters (gives appearance of gray blanket appaloosa). Variations include more stockings and more dapples. $30.10.

bottom row
1.) 134: 1963 – 87. *Running Foal.* Matte, bay/chestnut; black mane, tail, and hooves, stockings, bald face. $15.40.
2.) 849: 1991 – 93. *Running Foal.* Matte, chestnut pinto; flaxen mane and tail, left socks, star. $16.10.

Running Foal
top row
1.) 865: 1992 – 94. *Bluegrass Foal.* Matte, blue roan; black points. $16.10.
2.) 903: 1994 – 95. *Little Bub.* Matte, red bay; black points, black hooves. $15.10.

bottom
970: 1996 – current. *Korinth, Buckskin Foal.* Matte, light buckskin; black points, left fore and right hind socks, shaded muzzle, bald face. $13.30.

Running Foal
top row
1.) S 1982: Model Horse Congress (200). Matte, red roan; over-dappled type, chestnut mane, tail, legs. $134.50.
2.) S 1983: Mail Order (200). Matte, dapple gray; gray mane and tail, socks. Included Running Mare S 1983. $112.00.

bottom row
1.) S 1983: JC Penney (about 25). Matte, buckskin; black points, bald face. This was apparently shown incorrectly in the JC Penney catalog, so very few were actually made. $231.00.
2.) S 1984: Sears. *Running Horse Family Set.* Matte, bay; black points, dark gray or black hooves. Set included bay Black Beauty (Traditional) and Running Mare S 1984. $26.60.

Running Foal
top row
1.) S (year unknown): source unknown. Glossy, dapple gray; dapples all over, white mane and tail, pink hooves and shaded muzzle. Included Running Mare. $39.40.
2.) S 1987: Sears. Matte, dapple gray; white mane and tail, pink hooves and shaded muzzle. $22.40.
3.) S 1991: JC Penney. *Adorable Horse Foal Set.* Matte, rose gray; dark rose gray, darker mane, tail, hooves. Set included Grazing Foal, Lying Down Foal, and Scratching Foal S 1991. $20.30.

bottom row
1.) S 1992: JC Penney. *Frisky Foals Set.* Matte, black appaloosa; stockings, star and snip, blanket pattern on hindquarters with splash spots. Set included Action Stock Horse Foal, Proud Arabian Foal, and Nursing Foal S 1992. $18.90.
2.) S 1994: JC Penney. *Spirit of the East.* Matte, soft gray; light gray knees and hocks, striped mane and tail, pink shaded muzzle. Included Running Mare S 1994. $18.20.

Running Foal model (shown in Clocks and More Chapter):
930: 1963 – 65. *Running Foal.* Woodgrain; no markings. $91.70.

Flocked Running Mares and Foals
top row
1.) S 1985: JC Penney. *Fanciful Mare and Pony Set.* (Running Foal) Flocked, white; pink hair mane and tail, pink hooves. Included Running Mare S 1985 and brush. $40.60.
2.) S 1985: JC Penney. *Fanciful Mare and Pony Set.* (Running Mare) Flocked, white; pink mane and tail. Included Running Foal S 1985. $73.50.

bottom row
1.) S 1984: JC Penney. *Collector's Mare and Foal Set.* (Running Mare) Flocked, palomino; white hair mane and tail, blaze, stockings. Included Running Foal S 1984. $73.50.
2.) S 1984: JC Penney. *Collector's Mare and Foal Set.* (Running Foal) Flocked, palomino; white hair mane and tail, blaze, stockings. Included Running Mare S 1984 and brush. $39.20.

Running Mare

Mold #120; introduced in 1961.

Running Mare
top row
1.) 124: 1961 – 87. *Running Mare.* Matte or semi-gloss, bay/chestnut; black mane, tail and hooves, bald face, stockings; some have eyewhites. $23.10.
2.) 121: 1961 – 70. *Running Mare.* Matte, smoke/charcoal; white points, bald face, gray hooves, pink shaded muzzle. Color can vary from medium charcoal to very dark gray. $42.00.

bottom row
1.) 123: 1963 – 73. *Running Mare.* Glossy, dapple gray; gray mane and tail, bald face, stockings, most with dapples only on hindquarters. $50.40.
2.) 120: 1961 – 72. *Running Mare.* Matte, alabaster; light gray mane, tail, and hooves. $38.20.

Running Mare
top row
1, 2.) 920: 1963 – 65. *Running Mare.* Woodgrain; no markings, color varied light to dark (both shown). Also used on lamps. $175.00.

bottom
119: 1971 – 73. *Running Mare.* Matte, red roan; overdappled roaning, chestnut mane, tail, and legs. $84.00.

Running Mare
top row
1.) 3120: 1963 – 64. *Running Mare.* Glossy, Gold Charm; white points, bald face, pink hooves, muzzle, and ears. $959.00.
2.) 2120: 1963 – 64. *Running Mare.* Glossy, Florentine; white points, bald face, pink hooves, muzzle, and ears. $959.00.

bottom row
1.) 1120: 1963 – 64. *Running Mare.* Glossy, Copenhagen; white points, bald face, pink hooves, muzzle, and ears. $959.00.
2.) 4120: 1963 – 64. *Running Mare.* Matte, Wedgewood; white points, bald face, pink hooves, muzzle, and ears. $959.00.

Running Mare
top row
1.) 848: 1991 – 93. *Running Mare.* Matte, chestnut pinto; flaxen mane and tail, three stockings (not left hind), blaze on lower face only, tail tip is chestnut. $24.50.
2.) 902: 1994 – 95. *Wild Diamond.* Matte, bay; black points, hind socks. $21.70.

bottom
969: 1996 – current. *Karinthia, Buckskin Mare.* Matte, light buckskin; black points, three socks (not right hind), bald face, shaded muzzle. $19.40.

Running Mare
top row
1.) S 1979: JC Penney. Matte, buckskin; black points. Never officially released. $378.00.
2.) S 1982: Montgomery Wards. Matte, palomino; white mane and tail, stockings, gray hooves. Included leather bridle and English saddle. $108.50 ($126.00 complete).

bottom row
1.) S 1982: Model Horse Congress (200). Matte/semi-gloss, red roan; overdappled roaning, chestnut points. This version tended to have smaller dapples and a creamier base color. $98.00.
2.) S 1983: mail order companies (200). Matte, dapple gray; gray mane and tail, socks. Included Running Foal S 1983. $170.10.

Running Mare
top row
1.) S 1984: Sears. *Running Horse Family Set.* Matte, bay; black points. Set included bay Black Beauty (Traditional) and Running Foal S 1984. $47.60.
2.) S 1987: Sears. Matte, light dapple gray; white mane and tail, stockings, bald face. Included Running Foal S 1987. $46.20.

bottom row
1.) S 1994: JC Penney. *Spirit of the East.* Matte, soft gray; gray knees, hocks, ankles, mane, and tail (striped mane and tail), pink shaded muzzle. Included Running Foal S 1994. $30.80.
2.) S 1995: State Line Tack. *Special Delivery.* Matte, dark bay; black points, stockings, blaze, SLT painted brand on left hip. $40.60.

Running Stallion

Mold #210; introduced in 1968.

Running Stallion
top row
1.) 125: 1968 – 71. *Running Stallion.* Matte, alabaster; gray hooves; some have various pink or gray shadings on muzzle and stallion parts. $108.50.
2.) 126: 1968 – 71. *Running Stallion.* Glossy, charcoal; white points, and bald face. $158.50.

bottom row
1.) 128: 1968 – 74. *Running Stallion.* Matte, red roan; over-dappled roaning, natural hooves, reddish mane and tail. $87.50.
2.) 127: 1968 – 81. *Running Stallion.* Matte, black appaloosa; bald face, blanket over hindquarters with splash spots. $30.10.

Running Stallion
top row
1.) 129: 1971 – 76, 1978 – 80. *Running Stallion.* Matte, bay/chestnut; black mane and tail, bald face, stockings. $32.20.
2.) 879: 1993 – 94. *Rumbling Thunder.* Semi-gloss, dark dapple gray; black points. $26.60.

bottom
928: 1995 – 96. *Lone Star.* Matte, light dapple rose gray; dapples mostly on hindquarters, shoulders, and face; the gray has a pale rosy-tan cast to it. $22.90.

Running Stallion

top row

1.) S 1988: Just About Horses subscriber special (1500). *Running Stallion.* Matte, sorrel; flaxen mane and tail. Numbered. $80.50.
2.) S 1989: Black Horse Ranch (about 150). Matte, dark chestnut; black mane and tail, stockings. $87.50.

bottom row

1.) S 1990: Sears. *Appaloosa American Classic Set.* Matte, palomino appaloosa; stenciled blanket, spots, blaze or bald white face. Set included Appaloosa Performance Horse and Stud Spider S 1990. $40.60.
2.) S 1996: Breyer Tour Model. *Mighty Buck.* Matte, buckskin; black points, three socks (not left fore), bald face, shaded muzzle. Made for Breyer Tour events only. $26.30.

Running Stallion (Unicorns)

top row

1.) 210: 1982 – 88. *Unicorn.* Matte, alabaster; silver gray beard, mane, and tail, gold striped horn, gray hooves. Some had shaded gray muscles. $42.70.
2.) S 1985: JC Penney. *Sky Blue Unicorn.* Flocked, turquoise blue; added horn, blue hair mane and tail, brown glass eyes, some glitter across back. Included brush. $63.70 ($69.30 complete).

bottom row

1.) S 1994: Toys "R" Us. *Unicorn.* Matte, alabaster; silver beard, mane, and tail, silver on horn, gray hooves. $37.10.
2.) S 1995: Toys "R" Us. *Unicorn II.* Glossy, black; gold beard, and gold accented mane, tail, and horn. $35.00.

Saddlebred Weanling

Mold #62; introduced in 1973.

Saddlebred Weanling

top row

1.) 62: 1973 – 80. *Saddlebred Weanling.* Matte, chestnut; same color or slightly darker mane and tail, usually three socks (not right hind), blaze, gray hooves. Variations on socks (four) are known, as well as many variations on the blaze. $36.40.
2.) 701: 1985 – 87. *Collector's Rocking Horse.* Flocked, chestnut; four white socks, blaze, hair mane and tail, brown glass eyes, leather bridle, black hooves, yellow molded rocker. $85.40.

bottom row

1.) 818: 1990. *Saddlebred Weanling.* Matte, palomino/light chestnut pinto; white legs, mane, tail, narrow blaze. Commemorative Edition (5000), numbered. $70.00.
2.) 915: 1995 – 96. *Kentuckiana Saddlebred Weanling.* Matte, dark chestnut; sparsely resist dappled, three stenciled stockings (not left hind), striped hooves, wide blaze over muzzle. $17.80.

Saddlebred Weanling
top row
1.) S 1980: Just About Horses subscriber special. *Saddlebred Weanling.* Unpainted. $51.10.
2.) S 1984: Just About Horses (1000). *Saddlebred Weanling.* Matte, sorrel; flaxen mane and tail, stockings, star, gray hooves. $161.00.

bottom row
1.) S 1991: Breyer Signing Party Model. *Raven.* Semi-gloss, "plum" black; diamond star (variations can have a vague star or no star), look for the purplish hue from the different colored layers of paint. Given SR number 701091. $32.20.
2.) S 1992: Sears. *Future Champions Set.* Matte, bay pinto; black tail streaked with white. Included Brenda doll in show outfit, and leather halter and lead. $32.90 ($41.30 complete).

Saddlebred Weanling
top row
1.) S 1985: JC Penney. *My Companion Rocking Horse.* Flocked, white; pink hair mane and tail, glass eyes, pink rockers to make into rocking horse. Included brush, pink leather reins and saddle. $98.00 ($98.70 complete).
2.) S 1985: JC Penney. *My Favorite Rocking Horse.* Flocked, purple; lavender hair mane and tail, glass eyes, purple rockers to make into rocking horse. Included brush, dark purple leather reins and saddle. $98.00 ($98.70 complete).

bottom
S 1985: Sears. *Our Rocking Horse.* Flocked, black appaloosa; black hair mane and tail, blue glass eyes, black rockers to make into rocking horse. Included black leather reins and saddle. $98.00 ($98.70 complete).

Saddlebred Weanling
top
S 1995: QVC. *Parade of Breeds.* Matte, alabaster; light gray mane, tail, and shaded muzzle, slightly darker hooves. Set included Cantering Welsh Pony and Proud Arabian Mare S 1995. $25.20.

bottom
S 1996: JC Penney. *Gaited Breeds of America.* Matte, palomino; white mane and tail, star. Set included Five Gaiter and Midnight Sun S 1996. $20.00.

New for 1997:
982: 1997 – current. *Burnt Sienna, American Saddlebred Weanling.* Matte, red roan; speckled roaning, darker points and head, hind socks, bald face. $14.00.

San Domingo

Mold #67; introduced in 1978.

San Domingo

top row

1.) 67: 1978 – 87. *San Domingo.* Matte, chestnut pinto; mostly white, chestnut medicine hat, natural hooves. $28.00.
2.) 703: 1988 – 89. *Blanket Appaloosa.* Matte, dark gray appaloosa; darker/black points, blanket over hindquarters and half of barrel with splash spots. $28.70.

bottom row

1.) 829: 1990 – 92. *Comanche Pony.* Matte, palomino; white mane and tail, stockings, gray shaded muzzle. $27.30.
2.) 871: 1993. *Domino, The Happy Canyon Trail Horse.* Matte, black/dark gray pinto; black mane and tail, right eye is blue, left eye is tri-colored, natural hooves. Commemorative Edition (7500); numbered. $43.40.

San Domingo

top row

1.) 917: 1995 – 96. *Oxydol Rodeo Appaloosa.* Matte, alabaster; gray mottled muzzle, pink/natural hooves. $18.00.
2.) S 1985: Montgomery Ward. *Black Gold.* Matte/semi-gloss, black; no markings, natural hooves. $94.50.

bottom row

1.) S 1988: Model Horse Collectors Supply Co. (1000). *Wildfire.* Matte, chestnut pinto; very wild pinto pattern; white mane, dark chestnut tail. $60.90.
2.) S 1987: JC Penney. *Traditional Western Horse Collector Set.* Matte, bay; black mane, tail, knees, and hocks, hind stockings. Set included Adios and Foundation Stallion S 1987. $48.30.

San Domingo

top

S 1991: BreyerFest '91 Raffle Model (21). Glossy, Copenhagen; dapple blue, even on mane and tail, and smaller dapples on legs, gray hooves. $875.00.

bottom row

1.) S 1991: Sears (1000). *Spotted Bear.* Matte to semi-gloss, black pinto; cold cast porcelain; mostly white with dark gray patches, either hand painted or airbrushed, medicine hat pattern. $105.00.
2.) S 1994: BreyerFest '94 Dinner Model (2300+). *Bright Zip.* Matte, chestnut appaloosa; most of barrel has blanket, with white resist spots on shoulders/neck, and dark chestnut spots over most of body. $83.30.

New for 1997:

990: 1997. *Dakotah Indian Horse — "Thunder" Waykinyan Hoton.* Matte, black pinto; blaze, striped hooves, white lightning mark on cheek near throat. In production 1/97 through 6/97 only. $15.00.

991: 1997. *Dakotah Indian Horse — "Lightning" Waykinyan.* Matte, light bay/red dun pinto; darker points, blaze, striped hooves, red lightning mark on cheek near throat. In production 7/97 through 12/97 only. $15.00.

Scratching Foal

Mold #169; introduced in 1970.

Scratching Foal
top row
1.) 169: 1970 – 71. *Scratching Foal.* Matte, liver chestnut; darker or black mane and tail, various stockings. $88.20.
2.) 170: 1970 – 73. *Scratching Foal.* Matte/semi-gloss, red roan; overdappled roaning, chestnut points. $63.00.
3.) 168: 1970 – 86. *Scratching Foal.* Matte, black appaloosa; bald face, blanket pattern over hindquarters, some with solid black legs, some with stockings. $22.40.

bottom row
1.) S 1991: JC Penney. *Adorable Horse Foal Set.* Matte, alabaster; light gray mane, tail, knees and hocks. Set included Grazing Foal, Lying Down Foal, and Running Foal S 1991. $19.60.
2.) S 1995: Just About Horses subscriber special (2000). *Buster and Brandi Twin Appaloosa Foal Set.* Matte, bay appaloosa; blanket over most of barrel, right hind sock, blaze. Included Lying Down Foal S 1995. $39.90.

Sea Star

Mold #16; introduced in 1980.

Sea Star
top row
1.) 16: 1980 – 87. *Marguerite Henry's Sea Star.* Matte, dark chestnut; star, black hooves, darker mane and tail. This model was also included in set #2169 (Misty and Stormy). $12.60.
2.) 845: 1991 – 93. *Chincoteague Foal.* Matte, buckskin; gray-brown points, stripes on forelegs, star. $11.20.

bottom row
1.) 893: 1994 – current. *Scribbles Paint Horse Foal.* Matte, chestnut pinto; darker chestnut points, stripe, stockings, pink hooves. $11.20.
2.) S 1995: Toys "R" Us. *Geronimo and Cochise.* Matte, bay appaloosa; dark brown/black points, socks, white tail tip. Included Kelso (Classic) S 1995. $11.90.

New for 1997:
985: 1997 – current. *Sure Fire, Pinto.* Matte/semi-gloss, black pinto; minimal pinto, high white stockings, blaze, natural hooves. $5.00.

Secretariat

Mold #435; introduced in 1987.

Secretariat
top row
1.) 435: 1987 – 95. *Secretariat.* Matte, chestnut; star and strip, three socks (not left fore), darker mane and tail. $20.30.
2.) S 1990: Sears. *Race Horse Set.* Glossy, chestnut; three socks (not left fore), narrow stripe. Included Sham and Man O'War S 1990. $36.40.

bottom

S 1990: Breyer Signing Party model (3500). Glossy, Gold Charm; gold mane and tail, white narrow stripe, three socks (not left fore). $39.20.

Secretariat

top row

1.) S 1990: German Export. *Bermese, Her Majesty the Queen's Horse.* Matte, black; no markings. SR number 700435. $105.00.
2.) S 1992: Sears (less than 1000). *Secretariat.* Matte, chestnut; cold cast porcelain; three socks (not left fore) and narrow stripe. Numbered. $119.00.

bottom

S 1996: State Line Tack. *Irish Warrior.* Semi-gloss, black; three socks (not left fore) and narrow stripe. $30.00.

New for 1997:

S 1997: Breyer Spring Show Horse. *King of Hearts.* Matte, bay blanket appaloosa; black points, stripe, right front sock. Made for dealers who sponsor a Breyer show day (in production 2/97 through 7/97 only); given SR number 700197. $15.00.

Sham

Mold #410; introduced in 1984. Sculpted by Rich Rudish; this model was the first in the Artist Series.

Sham

top row

1.) 410: 1984 – 88. *Marguerite Henry's Sham.* Matte, red bay; black points, some had "wheat ear" on model's chest, and white spot on back of right ankle. In some catalogs it was called "Sham the Godolphin Arabian." $30.80.
 also S 1995: QVC. *Sham the Godolphin Arabian.* Matte, bay; same as #410, except it has '95 stamped on inner hind leg. $35.00.
2.) 411: 1988 – 89. *Prancing Arabian Stallion.* Matte, flea-bit gray; light gray points, shaded face, socks/stockings, pink/natural hooves. $29.40.

bottom row

1.) 812: 1989 – 91. *Prancing Arabian Stallion.* Matte, palomino; three socks (not left hind), white mane and tail, shaded gray muzzle, gray hooves. $27.30.
2.) 863: 1992 – 93. *Rana.* Matte, dark gray; grayish tan mane and tail, grayish-brown body color, stockings. $25.20.

Sham

top row

1.) 3162: 1994. *Arabian Stallion & Frisky Foal.* Matte, bay; resist dappled, black points. Included Classic Arabian Foal #3162; in production 1/94 through 6/94. $25.20.
2.) 3163: 1994. *Arabian Stallion & Frisky Foal.* Matte, bay-going-gray; dappled, black points. Included Classic Arabian Foal #3163; in production 7/94 through 12/94. $25.20.

bottom row

1.) S 1990: Sears. *Race Horse Set.* Glossy, red bay; white spot on back of right ankle. Included Secretariat and Man O'War (glossy chestnut) S 1990. $35.70.
2.) S 1991: JC Penney (less than 3000). *Galaxias.* Matte, dappled gray; cold cast porcelain; black points, hind socks. Dapples can be a light lavender color; numbered. $101.50.

Sham
top row
1.) S 1984: Kansas horse show. Matte, golden bay; black points. $147.00.
2.) S 1994: West Coast Model Horse Collectors Jamboree. Matte, chocolate sorrel; flaxen mane and tail, lighter lower legs. $79.80.

bottom row
1.) S 1991: BreyerFest '91 Raffle Model (21). Matte, Wedgewood; white mane, tail, and stockings, gray hooves. $945.00.
2.) S 1996: BreyerFest '96 Dinner Model (about 3700). *Tseminole Wind.* Matte, red bay pinto; mostly white mane, tail, and legs, black forelock and shaded muzzle, star and blaze, natural hooves, eye whites. $52.00.

New for 1997:
975: 1997 – current. *Best Choice, Arabian.* Matte, mahogany bay; black points, right front sock, other legs with stockings, broad irregular blaze, shaded muzzle, natural hooves. $15.00.

Sherman Morgan

Mold #430; introduced in 1987. Apparently part of this mold was lost or broken in 1992 or thereabouts; it is unclear whether Breyer can or will repair this mold for future runs.

Sherman Morgan
top row
1, 2.) 430: 1987 – 90. *Sherman Morgan.* Matte, chestnut; darker mane, tail, and hooves, right hind sock, stripe. Sculpted by Jeanne Mellin Herrick. $32.20.
3.) 835: 1991 – 92. *Prancing Morgan.* Matte, black; stripe on lower face, three stockings (not right hind). $37.80.

bottom row
1.) S 1992: Just About Horses subscriber special (1500). *Pride and Vanity.* Matte, alabaster; gray mane and tail. $86.10.
2.) S 1992: Sears (less than 1000). *Fashionably Late.* Matte, sorrel; cold cast porcelain, flaxen mane and tail, stockings. $154.00.

Shetland Pony

Mold #25; introduced in 1960.

Shetland Pony
top row
1.) 25: 1960 – 72. *Shetland Pony.* Glossy or Matte, alabaster; gray mane, tail, hooves. $25.90.
2, 3.) 22: 1960 – 73. *Shetland Pony.* Glossy, light chestnut pinto; white mane, chestnut tail with white tip, bald face, pink shading on muzzle, pink/natural hooves. Color varied from light to medium palomino/chestnut (variation shown). $24.50.

bottom row
1.) 21: 1960 – 73, 1976. *Shetland Pony.* Glossy or Matte, black pinto; white mane, black tail with white tip, bald face, pink shading on muzzle, pink/natural hooves. Glossy until 1968, 1969 and later models were matte. $21.70.
2.) 925: 1963 – 64. *Shetland Pony.* Matte, woodgrain; no markings. $126.00.

Shetland Pony
top row

1.) 23: 1973 – 88. *Shetland Pony.* Matte, bay; bald face, black points. $18.90.
2.) 3066: 1986 – 96. *Marguerite Henry's "Our First Pony" Gift Set.* Matte, black pinto; socks, white mane, black and white tail, pink hooves. "Midget"; included Classic Arabian and Mustang Foals #3066. $20.30.
   also S 1984 – 85: Sears. Matte, black pinto; same as #3066. Included leather halter and lead. $19.60 ($23.10 complete).
3.) 801: 1989 – 91. *Shetland Pony.* Matte, bay pinto; black mane and tail, natural hooves, blaze. $18.90.

bottom row

1.) 857: 1992 – 94. *Shetland Pony.* Matte, chestnut; flaxen mane and tail, blaze, three stockings (not right fore). $16.80.
2.) 944: 1996 – current. *Pine, Shetland Pony.* Matte, golden sorrel, or palomino; white mane and tail, socks, blaze, slightly darker knees and hocks, gray shaded muzzle and ears, hand painted eyes. $12.40.

Shire

Mold #95; introduced in 1972.

Shire
top row

1.) 95: 1972 – 73, 1975 – 76. *Shire.* Matte, dapple gray; dark gray points, white stockings. $73.50.
2.) 96: 1972 – 76, 1978 – 80. *Shire.* Matte, honey sorrel; stockings, dark brown/black mane and tail, blaze (stenciled or unstenciled). Shire with the stenciled face is earlier model. $49.00.

bottom row

1.) same as top row, 2. Variation of #96.
2.) S 1982 – 83: Montgomery Ward. Semi-gloss, dapple gray; darker points, bald face, stockings. Included Belgian S 1982 (black with yellow on red ribbons). $79.10.

Shire 2
top row

1.) S 1985: Riegseckers (300). Matte, bay; black points, bald face, stockings. $98.00.
2.) S 1985: Riegseckers (300). Matte, black; bald face, stockings. $98.00.

bottom

S 1985: Riegseckers (300). Matte, gray; darker points, bald face, stockings. $98.00.

Shire
top
S 1985: Riegseckers (300). Matte, palomino; mane and tail same color or slightly lighter than body. $98.00.

bottom
S 1992: Sears. *Drafters Set.* Matte, palomino; white mane and tail, stripe, stockings, gray shaded face. Set included Belgian and Roy the Belgian S 1992. $37.80.

Smoky

Mold #69; introduced in 1981. This mold is notorious for having balance problems with the early models produced; hence you might find many in poor shape from falls.

Smoky
top
69: 1981 – 85. *"Smoky" the Cow Horse.* Matte, medium gray; black or gray points, white socks and blaze, gray hooves. The 1985 dealer catalog showed left hind sock only (not all 4). $39.90.
also 2090: 1981 – 85. *"Smoky" the Cow Horse Gift Set.* Matte, gray; same as #69. Set included paperback book *Smoky the Cow Horse* by Will James. $50.00 complete.

bottom
S 1984: JC Penney. *Unicorn.* Flocked, white; black hooves, added gold striped horn, brown glass eyes, white hair mane, tail, and beard. $72.10.

New for 1997:
993: 1997. *Shenandoah, Mustang.* Matte, buckskin; black points, bald/blaze face, right front sock. Breyer held a contest to determine colors for the 1997 release of this mold. Erin Logan won the junior division with this submission. $14.00.
994: 1997. *Remington, Pinto.* Matte, bay pinto; black points, apron face, socks, natural hooves. Debra Omel won the adult division of the color contest with this eye-catching pinto. $14.00.

Stock Horse Foal (Rough Coat)

Mold #18; introduced in 1978.

Stock Horse Foal (Rough Coat)
top row
1.) 18: 1978 – 82. *Stock Horse Foal.* Matte, black appaloosa; blanket over hindquarters. $16.10.
2.) 17: 1979 – 82. *Stock Horse Foal.* Matte, brown appaloosa; small blanket over hindquarters. $16.10.
3.) 29: 1983 – 87. *Phantom Wings, Misty's Foal.* Matte, palomino pinto; white "wing" shaped markings over withers, stockings, white mane, tail is body color. Also part of the Assorted Mare and Foals set (JC Penney 1983). See Proud Arabian Mare S 1983 for details. $15.40.

bottom row
1.) 846: 1991 – 93. *Rough Diamond.* Matte, dark brown pinto; white mane and tail, star and narrow stripe. $12.60.
2.) 875: 1993 – 94. *Woodsprite.* Matte, bay; black points, star. $12.60.
3.) 895: 1994 – 95. *Bright Socks.* Matte, black pinto; white mane, tail, and muzzle, high stenciled hind stockings, fore socks. $12.60.
4.) S 1993: JC Penney. *Breyer Three Generations Appaloosa Set.* Matte, chestnut appaloosa; darker mane and tail, few or no spots. Set included Adios and Quarter Horse Yearling S 1993. $15.40.

New for 1997:
984: 1997 – current. *Duke, Pinto.* Matte, chestnut pinto; splash overo, black mane and tail, chestnut brown over top half of body, natural hooves, chestnut brown "stripe" down face. $6.00.

Stock Horse Foal

Mold #228; introduced in 1983.

Stock Horse Foal
top row
1.) 234: 1983 – 86. *Appaloosa Stock Horse Foal.* Matte, gray appaloosa; blanket over barrel and hindquarters, socks, star, black mane and tail. Shown with no socks or star in 1985 dealer catalog. $18.90.
  also S 1983: Sears. *Stock Horse Family.* Matte, gray blanket appaloosa; black points, some with bald faces and some solid; same as #234. Included matching Stock Horse Mare and Stock Horse Stallion S 1983. $23.80.
2.) 228: 1983 – 88. *Bay Quarter Horse Stock Foal.* Matte, bay; black points, hind socks. 1985 – 87 dealer catalog showed hind socks only (socks and stockings can vary), darker points. In 1987 this was called American Quarter Horse Foal. $18.90.
3.) 231: 1983 – 88. *Pinto Stock Horse Foal.* Matte, black pinto; socks, gray hooves, stripe. In 1984 – 85 catalogs it was called Paint Stock Horse Foal, and in 1987 it was American Paint Horse Foal. $18.90.

bottom row
1.) 224: 1987 – 88. *American Buckskin Stock Horse Foal.* Matte, buckskin; black points, shaded muzzle, no dorsal stripe. Normally solid faced, but bald face variation shown. $18.90.
2.) 809: 1989 – 90. *Paint Horse Foal.* Matte, dark chestnut pinto; slightly darker mane and tail, narrow blaze, hind, smallish white patches. $18.90.
3.) 844: 1991 – 92. *Paint Horse Foal.* Matte, light chestnut pinto; blaze, hind socks, smallish white patches. $17.50.

Stock Horse Foal
top row
1.) 861: 1992 – 94. *Family Appaloosa Foal.* Matte, red bay appaloosa; black points, stripe, three socks (not left fore). $16.10.
2.) S 1983: Montgomery Ward. *Palomino Horse and Foal Set.* Matte, palomino; white mane, tail, stockings, bald face. Included Foundation Stallion S 1983. $48.30.
3.) S 1983 – 84: JC Penney. *Quarter Horse Mare and Foal Set.* Matte, buckskin; identical to #224 (except some are bald faced). Included Lady Phase S 1983. $29.40.

bottom row
1.) S 1992: Sears. *Spirit of the West Gift Set.* Matte, dark bay pinto; blaze, three stockings (not left fore). Included Lady Phase S 1992. $22.40.
2.) S 1992: Black Horse Ranch (1500). *Night Vision.* Matte, dark bay snowflake appaloosa; black points, hind socks, with lavender splash spots. $23.10.
3.) S 1993: Toys "R" Us. *Watchful Mare and Foal.* Matte, soft gray; slightly darker points, pink shaded nose. Included Lady Phase S 1993. $18.20.

New for 1997:
999: 1997 – current. *Golden Joy, Paint.* Matte, palomino pinto; white mane and tail, blaze, hind socks, darker shaded front legs, hocks, and muzzle. $9.00.

Stock Horse Mare

Mold #227; introduced in 1982; modified to correct balance problem in 1983 (moved foreleg position). Over the years, the catalogs have given various sizes—12" x 9", 11¾" x 9", or 12" x 8½", for example.

Stock Horse Mare
top row
1.) 227: 1983 – 86. *Sorrel Quarter Horse Stock Mare.* Matte, sorrel; flaxen mane and tail, right hind sock, stripe. Some did not have a sock. $25.90.
2.) 227: 1982. *Sorrel Quarter Horse Stock Mare.* Matte, sorrel (leg up version); flaxen mane and tail, right hind sock, stripe. $29.40.

bottom row
1.) 230: 1983 – 88. *Overo Paint Stock Horse.* Matte, bay pinto; black mane and tail, darker knees and hocks, socks, gray or natural hooves. In 1987 this was called American Paint Horse Mare. $25.90.
2.) 230: 1982. *Overo Paint Stock Horse Mare.* Matte, bay pinto (leg up version); black points, front stockings, gray/black hooves, black points. $29.40.

Stock Horse Mare
top row
1, 3.) 233: 1983 – 88. *Appaloosa Stock Horse Mare.* Matte, black appaloosa; stripe or star, stenciled blanket over hindquarters, spatter spots, socks, gray hooves. In the 1987 catalog, this was called American Appaloosa Stock Horse Mare. $25.20.
2.) 233: 1982. *Appaloosa Stock Horse Mare.* Matte, black appaloosa (leg up version); stripe or star, stenciled blanket over hindquarters, spatter spots, socks, gray hooves. Number of socks may vary, and a variation is shown without spots. $29.40.

bottom row
1.) 222: 1987 – 88. *American Buckskin stock Horse Mare.* Matte, buckskin; black points, no dorsal stripe. $27.30.
2.) 808: 1989 – 90. *Paint Horse Mare.* Matte, dark chestnut pinto; darker mane and tail, hind stockings/socks, long star, gray hooves. $25.90.

Stock Horse Mare
top row
1.) 852: 1991 – 92. *Appy Mare.* Matte, red roan/leopard appaloosa; chestnut points, small chestnut speckles, socks. $25.20.
2.) 954: 1996 – current. *Goin For Approval, Appaloosa.* Matte, chestnut snowflake appaloosa; darker mane and tail, hind socks, blaze, snowflakes on shoulders and quarters. Represents the champion Appaloosa stallion; variation shown with well defined spots. $20.20.

bottom row
Same as top row, 2.

Stock Horse Mare
top row
1.) S 1983: Sears. *Stock Horse Family.* Matte, gray appaloosa; black points, bald face, blanket over hindquarters with splash spots. Included Stock Horse Foal and Stock Horse Stallion S 1983. $37.10.
2.) S 1984: Sears. *Collectible Stock Horse Family.* Matte, buckskin; black points, creamier color than #222. Set included matching Action Stock Horse Foal and Stock Horse Stallion S 1984. $31.50.

bottom row
1.) S 1984, 85: JC Penney. *Pinto Mare and Foal Set.* Matte, black pinto; socks/stockings, white muzzle. Included matching Action Stock Horse Foal S 1984. $38.50.
2.) S 1986: JC Penney. *Breyers Traditional Collector's Family Set.* Matte, bay roan peppercorn appaloosa; bay base-color with chestnut spots, star, chestnut shading on face. Set included matching Action Stock Horse Foal and Stock Horse Stallion S 1986. $31.50.

Stock Horse Stallion
Mold #226; introduced in 1981.

Stock Horse Stallion
top row
1.) 232: 1981 – 86. *Appaloosa Stock Horse Stallion.* Matte, bay blanket appaloosa; blanket over most of barrel and hindquarters with splash spots, black points, socks, gray hooves. $29.40.
2.) 226: 1981 – 88. *Bay Quarter Horse Stock Stallion.* Matte, bay; black points. This was called Bay Quarter Horse Stallion in the 1985 and 1986 dealer catalogs, and mislabeled as New #221 in the 1987 dealer catalog. $28.00.

bottom
229: 1981 – 88. *Tobiano Pinto Stock Horse Stallion.* Matte, black pinto; socks, gray hooves. In the 1987 catalog, this was called American Paint Horse Stallion. $28.00.

Stock Horse Stallion Variations
229: *Tobiano Pinto Stock Horse Stallion* pinto pattern variations.

Stock Horse Stallion
3096: 1984 – 85. *Kelly Reno and Little Man Gift Set.* Matte, palomino; white mane and tail, blaze, gray hooves. Set included Kelly Reno doll, leather bridle, red bareback pad. $57.40 ($72.10 complete).

Stock Horse Stallion
top row
1.) 221: 1987 – 88. *American Buckskin Stock Horse Stallion.* Matte, buckskin; black points, no dorsal stripe. The 1987 dealer catalog had this mislabeled as American Quarter Horse Stallion #226. $28.00.
2.) 807: 1989 – 90. *Paint Horse Stallion.* Matte, liver chestnut pinto; darker mane and tail, hind socks, smallish white patches. $28.00.

bottom row
1.) 842: 1991 – 92. *Skipster's Chief, Famous Therapeutic Riding Horse.* Matte, sorrel; flaxen mane and tail, stockings, blaze. $25.90.
2.) 938: 1995 – 96. *Shane, American Ranch Horse.* Matte, black roan; black points, hind socks, stripe and snip, Rocking R brand on left shoulder (painted on). $20.00.

Stock Horse Stallion
top
S 1983: Sears. *Stock Horse Family.* Matte, gray appaloosa; black points, bald face, blanket over hindquarters with splash spots. Set included Stock Horse Foal and Stock Horse Mare S 1983. $40.60.

bottom
S 1984: JC Penney. *Stallion Mare and Foal Set.* Matte, light gray; soft rose shading in mane and tail, gray muzzle, knees, and hocks. The set name was misleading; there was only the Stock Horse Stallion and Action Stock Horse Foal (bay) S 1984. $43.40.

Stock Horse Stallion
S 1984: breeder, Just About Horses and other retailers. *Sam I Am.* Matte, dark bay pinto; black points, left hind stocking, gray hooves, wide blaze and pink nose. Came with application for share in ownership. $108.50.

Stock Horse Stallion
top row
1.) S 1984: Sears. *Collectible Stock Horse Family.* Matte, buckskin; black points, shaded muzzle. Set included matching Action Stock Horse Foal and Stock Horse Mare S 1984. $35.70.
2.) S 1984: JC Penney. *Brown and White Pinto Stock Horse.* Matte, bay pinto; black points, stockings. $37.80.

bottom row
1.) S 1986: JC Penney. *Breyers Traditional Collector's Family Set.* Matte, bay roan peppercorn appaloosa; bay base-color, black points with chestnut spots, blaze. Set included matching Action Stock Horse Foal and Stock Horse Mare S 1986. $35.70.
2.) S 1995: JC Penney. *Race Horses of America.* Matte, dappled chestnut; three socks (not left fore), shaded muzzle. Set included Pacer and Phar Lap S 1995. $33.60.

New for 1997:
992: 1997 – current. *Docs Keepin Time, Quarter Horse.* Semi-gloss, black; diamond star. Represents the horse that starred in the 1994 film *Black Beauty.*

Stormy

Mold #19; introduced in 1977.

Stormy
top
19: 1977 – current. *Marguerite Henry's Stormy.* Matte, chestnut pinto; stockings, crescent-shaped star. This was also included in #2169, Misty and Stormy Gift Set. $10.00.

bottom
S 1984: Sears. *Marguerite Henry's Stormy and Misty.* Flocked, chestnut pinto; white hair mane and tail, brown glass eyes, stockings, crescent-shaped star. Set included Misty S 1984. $33.60.

Stormy
S 1995: Toys "R" Us. *Buckaroo and Skeeter.* Matte, bay pinto; stockings, crescent-shaped star. Included Classic Arabian Mare S 1995; Medallion Series. $13.30.

Stud Spider
top row
1.) 916: 1995 – 96. *Mister Mister Champion Paint*. Matte, chestnut pinto; dark patch by mouth on right side, right foreleg solid chestnut, other legs have varied white markings. $19.10.
2.) S 1980: Just About Horses subscriber special. *Stud Spider*. Unpainted. $46.20.

bottom row
1.) S 1986: Your Horse Source (1000). Matte, bay/chestnut; black points (on most) and hind socks. $60.20.
2.) S 1990: Sears. *Appaloosa-American Classic Set*. Matte, blue roan leopard appaloosa; black points, left hind stocking, gray body color, with vague blanket over hindquarters and black splash spots to shoulders. Set included Appaloosa Performance Horse and Running Stallion S 1990. $47.60.

New for 1997:
976: 1997 – current. *Smooth Copper, Quarter Horse*. Matte, shaded light bay; black points, right hind and left fore socks. $15.00.
S 1997: Breyerfest '97 Dinner Model. *Bold*. Matte, palomino; white mane and tail, blaze (narrow at top, wide on muzzle), shaded muzzle, left hind sock. Portrait of the 1995 Police Horse of the Year. $49.00.

Stud Spider
Mold #66; introduced in 1978.

Stud Spider
top row
1.) 66: 1978 – 89. *Stud Spider*. Matte, black appaloosa; stenciled blanket pattern over most of barrel and hindquarters, front right stocking, thin star. Called just "Appaloosa" in the 1985 – 86 dealer catalogs. $30.80.
also 3080: 1978 – 83. *Stud Spider Gift Set*. Matte, black blanket appaloosa; same as #66. Set included booklet "Let's Go to the Races with the Appaloosa" by Jim Brolin, and carrying case. $41.30 complete.
2, 3.) 88: 1979 – 81. *Overo Paint*. Matte, chestnut pinto; darker mane and tail, bald face, stockings. Variation shown. $32.90.

bottom row
1.) 823: 1990 – 91. *Blanket Appaloosa*. Matte, chestnut appaloosa; stockings, well defined blanket with small spatter spots, narrow blaze, black mane and tail. $28.00.
2.) 859: 1992 – 94. *Family Appaloosa Stallion*. Matte, bay appaloosa; hind socks, star, black points, blanket pattern over hindquarters and part of barrel points, stenciled spots, blanket. $25.20.

Thoroughbred Mare
Mold #3155MA; introduced in 1973.

Thoroughbred Mare (Traditional)
top row
1.) 3155: 1973 – 84. *Thoroughbred Mare and Foal Gift Set*. Matte, dark chestnut/bay; black mane and tail. Set included Nursing Foal #3155, and carrying case. $35.00.
2.) 3180: 1994 – current. *Medicine Hat Mare and Foal Gift Set*. Matte, chestnut pinto; mostly white, light chestnut "hat," chest, and rump. Included Nursing Foal #3180. $16.60.

bottom row
1.) S 1982 – 83: Sears. *Pinto Mare and Suckling Foal*. Matte, bay pinto; black points, varying socks. Included Nursing Foal S 1982. $54.60.
2.) S 1996: JC Penney. *Pride and Joy*. Matte, light chestnut; socks. Included Nursing Foal S 1996. $18.00.

Touch of Class

Mold #420; introduced in 1986.

Touch of Class
top row

1.) 420: 1986 – 88. *Touch of Class.* Matte, bay; black points, wide blaze, gray hooves. $27.30.
2.) 813: 1989 – 90. *Thoroughbred Mare.* Matte, black; socks, blaze, gray hooves. $27.30.
3.) 843: 1991 – 92. *Selle Francais.* Matte, dark chestnut; darker mane and tail, blaze, stockings, gray hooves. $21.70.

bottom row

1.) 877: 1993 – 94. *Guinevere.* Matte, reddish bay; black points, star, black muzzle. $21.70.
2.) 952: 1996 – current. *Rox Dene, Show Hunter.* Matte, light dapple gray; darker knees, hocks, muzzle, and shaded body. $18.40.

Trakehner

Mold #54; introduced in 1979.

Trakehner
top row

1.) 54: 1979 – 84. *Trakehner.* Matte, bay; black points. Brand on left thigh. $38.50.
2.) 817: 1989. *Abdullah Champion Trakehner.* Matte, light dapple gray; generally light, especially around barrel, gray mane, tail, and hooves, shaded muzzle, two dark spots on right neck. Limited Edition. $38.50.

bottom

912: 1995 – 1996. *Hanover Trakehner.* Matte, liver chestnut; hind socks, blaze, lighter mane and tail (some have faint fore socks as well). $20.00.

Trakehner
top row

1.) S 1987: Just About Horses subscriber special (1500). *Trakehner.* Matte, chestnut; darker mane and tail, stockings. $77.70.
2.) S 1987: Small World (about 400). Matte, bay; black points, socks, star. $90.30.

bottom row

1.) S 1980: Just About Horses subscriber special. *Trakehner.* Unpainted. $49.70.
2.) S 1995: Breyer Tour Model. *Kaleidoscope the Pinto Sporthorse.* Matte, red bay pinto; black tail, black and white mane, blaze, white legs, shaded muzzle. $28.00.

Trakehner
S 1996: USET Festival of Champions (1000). *Calypso.* Matte, light bay; black points, three socks (not left fore), blaze, striped hooves. $37.70.

Western Horse

Mold #57; introduced in 1950. Like many of the early molds, there is much conflicting information about which models are which. These descriptions are as accurate as possible.

Western Horse
number unknown: before 1960. *Western Horse.* Semi-gloss, chocolate brown; plastic itself is brown, almost bronzish, with brown or black slip-on saddle, plastic reins. $125.70 ($147.70 complete).

Western Horse
top row
1, 2.) 59: 1951 – 63. *Western Horse.* Glossy, white; gray hooves, gold chain reins, gold bridle and harness, black plastic snap-girth saddle. $38.20 ($44.80 complete).
3.) 57: 1950 – 70. *Western Horse.* Glossy, palomino; stockings, gray hooves, gold chain reins, gold bridle and harness, reddish-brown plastic snap-girth saddle. Some might have had grooming kits. $27.30 ($49.00 complete).

bottom row
1.) 57: about 1970 – 91. *Western Horse.* Matte, palomino; stockings, gray hooves, gold chain reins, gold bridle and harness, sepia shaded plastic slip-on saddle. Some might have the brown snap-girth saddles. $17.00 ($19.60 complete).
also S 1995: QVC. *Western Horse.* Matte, palomino; very similar to #57 (late matte models) except for added "'95" next to mold mark. $30.80 ($38.60 complete).
2.) 960: 1996 – current. *Royal Te, Appaloosa.* Matte, bay blanket appaloosa; black points, three socks (not left fore), black saddle with gold trim, gold bridle and breast collar and chain reins. $14.70 ($18.70 complete).

Western Horse

top row

1.) 58: 1956 – 60. *Western Horse.* Glossy, black; gold hooves, and bridle and harness, black snap-girth saddle. $78.80 ($108.50 complete).

also 50: 1959 – 62. *Western Horse.* Glossy, black; gold hooves, bridle, and breastcollar, gold chain reins, black plastic snap-girth saddle. $78.80 ($108.50 complete).

2.) 58: 1956 – 60. *Black Beauty.* Glossy, black; bald face, socks, white tail tip, silver bridle, black snap-girth saddle. $78.80 ($108.50 complete).

bottom

55: 1954 – 76. *Western Horse.* Glossy, black pinto; stockings, gray hooves, gold chain reins, gold bridle and harness, black snap-girth saddle; later models had slip-on gray shaded saddles (shown).

also, some later models might have been matte, but this is questionable. $23.30 ($30.80 complete).

Western Horse

top row

1, 2.) 56: 1956 – 67. *Western Horse.* Glossy, palomino or chestnut pinto; stockings, gray hooves, gold chain reins, gold bridle and harness, reddish snap-girth saddle. Both colors used this number and in general, collectors consider these to be variations of the same model. $25.70 ($32.90 complete).

bottom row

1.) 864: 1992 – 94. *Tic Toc.* Matte, alabaster; gray hooves, mane and tail, black saddle with gold trim, gold conchas on harness, gold bridle and chain reins. $20.00 ($23.10 complete).

2.) S 1990: Just About Horses subscriber special (1525). *Western Horse.* Matte, chestnut pinto; white mane, chestnut tail with white tip, gold bridle, brown saddle. "JAH 1990" hand written on belly. $57.10 ($63.70 complete).

Western Pony

Mold #45; introduced in the early 1950s.

Western Pony

top row

1.) 40: before 1956. *Western Pony.* Semi-gloss, plum brown; socks (painted on), probably made of brown plastic; diamond star, black snap-girth saddle. $77.10 ($87.50 complete).

2.) 42: 1956 – 67. *Western Pony.* Glossy, chestnut pinto; chestnut tail with white tip, white mane, stockings, bald face, gold chain reins, brown snap-girth saddle. $26.80 ($29.40 complete).

3.) 43: 1956 – 67. *Western Pony.* Glossy, palomino; bald face, stockings, gold bridle and harness, reddish-brown snap-girth saddle. This model was also available with a grooming kit (see the variation for #45); some early models had gold eyes. $24.50 ($36.40 complete).

bottom row

1, 2.) 41: 1956 – 76. *Western Pony.* Glossy/Matte, black pinto; stockings, bald face, black and white mane and tail, gold chain reins, gold trim, gray shaded plastic slip on saddle, gray hooves. Variation shown with shoulder spot; notice the differences in the facial markings and the socks. $22.10 ($24.50 complete).

3.) 44: 1958 – 63. *Western Pony.* Glossy, black; gold hooves and trim, black saddle with gold trim, snap-girth. $50.80 ($58.10 complete).

Western Pony
top row
1.) 40: 1956 – 63. *Black Beauty.* Glossy, black; socks, star, white tail tip, black snap-girth saddle with gold trim. $57.90 ($68.60 complete).
2.) 945: 1963 – 65. *Western Pony.* Matte/semi-gloss, woodgrain; no markings, came without saddle as well, just reins. $160.20 ($164.50 complete).

bottom row
1, 2.) 45: 1958 – 71. *Western Pony.* Glossy, alabaster; gray hooves, gold bridle, black snap-girth saddle. Also shown is a variation with the grooming kit, was also used for Lucky Ranger; some models might have gold eyes. $25.90 ($33.60 complete with saddle, $46.90 with rider).
3.) 910: 1995 – 1996. *Cisco Western Pony with Saddle.* Matte, buckskin; bald face, black points, socks, black saddle with gold trim, gray hooves and shaded muzzle. $18.00 ($20.00 complete).

Western Pony
42: *Western Pony* variations with riders.

Western Pony model not shown:
43: 1968 – 73. *Western Pony.* Matte, palomino; very similar to the glossy version except for finish. $17.50.

New for 1997
998: 1997 – current. *Gambler, Western Pony.* Matte, palomino; painted eyes, white mane and tail, bald face, socks, gray shaded muzzle and hooves, gold tack and black saddle. $14.00 complete.

Western Prancing Horse
Mold #110; introduced in 1961.

Western Prancing Horse
top row
1.) 113: 1961 – 66. *Western Prancing Horse.* Glossy, black pinto; socks, bald face, gray shaded plastic slip on saddle, gold chain reins. $65.30 ($77.70 complete).
2.) 114: 1961 – 71. *Western Prancing Horse.* Matte, bay; black points, socks, bald face, sepia shaded plastic saddle, gold chain reins. $38.50 ($45.50 complete).

bottom row
1.) 111: 1961 – 73. *Western Prancing Horse.* Matte, buckskin; black points, bald face, sepia shaded plastic saddle. $40.20 ($45.50 complete).
2.) 115: 1961 – 73. *Western Prancing Horse.* Glossy, leopard appaloosa; black points, black speckles, gold bridle, gray shaded plastic saddle. $31.90 ($38.50 complete).

Western Prancing Horse
top row
1, 2.) 110: 1961 – 76. *Western Prancing Horse.* Matte, smoke; stockings, white mane and tail, bald face, gray hooves, gray shaded saddle. Dark and light color variations were common. $32.30 ($37.80 complete).
3, 4.) 112: 1961 – 85. *Western Prancing Horse.* Matte, palomino; white mane and tail, stockings, gray hooves, gold chain and bridle, sepia slip-on plastic saddle. Dark and light color variations were common. $20.10 ($24.50 complete).

bottom row
1.) 1120: 1983 – 85. *Brenda Western Gift Set.* Matte, chestnut pinto; white mane and tail, bald face, socks, gray hooves, gold bridle, gold chain reins, sepia shaded slip-on saddle. Set included Western dressed Brenda doll with plastic hat. $30.80 ($41.30 complete).
2.) 889: 1994 – 95. *Ranger Cow Pony.* Matte, dun; brown points, socks, white blaze, semi-gloss brown plastic saddle, black bridle. $16.60 ($21.80 complete).

Western Prancing Horse
968: 1996 – current. *Vigilante, Western Prancer.* Semi-gloss, black; right front sock, natural hooves, brown saddle, gold bridle and chain reins. $14.00 ($18.40 complete).

Fine Porcelain Series

In 1992 Breyer began a new line of fine porcelain horse figurines. These horses rival the finest available from other sources and are truly works of art. Collectors would like to see these molds used to produce plastic models, but it is unclear whether this is possible. All of these porcelains are very limited in availability, and are prized in all collections. Sculpted by Kathleen Moody.

Porcelain Icelandic Horse

Mold #79192; introduced in 1992.

Porcelain Icelandic Horse

79192: 1992. *Fine Porcelain Icelandic Horse.* Matte, buckskin pinto; dark brown hocks and tail, forelock and top of mane, and partial dorsal stripe, white front legs, star and partial stripe, hind socks. Limited to production of 2,500. $148.50.

Porcelain Shire

Mold #79193; introduced in 1993.

Porcelain Shire

79193: 1993. *Fine Porcelain Shire.* Matte, bay; black points, broad blaze, three stockings (not left fore), silver horse shoes. Limited to production of 2,500. $163.80.

Porcelain Spanish Barb

Mold #79194; introduced in 1994.

Porcelain Spanish Barb

79194: 1994. *Fine Porcelain Spanish Barb.* Matte, grulla; brown points, primitive bars on legs, broken blaze, right fore sock. Limited to production of 2,500. $139.50.

Porcelain Arabian Mare in Costume
Mold #79195; introduced in 1995.

Porcelain Arabian Mare in Costume
79195: 1995. *Fine Porcelain Premier Arabian Mare.* Matte, light gray; gray shaded body, tail, mane, and legs, wearing traditional Arabian costume. Limited to production of 2,500. $180.30.

Porcelain Saddlebred in Parade Tack
Mold #79196; introduced in 1996.

Porcelain Saddlebred in Parade Tack
79196: 1996. *All American Saddlebred in Parade Costume.* Matte, orange/palomino; cream shaded mane and tail, stockings, blaze, silver hooves, silver and black costume with red roses and red and blue ribbons; Tapaderos are separate pieces. Limited to production of 2,500. $164.90.

Porcelain Circus Ponies
Mold #79296; introduced in 1996 (actually released in 1997).

Porcelain Circus Ponies in Costume
79296: 1996. *Circus Ponies in Costume.* Matte, white/gray; red and gold bridles and gear, red plumes at poll and at withers. These two horses are a set. Limited to production of 2,500 sets. $167.00.

Porcelain Great Horse in Armor (not shown)
Mold #79197; new mold for 1997.

79197: 1997. *The Great Horse in Armor.* Matte, black; armored. Limited to production of 2,500. $155.00.

Introduced in 1973 with the Arabian Family, Breyer has been slowly increasing the number of molds in this scale. In this guide "Classic Series" denotes all molds in the classic scale, including Hobo, the Polo Pony, the Rearing Stallion, and the Bucking Bronco. These four molds are *usually* classified by others as Traditional — even though they are generally acknowledged to be Classic scale. So because this guide uses *scale* as the first criteria for classification, they are listed in this section.

Most Classic molds have stayed in production fairly consistently, going through the normal variety of colors. Several series have been made (Race Horse, After School Herd, Miniature Collection, B Ranch, and more) and have had a good mix of molds used in them.

Many people consider that Classic models are easier to collect than Traditionals for two reasons: First, they take up less shelf space; and second, they are usually less expensive than the Traditional models.

Several of the Classic molds were derived from Hagen-Renaker figurines.

Andalusian Foal

Mold #3060FO; introduced in 1979.

Andalusian Foal
top row
1.) 3060: 1979 – 93. *Classic Andalusian Family.* Matte, dark chestnut; stockings, bald face, darker mane and tail. Set included Andalusian Mare and Stallion #3060 and carrying case. $9.10.
2.) 3346: 1992 – 93. *Hanoverian Family.* Matte, bay; black points. Set included Keen and Ginger #3346. $9.80.
3.) 3160: 1993. *Proud Mare and Newborn Foal.* Matte, apricot dun; grayish shading, left hind sock. Included Traditional Lady Roxana #3160. $9.80.
4.) 3161: 1993. *Proud Mare and Newborn Foal.* Matte, dark bay; black points, left hind sock. Included Traditional Lady Roxana #3161. $9.80.

bottom row
1.) 2005: 1996 – current. *Precious Beauty Foal & Gift Set.* Matte, bay blanket appaloosa; black points, four socks, natural hooves. Included Ginger #2005. $6.70.
2.) S 1984: Sears. *Classic Andalusian Family.* Matte, bay; black points; virtually identical to #3346. Set included Andalusian Mare and Stallion S 1984. $11.20.
3.) S 1994: Toys "R" Us. *Spanish-Norman Family.* Matte, gray; black points. Set included Ginger and Andalusian Stallion S 1994; given SR number 700294. $9.80.
4.) S 1996: Sears Wish Book. *Classic Beauty Gift Set.* Matte, light gray; shaded, socks, bald face, natural/pink hooves. Set included Classic Black Beauty S 1996. $9.00.

Andalusian Mare

Mold #3060MA; introduced in 1979.

Andalusian Mare
top
3060: 1979 – 93. *Classic Andalusian Family.* Matte, dapple gray; darker points, socks. Set included Andalusian Stallion and Foal #3060 and carrying case. $11.90.

bottom
S 1984: Sears. *Classic Andalusian Family.* Matte, alabaster; light gray points, hooves. Set included Andalusian Stallion and Foal S 1984 and carrying case. $14.70.

New for 1997:
289: 1997 – current. *Chaval.* Matte, shaded red roan/chestnut; darker points. B-Ranch series; included ribbon. $7.00.

Andalusian Stallion

Mold #3060ST; introduced in 1979.

Andalusian Stallion

top

3060: 1979 – 93. *Classic Andalusian Family.* Matte, alabaster; very pale gray mane and tail, gray or pink hooves. Set included Andalusian Mare and Foal #3060 and carrying case. $10.50.

bottom row

1.) S 1984: Sears. *Classic Andalusian Family.* Matte, dapple gray; gray points, stockings. Set included Andalusian Mare and Foal S 1984 and carrying case. $16.10.

2.) S 1994: Toys "R" Us. *Spanish-Norman Family.* Matte, red roan; darker points, shaded body, gray hooves. Set included Ginger and Andalusian Foal S 1994; given SR number 700294. $11.90.

Arabian Foal

top row

1.) 3162: 1994. *Arabian Stallion and Frisky Foal Set.* Matte, gray; black or dark gray points, hind socks. $7.70.

2.) 3163: 1994. *Arabian Stallion and Frisky Foal Set.* Matte, light bay; black points, shaded muzzle. $7.70.

3.) S 1984 – 85: Sears. *Classic Arabian Family.* Matte, red bay; black points. Set included Arabian Stallion and Mare S 1984. $16.10.

4.) S 1988: Signing Parties, and other retailers. *Foal's First Day.* Matte, light bay; darker/black points, stockings, gray or black hooves, white tail tip. Set included Johar S 1988 (rose gray); signing parties offered only the models, some sets were sold by the Enchanted Doll House with a cookie tin. $16.10 ($44.10 complete).

bottom row

1.) S 1988: British export (200 – 250 made). *Classic Arabian Family.* Matte, dapple gray; medium gray points, socks, blaze. Set included dapple gray Arabian Stallion and Mare S 1988. $32.90.

2.) S 1988, 90: JC Penney. *Breyer Classic Collector's Arabian Family Set.* Matte, black; socks, snip, gray hooves. Set included black Arabian Stallion and Mare S 1988. $14.70.

3.) S 1993: Toys "R" Us. *Drinkers of the Wind.* Matte, rose gray; darker/gray points, right hind sock; given SR number 700693. Set included Arabian Stallion and Johar S 1993. $11.10.

New for 1997:

3097: 1997 – current. *Arabian Mare and Foal.* Matte, bay; resist dappled, black points, stripe, stockings. $4.00.

S 1997: State Line Tack. *1997 Pinto Family* (temporary name). Matte, black pinto; white right leg, blaze. Set included Black Beauty (Classic) and Ginger S 1997. $7.20

Arabian Foal

Mold #3055FO; introduced in 1973.

Arabian Foal

top row

1.) 4000: 1973 – 82. *Arabian Foal.* Matte, alabaster; light gray mane, tail, and hooves. Sold in blister packs. $17.20.

2.) 4000: 1973 – 82. *Arabian Foal.* Matte, black; socks/stockings, black hooves, bald face. Sold in blister packs. $14.10.

3.) 4000: 1973 – 82. *Arabian Foal.* Matte, chestnut; socks/stockings, bald face. Sold in blister packs. $14.10.

4.) 4000: 1973 – 82. *Arabian Foal.* Matte, gray; socks, darker points, bald face. Sold in blister packs. $17.20.

bottom row

1.) 3055: 1973 – 91. *Classic Arabian Family.* Matte, light chestnut; darker mane and tail, stockings, bald face, gray hooves. Set included Arabian Stallion and Mare #3055 and carrying case. $9.80.

2.) 3066: 1987 – 96. *Marguerite Henry's "Our First Pony" Set.* Matte, bay pinto; stockings, black knees, hocks, and top half of mane, lower mane and most of tail white, stripe, pink hooves. Set included Traditional Shetland Pony and Classic Mustang Foal #3066; 1987 sets were produced with black pinto Arabian Foal. $5.00.

3.) 3056: 1992 – 94. *Desert Arabian Family.* Matte, red bay; black points, right hind sock. Set included Arabian Stallion and Mare #3056 and carrying case. $6.30.

Arabian Mare

Mold #3055MA; introduced in 1973.

Regular Run Arabian Mare Models (Classic)
top
3055: 1973 – 91. *Classic Arabian Family.* Matte, chestnut; darker mane and tail, stockings, stripe. Set included Arabian Stallion and Foal #3055 and carrying case. $11.90.

bottom
3056: 1992 – 94. *Desert Arabian Family.* Matte, bay; black points, hind socks, stripe, snip. Set included Arabian Stallion and Foal #3056 and carrying case. $11.20.

Special Run Arabian Mare Models (Classic)
top row
1.) S 1984 – 85: Sears. *Classic Arabian Family.* Matte, alabaster; shaded mane, tail, knees, hocks, ankles, and muzzle. Set included Arabian Stallion and Foal S 1984 and carrying case. $23.10.
2.) S 1988: Export (200 – 250 made). *Classic Arabian Family.* Matte, dapple gray; darker points, stockings, pink hooves. Set included dapple gray Arabian Stallion and Foal S 1988. $44.80.

bottom row
1.) S 1988, 90: JC Penney. *Breyer Classic Collector's Arabian Family Set.* Matte, black; front socks, broad blaze. Set included black Arabian Stallion and Foal S 1988. $26.60.
2.) S 1995: Toys "R" Us. *Buckaroo and Skeeter.* Matte, buckskin; socks, white nose, mostly flaxen mane and tail with black stripes, black forelock. "Buckaroo"; set included Stormy S 1995. Medallion Series. $17.50.

New for 1997:
3097: 1997 – current. *Arabian Mare and Foal.* Matte, light bay; resist dappled, black points, stripe, hind stockings, front socks. $8.00.

Arabian Stallion

Mold #3055ST; introduced in 1973.

Regular Run Arabian Stallion Models (Classic)
top
3055: 1973 – 91. *Classic Arabian Family.* Matte, sorrel; socks, flaxen mane and tail. Set included Arabian Mare and Foal #3055 and carrying case. $12.60.

bottom
3056: 1992 – 94. *Desert Arabian Family.* Matte, bay; red bay, black points, star, left hind sock. Set included Arabian Mare and Foal #3056 and carrying case. $10.50.

Special Run Arabian Stallion Models (Classic)
top row
1.) S 1984 – 85: Sears. *Classic Arabian Family.* Matte, bay; lighter brown bay, black points, diamond star, three or four socks. Set included Arabian Mare and Foal S 1984 and carrying case. $23.10.
2.) S 1988: Export (200 – 250 made). *Classic Arabian Family.* Matte, dapple gray; gray points, socks/stockings. Set included dapple gray Arabian Mare and Foal S 1988. $42.70.

bottom row
1.) S 1988, 90: JC Penney. *Breyer Classic Collector's Arabian Family Set.* Matte, black; socks, snip, gray hooves. Set included black Arabian Mare and Foal S 1988. $26.60.
2.) S 1993: Toys "R" Us. *Drinkers of the Wind.* Matte, gray; black points, four socks, shaded muzzle; given SR number 700693. Set included Johar and Arabian Foal S 1993. $13.30.

New for 1997:
2007: 1997 – current. *Tyler and Hillary, B-Ranch Gift Set.* Matte, chestnut pinto; mostly white, small chestnut patches, chestnut head with star, chestnut tail. Set included Western saddle and bridle, ribbon, and Western-dressed Hillary. $10.00 ($15.00 complete).

Arabian Family
Bedouin Family (Classic Arabian Models)
3057: 1995 – 96. *Bedouin Family Gift Set.*
1.) Arabian Mare. Matte, black; mane and tail have lighter streaking, socks, and half-apron face marking. $9.20.
2.) Arabian Foal. Matte, bay; black points, socks, stripe, white muzzle, black points, white tail tip, pink hooves. $4.80.
3.) Arabian Stallion. Matte, bay; black points, socks, white tail tip, striped mane, blaze that wraps under chin, pink hooves. $9.20.

Black Beauty

Mold #3040BB; introduced in 1980.

Black Beauty (Classic)
top row
1.) 3040: 1980 – 93. *Black Beauty Family.* Matte, black; right fore stocking, star. Set included Ginger, Duchess, and Merrylegs #3040 and carrying case. $9.10.
2.) 3345: 1990 – 93. *King of the Wind Set.* Matte, bay; black points. "Lath"; set included Black Stallion and Duchess #3345. $9.80.
3.) S 1990: Export. *Iltschi.* Matte, black; socks, long diamond star, black or dark gray hooves. Sometimes called the Karl May Set, sold separately or with Ginger S 1990. $33.60.

bottom row
1.) S 1994: Mid-year release. *Black Beauty.* Glossy, black; right fore sock, diamond star. Included Brenda doll, halter and lead. $24.50.
2.) S 1996: Sears Wish Book. *Classic Beauty Gift Set.* Matte, flea-bit gray; light gray mane tail, knees, and hocks, pink/natural hooves. Set included Andalusian Foal S 1996. $16.00.

Classic Black Beauty model not shown:
S 1984: JC Penney (less than 1,500 made). *One Horse Open Sleigh.* Flocked, dapple gray; black or dark gray hair. Set included leather harness, black wooden sleigh with red trim, a man and woman doll (porcelain) dressed for winter. The wood base was covered with white felt to look like snow. A plastic display case was also provided. This set was part of the Miniature Collection. $80.50 ($203.00 complete).

New for 1997:
S 1997: State Line Tack. *1997 Pinto Family* (temporary name). Matte, bay pinto; white right leg, black lower left leg with sock. Set included Arabian Foal (Classic) and Ginger S 1997. $12.00.

Black Stallion

Mold #3030BS; introduced in 1983.

Black Stallion (Classic)
top
3030: 1983 – 93. *The Black Stallion Returns Set.* Matte, black; natural hooves. "The Black" from Walter Farley's books; set included Sagr and Johar #3030. $9.80.

bottom
3345: 1990 – 93. *King of the Wind Set.* Matte, blood bay; black points, white spot on right hind ankle. "Sham"; set included Duchess and Black Beauty #3345. $9.80.

The Country Doctor

19842: 1984 – 87. *The Doctor's Buggy.* Flocked, bay; black hair mane and tail, three socks (not left hind), black points. Buggy is black with yellow pin striping, made of wood and metal, and had red upholstery; included a doctor doll, leather harness, wood base, plastic display case; part of the Miniature Collection. $79.10 ($182.00 complete).

Bucking Bronco

Mold #190; introduced in 1961.

Regular Run Bucking Bronco Models
top row
1.) 191: 1961 – 67. *Bucking Bronco.* Matte, gray; darker mane and tail, stockings, bald face. $93.80.
2.) 190: 1966 – 73 1975 – 76. *Bucking Bronco.* Matte, black; stockings, bald face. Called Black Bucking Horse in 1976 catalog. $42.00.

bottom row
1.) 192: 1967 – 70. *Bucking Bronco.* Matte, bay; stockings, black mane and tail, gray hooves, bald face. $13.60.
2.) 932: 1995 – 96. *Dakota Bucking Bronco.* Matte, palomino; hind socks/stockings, white mane and tail, gray shaded muzzle, resist dappling. $82.60.

Special Run Bucking Bronco Models
top row

1.) S 1988: Bentley Sales Company (400). *Bucking Bronco.* Matte, gray; black mane and tail. $72.80.
2.) S 1988: Bentley Sales Company (400). *Bucking Bronco.* Matte, red roan; reddish-gray points, stockings. $72.80.
3.) S 1988: Bentley Sales Company (400). *Bucking Bronco.* Matte, chestnut; darker chestnut points, stockings. $72.80.

bottom row

1.) S 1988: Bentley Sales Company (400). *Bucking Bronco.* Matte, black leopard appaloosa; light gray mane and tail, shaded knees and hocks, stockings, black speckles. $72.80.
2.) S 1992: Made as a Breyer Show Special. *Bucking Bronco.* Matte, black pinto; apron face, three stockings (not left fore). Given SR number 700192. $32.90.

Ginger

Mold #3040GI; introduced in 1980.

Ginger
top row

1.) 3040: 1980 – 93. *Black Beauty Family.* Matte, chestnut; darker mane, tail, and hooves, stripe, and snip. Set included Ginger, Duchess, and Merrylegs #3040, and carrying case. $11.90.
2.) 3234: 1990 – 91. *A Pony For Keeps.* Matte, alabaster; gray points. "Another"; set included Keen, Mustang Stallion, and Merrylegs #3234. $11.20.
3.) 3346: 1992 – 93. *Hanoverian Family.* Matte, light bay; black points, faint dorsal stripe, socks, natural hooves, stripe. Set included Keen and Andalusian Foal #3346. $11.20.

bottom row

1.) 2005: 1996 – current. *Precious Beauty Foal & Gift Set.* Matte, chestnut leopard appaloosa; light chestnut mane and tail, gray-ish-tan hooves. Included Andalusian Foal #2005. $10.90.
2.) S 1990: Export. *Hatatitla.* Matte, bay; black points. Sometimes called the Karl May Set, sold separately or with Black Beauty S 1990. $32.20.
3.) S 1994: Toys "R" Us. *Spanish-Norman Family.* Matte, alabaster; white mane and tail, grayish-tan hooves, shaded muzzle and ears; given SR number 700294. Set included Andalusian Stallion and Foal S 1994. $13.30.

Duchess

Mold #3040DU; introduced in 1980.

Duchess
top row

1.) 3040: 1980 – 93. *Black Beauty Family.* Matte, bay; black points. Set included Black Beauty, Ginger, and Merrylegs #3040, and carrying case. $10.80.
2.) 3345: 1990 – 93. *King of the Wind Set.* Matte, alabaster; gray mane and tail, darker hooves, shaded muzzle. "Lady Roxana"; set included Black Stallion and Black Beauty #3345. $10.80.

bottom

1.) 3347: 1992 – 94. *Trakehner Family.* Matte, light dapple gray; gray points, stockings/socks, shaded muzzle. Set included Jet Run and Mustang Foal #3347. $10.80.

Duchess model not shown:
19843: 1984 – 87. *Family to Church on Sunday.* Flocked, bay; black hair mane and tail, three socks, and a blaze. Included matching Jet Run, leather and metal harness, black metal and wood surrey with pin striping and red wheels, ceramic dolls dressed for church, wood base, clear plastic display case. $63.90 ($259.00 complete).

New for 1997:
S 1997: State Line Tack. *1997 Pinto Family* (temporary name). Matte, black pinto; natural hooves. Set included Arabian Foal (Classic) and Black Beauty (Classic) S 1997. $12.60.

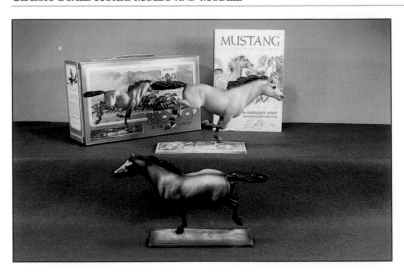

Hobo

Mold #625; introduced in 1975.

Hobo
top

3085: 1975 – 81. *Hobo of Lazy Heart Ranch Gift Set.* Matte, buckskin; darker legs, black mane and tail, shaded muzzle, natural hooves, white stripe; sepia shaded stand. Set included Marguerite Henry's "Mustang" in paperback, and carrying case. $37.80.

also 625: 1975 – 80. *Hobo the Mustang of Lazy Heart Ranch.* Matte, buckskin; same as model from #3085. In 1976 catalogs was called Hobo, and in 1977 – 79 was labeled Hobo Mustang. $44.80.

bottom

S 1993: Breyerfest '93 Raffle model (21). *Nevada Star.* Matte, gray; color called "Silver Dust," has a slightly metallic sheen, black points, lighter face, dorsal stripe, grulla markings; stand is more heavily shaded than #625s. $644.00.

Hobo
top row

1.) S 1995: Mid-year release. *Riddle Passing Through Time, Phase 1.* Matte, bay blanket appaloosa; black points, hind socks, light brown stand. $20.30.

2.) S 1995: Mid-year release. *Riddle Passing Through Time, Phase 2.* Matte, leopard appaloosa; chestnut points and shaded face, natural hooves, chestnut spots, medium brown stand. $20.30.

bottom

S 1995: Mid-year release. *Riddle Passing Through Time, Phase 3.* Matte, leopard appaloosa; gray mane and tail, slightly shaded face, black and brown spots, dark brown stand. $20.30.

Jet Run

Mold #3035JR; introduced in 1980.

Jet Run
top row

1.) 3035: 1980 – 93. *U.S. Equestrian Team Gift Set.* Matte, bay; black points, white star. Set included Keen and Might Tango #3035, and carrying case. $11.90.

2.) 3347: 1992 – 94. *Trakehner Family.* Matte, dark red chestnut; right hind sock, star. Set included Duchess and Mustang Foal #3035. $11.20.

bottom row

1.) S 1987: Sears. *US Olympic Team.* Matte, chestnut; darker mane and tail, fore socks. Set included Keen and Might Tango S 1987. $18.90.

2.) S 1989 – 90: Sears (89) and also Export (90). *German Olympics Set.* Matte, bay; black points, snip, left hind sock, gray hooves, "Rembrandt"; set included Keen and Might Tango S 1989; Export set was called "German Olympic Team." $19.60.

Jet Run model not shown:

19843: 1984 – 87. *Family to Church on Sunday.* Flocked, bay; black hair mane and tail, three socks, and a blaze. Included matching Duchess, leather and metal harness, black metal and wood surrey with pin striping and red wheels, ceramic dolls dressed for church, wood base, clear plastic display case. $63.90 ($259.00 complete).

Johar

Mold #3030JO; introduced in 1983.

Johar

top row

1.) 3030: 1983 – 93. *The Black Stallion Returns Set.* Matte, alabaster; gray mane, tail, and hooves. Set included the Classic Black Stallion and Johar #3030. $10.50.

2.) S 1988: Breyer Signing Parties and other retailers. *Foal's First Day.* Matte, rose gray; darker points. Set included Arabian Foal S 1988; signing parties offered only the models, some sets were sold by the Enchanted Doll House with a cookie tin. $26.60 ($44.10 complete).

bottom row

1.) S 1993: Toys "R" Us. *Drinkers of the Wind.* Matte, flea-bit gray; light gray points and hooves, chestnut speckles; given SR number 700693. Set included Arabian Stallion and Foal S 1993. $14.70.

2.) S 1995: Mid-year release. *Eagle and Pow Wow.* Matte, black pinto; white legs, belly, and chest (splash overo pattern), and white muzzle. Included doll in Native American costume, saddle blanket, and leather halter and lead rope. $27.30 ($32.20 complete).

Johar model not shown:

19841: 1984 – 87. *Drive on a Sunny Day.* Flocked, chestnut; bobbed tail, three socks (not left hind) broad blaze, hair mane and tail. The 1984 dealer catalog showed the Classic Man O'War flocked and haired, while the 1985 dealer catalog showed Johar with same markings; set included leather harness, black metal and wood buggy with yellow trim and yellow wheels, wooden base, plastic display cover; signed and numbered; designed and crafted by the Riegsecker Family and Amish. $103.40 ($205.00 complete).

Kelso

Mold #601; introduced in 1975.

Regular Run Kelso Models

top row

1.) 601: 1975 – 90. *Kelso.* Matte/semi-gloss, dark bay/brown; right hind sock (some do not have the sock). $17.50.

2.) 251: 1991 – 92. *Norita.* Matte, dapple gray; medium gray points, socks/stockings, bald face, gray hooves. $16.10.

3.) 257: 1993 – 94. *Jeremy.* Matte, brown; star and stripe, socks, pink hooves. $15.40.

bottom row

1.) 3348: 1994 – 96. *Fine Horse Family.* Matte, roan; chestnut points, blaze on lower face over nose. Set included Silky Sullivan and Mustang Foal #3348. $9.80.

2.) 263: 1995 – 96. *Black Jack.* Matte, black pinto; white mane and tail, left foreleg white, right hind stocking, other legs with socks, blaze, pink shaded muzzle; included neck ribbon. $14.00.

Keen

Mold #3035KE; introduced in 1980.

Keen

top row

1.) 3035: 1980 – 93. *U.S. Equestrian Team Gift Set.* Matte, chestnut; right hind sock/stocking, darker mane and tail, stripe. Set included Jet Run and Might Tango #3035, and carrying case. $11.60.

2.) 3346: 1992 – 93. *Hanoverian Family.* Matte, black; star, narrow blaze, three socks (not left hind). Set included Ginger and Andalusian Foal #3346. $11.50.

bottom row

1.) S 1987: Sears. *U.S. Olympic Team Set.* Matte, gray; stockings, gray hooves. Set included Jet Run and Might Tango S 1987. $18.90.

2.) S 1989, 90: Sears, Export. *German Olympic Set.* Matte, red bay; black points, hind socks, blaze, gray hooves. "Ahlerich"; set included Jet Run and Might Tango S 1989. Export set was called "German Olympic Team." $18.20.

Keen model not shown:

19846: 1984, 87. *Delivery Wagon.* Flocked, chestnut; three socks (not left fore), blaze, flaxen mane and tail. First this member of the Miniature Collection was a special run (for Montgomery Ward), then it was offered in regular catalogs. The set included a leather and metal harness, a green wood and metal wagon with silver pin striping and red wheels, and a doll. $79.60 ($182.00 complete).

Special Run Kelso Models
top row
1.) S 1987: Hobby Center Toys. *Triple Crown Winners Set 1.* Matte, chestnut; darker mane and tail, left hind sock. "Citation"; set included Terrang and Silky Sullivan S 1987. $25.90.
2.) S 1992: Sears. *Draw Horses with Sam Savitt.* Matte, bay; black points, socks, pink hooves. Set included book "Draw Horses with Sam Savitt." $27.30 ($42.70 complete).

bottom row
1.) S 1993: Aristoplay. *Denver and Blaze — Dutch Warmbloods.* Matte, mahogany bay; black points, blaze. Sold with the game "Herd Your Horses" and separately; included Quarter Horse Foal S 1993. $19.60.
2.) S 1995: Toys "R" Us. *Geronimo and Cochise.* Matte, light bay appaloosa; three socks (not left fore), darker points except tail which is grayish-brown and white. "Cochise"; came in "Geronimo and Cochise, Medallion Series" set with Sea Star (Traditional scale) S 1995. $18.90.

New for 1997:
287: 1997 – current. *Vanity.* Matte, bay pinto; black points, white right legs, left socks, broad blaze. B-Ranch series; included ribbon. $7.00.

Lipizzan Stallion

Mold #620; introduced in 1975.

Lipizzan Stallion
top row
1, 2.) 620: 1975 – 80. *Lipizzan Stallion.* Matte, alabaster; pink/natural hooves, some have slight shaded gray mane and tail. Photo shows variation (shaded ears, etc.). $29.40.

bottom row
1.) 209: 1984 – 87. *Pegasus.* Matte, alabaster; included wings; pink hooves. Wings fit in slots on back. $44.80.
2.) S 1985: JC Penney. *Pegasus Flying Horse.* Flocked, light blue; blue hair mane and tail, sky blue hooves, some glitter on the white wings. $78.40.

Lipizzan Stallion
top
S 1993: World of Horses. *Lipizzan Stallion.* Matte, alabaster; lightly shaded. $30.10.

bottom row
1.) S 1996: Toys "R" Us. *Unicorn III.* Semi-gloss, pearly white; added horn. $25.00.
2.) S 1996: Toys "R" Us. *Unicorn III.* Glossy, black; added horn. $25.00.

Man O'War

Mold #602; introduced in 1975.

Man O'War (Classic)
top row

1, 2.) 602: 1975 – 90. *Man O'War*. Matte, red chestnut; darker mane and tail, broken stripe or just star. The 1985 and 86 dealer catalogs had the Man O'War and Terrang labels switched. $16.80.

3.) 252: 1991 – 92. *Pepe*. Matte, light chestnut; darker mane and tail, stockings. $16.10.

bottom row

1.) 258: 1993 – 94. *King*. Matte, dark chestnut; left hind sock. $15.40.

2.) 264: 1995 – 96. *Apache*. Matte, gray; darker gray points, shaded face, blaze, pink hooves, included neck ribbon. $11.30.

3.) S 1988: Hobby Center Toys. *Triple Crown Winners Set II*. Matte, chestnut; long diamond star. "Affirmed"; set included Swaps and Terrang S 1988. $26.60.

New for 1997:

288: 1997 – current. *Tumbleweed*. Matte, light bay; shaded, black mane and tail, black shaded knees, hocks, ankles, hooves, and muzzle. B-Ranch series; included ribbon. $7.00.

Mesteno Series Models

Mold #480 (Mesteno); introduced in 1992. Mold #4810FO (Mesteno the Foal) and #4810MO (Mesteno's Mother); introduced in 1993. Mold #4811ME and #4811SO (The Challengers — Mesteno and Sombra); introduced in 1994. Mold #4812ME (Charging Mesteno) and #4812RO (Rojo); introduced in 1995. Mold #481 (Reflections Mesteno); introduced in 1996.

Mesteno Series
top row

1.) Mesteno. 480: 1992 – current. *Mesteno, the Messenger*. Matte, dark buckskin; dark brown points. $12.60.

2.) Fighting Mesteno. 4811: 1994 – current. *The Challengers — Mesteno and Sombra*. Matte, dark buckskin; black points, some striping on legs. Set included Sombra; also sold in JC Penney catalog (1994) with Challenger print by Roland Cheney. $13.20 ($24.50 with print).

3.) Sombra. 4811: 1994 – current. *The Challengers — Mesteno and Sombra*. Matte, grulla; black points, some striping on legs. Set included Fighting Mesteno; also sold in JC Penney catalog (1994) with Challenger print by Roland Cheney. $13.20 ($24.50 with print).

bottom row

1.) Mesteno the Foal. 3350: 1996 – current. *Misty II, Black Mist, and Twister*. Matte, palomino; gray shaded muzzle, natural hooves. Set included Ruffian and Swaps #3350. $5.30.

2.) Mesteno's Mother. 4810: 1993 – current. *The Dawning — Mesteno and Mother*. Matte, buckskin; black points, some striping on upper legs. $12.20.

3.) Mesteno the Foal. 4810: 1993 – current. *The Dawning — Mesteno and Mother*. Matte, light dun; black mane, and shaded muzzle, stockings/lighter legs, gray hooves. $6.70.

Merrylegs

Mold #3040ML; introduced in 1980.

Merrylegs
top row

1.) 3040: 1980 – 93. *Black Beauty Family*. Matte, dapple gray; white mane and tail, gray hooves, lighter lower legs and face. Set included Ginger, Duchess, and Might Tango #3040. $10.50.

2.) 3234: 1990 – 91. *A Pony For Keeps*. Matte, alabaster; white mane and tail, gray hooves, gray shading on muzzle. "Lady Jane Grey"; set included Ginger, Might Tango, and Mustang Stallion #3234. $9.80.

bottom row

1.) 898: 1994 – 95. *Martin's Dominique Champion Miniature Horse*. Semigloss, black; three socks (not left fore), hooves are natural or striped. As a miniature horse, this model is almost scaled properly to be part of the Traditional Series. $12.30.

2.) 947: 1996 – current. *Bond Snippet, Miniature Horse*. Matte, chestnut pinto; chestnut tail, chestnut and white mane, star. $9.70.

3.) S 1992: Sears. *Horses Great and Small*. Matte, palomino; socks, white mane and tail, gray hooves and shaded muzzle. Set included Traditional Cantering Welsh Pony and Clydesdale Stallion S 1992. $16.10.

Merrylegs model not shown:

19845: 1987. *Joey's Pony Cart*. Flocked, black pinto; socks, black hooves, white mane, tail, blaze. Set included leather and metal harness, wood and metal cart, and doll; part of Miniature Collection. $77.00 ($154.00 complete).

Mesteno Series
top row
1.) Charging Mesteno. 4812: 1995 – current. *The Progeny Gift Set — Mesteno and His Yearling.* Matte/semi-gloss, dark buckskin; dark brown or black points, some striping on legs. Set included Rojo #4810. $13.40.
2.) Reflections Mesteno. 481: 1996 – current. *Reflections Mesteno.* Matte, buckskin; black points, leg bars. $12.60.

bottom
Rojo. 4812: 1995 – current. *The Progeny Gift Set — Mesteno and His Yearling.* Matte, light red dun; light chestnut mane and tail, grayish knees, hocks, and ankles, red striping on legs. Set included Charging Mesteno #4810. $9.80.

New for 1997:
Fighting Mesteno. 989: 1997 – current. *Runaway, Mustang Kiger, BLM Adopt-A-Horse.* Matte, cocoa dun; cream or off-white body with brown shading, brown points, primitive stripes on legs, shaded face, snip, left hind sock. $10.00.

Might Tango
Mold #3035MT; introduced in 1980.

Might Tango
top row
1.) 3035: 1980 – 91. *U.S. Equestrian Team Gift Set.* Matte, dapple gray; socks, darker points. Set included Jet Run and Keen #3035 and carrying case. $12.60.
2.) 3234: 1990 – 91. *A Pony For Keeps.* Matte, light dapple gray; gray points, socks. "Blue"; set included Merrylegs, Might Tango, and Mustang Stallion #3234. $13.30.

bottom row
1.) S 1987: Sears. *US Olympic Team Set.* Matte, bay; black points, hind socks. Set included Jet Run and Keen S 1987. $21.70.
2.) S 1989 – 90: Sears, Export. *German Olympic Set.* Matte, bay; black mane, tail, hocks, and forelegs, star, right hind or both hind socks. "Orchidee"; set included Jet Run and Keen S 1989. The export set was called "German Olympic Set." $22.40.

Mustang Foal
Mold #3065FO; introduced in 1976.

Mustang Foal
top row
1.) 3065: 1976 – 90. *Mustang Family.* Matte, chestnut; darker mane and tail, bald face, stockings, gray hooves. Set included Mustang Stallion and Mare #3065 and carrying case. $9.10.
2.) 3066: 1987 – 96. *Marguerite Henry's "Our First Pony" Set.* Matte, black pinto; stockings black and white mane and tail. Set included Traditional Shetland Pony, Classic Arabian, and Mustang Foals #3066. $9.10.
3.) 3347: 1992 – 94. *Trakehner Family.* Matte, bay; right hind sock, star. Set included Duchess and Jet Run #3347. $9.10.
4.) 3348: 1994 – 96. *Fine Horse Family.* Matte, roan; dark chestnut mane, lighter tail, blaze, hind socks. Set included Kelso and Silky Sullivan #3348. $5.00.

bottom row
1.) 3349: 1995 – current. *Appaloosa Mustang Family Gift Set.* Matte, bay appaloosa; darker points, narrow blaze, three stockings (not right fore), blanket over hindquarters and barrel. Set included Mustang Mare and Stallion #3349. $5.00.
2.) S 1985: Sears. *Mustang Family.* Matte, chestnut pinto; socks, gray hooves. Set included Mustang Mare and Stallion S 1985. $12.60.
3.) S 1992: JC Penney. *Breyer Mustang Family.* Matte, grulla; chestnut mane and tail, hind socks, knee/hock stripes. Set included Mustang Mare and Stallion S 1992. $12.60.

Mustang Mare

Mold #3065MA; introduced in 1976.

Mustang Mare
top row
1.) 3065: 1976 – 90. *Mustang Family.* Matte, chestnut pinto; chestnut mane and tail, gray hooves. Set included Mustang Stallion and Foal #3065 and carrying case. $14.00.
2.) 3349: 1995 – current. *Appaloosa Mustang Family Gift Set.* Matte, black appaloosa; blanket on hindquarters only, left hind sock, narrow blaze, natural hooves. Set included Mustang Stallion and Foal #3349. $9.10.

bottom row
1.) S 1985: Sears. *Mustang Family.* Matte, bay/chestnut; black mane and tail, socks. Set included Mustang Foal and Stallion S 1985. $21.00.
2.) S 1992: JC Penney. *Breyer Mustang Family.* Matte, bay; black points, right hind sock. Set included Mustang Stallion and Foal S 1992. $18.90.

Mustang Stallion

Mold #3065ST; introduced in 1976.

Mustang Stallion
top row
1.) 3065: 1976 – 90. *Mustang Family.* Matte, chestnut; flaxen mane and tail, socks, gray hooves. Set included Mustang Mare and Foal #3065 and carrying case. $12.60.
2.) 3234: 1990 – 91. *A Pony For Keeps.* Matte, chestnut; flaxen mane and tail, gray to black lower legs, shaded muzzle. "Jefferson"; set included Might Tango, Ginger, and Merrylegs #3234. $12.60.
3.) 3349: 1995 – current. *Appaloosa Mustang Family Gift Set.* Matte, dun appaloosa; most of body and neck is light gray or white, spots on hindquarters only, left hind sock, gray mane and tail, shaded face. Set included Mustang Mare and Foal #3349. $9.10.

bottom row
1.) S 1985: Sears. *Mustang Family.* Matte, buckskin; black points, knee stripes, no dorsal stripe. Set included Mustang Mare and Foal S 1985. $20.30.
2.) S 1992: JC Penney. *Breyer Mustang Family.* Matte, buckskin; black points, knee stripes, dorsal stripe, gray shaded muzzle. Some had shoulder stripe as well; set included Mustang Mare and Foal S 1992. $18.90.

Polo Pony

Mold #626; introduced in 1976.

Polo Pony
top
626: 1976 – 82. *Polo Pony.* Matte, bay; black points, early ones with socks, molded woodgrain base. $42.70.

bottom
S 1994: Breyer Show Special. *Silver Comet.* Matte, light dapple gray; darker gray knees, hocks, and shaded muzzle, socks, natural hooves, molded woodgrain base. $27.30.

Quarter Horse Foal

Mold #3045FO; introduced in 1974.

Regular Run Quarter Horse Foal Models
top row
1.) 3045: 1974 – 93. *Quarter Horse Family.* Matte, light bay; black points, some had socks. Set included Classic Quarter Horse Stallion and Mare #3045, and carrying case. $9.80.
2.) 4001: 1975 – 82. *Quarter Horse Foal.* Matte, red bay; black points, socks, gray hooves. $15.40.
3.) 4001: 1975 – 82. *Quarter Horse Foal.* Matte, black; stockings, bald face, gray hooves. $15.40.

bottom row
1, 2.) 4001: 1975 – 82. *Quarter Horse Foal.* Matte, palomino; socks, gray hooves, white mane and tail. $15.40.

Special Run Quarter Horse Foal Models
top row
1.) S 1984: Montgomery Ward. *Appaloosa Family.* Matte, black appaloosa; blanket on hindquarters only, splash spots. Set included Classic Quarter Horse Stallion and Mare S 1984 and carrying case. $18.90.
2.) S 1986: Sears. *Collector's Edition Appaloosa Family.* Matte, chestnut appaloosa; darker mane and tail, blanket pattern on hindquarters only, splash spots. Set included Classic Quarter Horse Stallion and Mare S 1986 and carrying case. $16.10.

bottom row
1.) S 1991: JC Penney. *Breyer Quarter Horse Family.* Matte, alabaster; gray mane, tail, and hooves. Set included Classic Quarter Horse Stallion and Mare S 1991. $16.10.
2.) S 1993: Aristoplay, and other mail order sources. *Denver and Blaze.* Matte, red bay; black points, narrow blaze. Sold with "Herd Your Horses" game or separately; set included Kelso S 1993. $12.60.

Quarter Horse Mare

Mold #3045MA; introduced in 1974.

Quarter Horse Mare (Classic)
top row
1.) 3045: 1974 – 93. *Quarter Horse Family.* Matte, bay; black points, socks, gray hooves. Set included Classic Quarter Horse Stallion and Foal #3045 and carrying case. $12.30.
2.) S 1984: Montgomery Ward. *Appaloosa Family.* Matte, black appaloosa; blanket pattern on hindquarters, splash spots. Set included Classic Quarter Horse Stallion and Foal S 1984 and carrying case. $20.30.
3.) S 1986: Sears. *Collector's Edition Appaloosa Family.* Matte, chestnut appaloosa; darker mane and tail, blanket pattern on hindquarters, splash spots. Set included Classic Quarter Horse Stallion and Foal S 1986 and carrying case. $19.60.

bottom row
1.) S 1989: Export and various mail order companies. Matte, chestnut pinto; darker mane and tail, socks. $23.10.
2.) S 1991: JC Penney. *Breyer Quarter Horse Family.* Matte, dark chestnut/bay; black/darker points, hind socks. Set included Classic Quarter Horse Stallion and Foal S 1991. $18.90.

Quarter Horse Stallion

Mold #3045ST; introduced in 1974.

Quarter Horse Stallion (Classic)
top row

1.) 3045: 1974 – 93. *Quarter Horse Family.* Matte, palomino; white mane and tail, various socks, gray hooves. Set included Classic Quarter Horse Mare and Foal #3045 and carrying case. $12.60.

2.) S 1984: Montgomery Ward. *Appaloosa Family.* Matte, black appaloosa; blanket pattern on hindquarters, splash spots. Set included Classic Quarter Horse Mare and Foal S 1984 and carrying case. $19.60.

3.) S 1986: Sears. *Collector's Edition Appaloosa Family.* Matte, chestnut appaloosa; blanket pattern on hindquarters, splash spots. Set included Classic Quarter Horse Mare and Foal S 1986 and carrying case. $18.90.

bottom row

1.) S 1989: Montgomery Ward. *Appaloosa Family.* Matte, black appaloosa; blanket extending over most of barrel, fore socks. $20.30.

2.) S 1991: JC Penney. *Breyer Quarter Horse Family.* Matte, dark chestnut/bay; darker points, right hind sock. Set included Classic Quarter Horse Mare and Foal S 1991. $18.90.

Rearing Stallion

Mold #180; introduced in 1965.

Regular Run Rearing Stallion Models
top row

1.) 185: 1965 – 80. *Rearing Stallion.* Matte, bay; black mane, tail, and hooves, bald face, stockings. $18.90.

2.) 183: 1965 – 85. *Rearing Stallion.* Matte, palomino; white mane and tail, stockings, bald face, pink/natural hooves. $17.50.

3.) 180: 1965 – 76, 78 – 85. *Rearing Stallion.* Matte, alabaster; gray hooves, shaded pink muzzle. $17.50.

bottom row

1.) 890: 1994 – 95. *Promises, Rearing Stallion.* Matte, dark bay pinto; brown bay, black mane and tail, front socks, hind legs white, natural hooves. $15.40.

2.) 957: 1996 – current. *Midnight, Bronco.* Semi-gloss, black; Circle M brand painted on right hip (white). $10.40.

Special Run Rearing Stallion Models
top

S 1995: Mid-year release. *Willow and Shining Star.* Matte, bay blanket appaloosa; dark bay, black points, gray hooves, white star and multicolored decoration on right side of neck. Included black and red leather halter, and Native American dressed doll; given SR number 703495. $32.30 ($44.80 complete).

bottom row

1.) S 1993: Breyer Show Special. *Little Chaparral.* Matte, buckskin pinto; black knees, tail, and upper mane, hind legs are white, blaze, pink hooves; given SR model number 700293. $28.70.

2.) S 1993: West Coast Model Horse Collector's Jamboree. *Rearing Stallion.* Matte, buckskin; black points, no dorsal stripe. $57.40.

Ruffian

Mold #606; introduced in 1977.

Ruffian
top row
1.) 606: 1977 – 90. *Ruffian.* Matte, dark bay; left hind sock, star. $16.80.
2.) 256: 1991 – 92. *Lula.* Matte, bay; black points, hind socks. $15.40.
3.) 262: 1993 – 94. *Colleen.* Matte, chestnut; flaxen mane and tail, three stockings (not right fore), blaze, gray shaded muzzle. $13.30.

bottom row
1.) 268: 1995 – 96. *Patches.* Matte, bay pinto; right hind stocking, other legs white, elongated star, striped hooves, included neck ribbon. $11.30.
2.) 2003: 1995 – 96. *Glory and Plank Jump Gift Set.* Matte, dun/buckskin; black points, socks, blaze. Set included blue, white, and yellow plank jump. $15.40.
3.) 3350: 1996 – current. *Misty II, Black Mist, and Twister.* Matte, chestnut pinto; white legs, narrow blaze, shaded muzzle, natural hooves. Set included Mesteno the Foal and Swaps #3350. $9.50.

New for 1997:
292: 1997 – current. *Whispers.* Matte, gray appaloosa; extensive blanket, gray mane, lower tail, and hooves, gray over shoulders, neck, and head, blaze. B-Ranch series; included ribbon. $7.00.

Sagr

Mold #3030SA; introduced in 1983.

Sagr
3030: 1983 – 93. *The Black Stallion Returns Set.* Matte, sorrel; flaxen mane and tail, socks, gray hooves. Set included Classic Black Stallion and Johar #3030. $13.30.

Silky Sullivan

Mold #603; introduced in 1975.

Silky Sullivan 1 (Classic)
top row
1.) 603: 1975 – 90. *Silky Sullivan.* Matte, brown; darker mane and tail, star, some with left fore sock. $16.80.
2.) 253: 1991 – 92. *T-Bone.* Matte, black roan; black points and speckles. $14.70.

bottom row
1.) 259: 1993 – 94. *Andrew.* Matte, gray; darker points (or just mane and tail), dorsal stripe, hind socks. $13.30.
2.) 3348: 1994 – 96. *Fine Horse Family.* Matte, dark chestnut/bay; darker/black points, star, three socks, pink hooves. Set included Kelso and Mustang Foal #3348. $9.50.

Silky Sullivan 2 (Classic)

top row

1.) 265: 1995 – 96. *Spice.* Matte, bay appaloosa; black points, diamond star, hind socks, natural hooves, blanket over hindquarters with splash spots, included neck ribbon. $11.30.

2.) 2004: 1995 – 96. *Buck and Hillary Gift Set.* Matte, buckskin; cream body color with dark gray or black mane and tail, shaded muzzle. Included jump and doll. $14.20.

bottom

S 1987: Hobby Center Toys. *Triple Crown Winners Set I.* Matte, chestnut; darker mane and tail. "Whirlaway"; set included Kelso and Terrang S 1987. $26.60.

Swaps

Mold #604; introduced in 1975.

Swaps (Classic)

top row

1.) 604: 1975 – 90. *Swaps.* Matte, chestnut; darker mane and tail, right hind sock and light gray hoof, otherwise darker hooves. $17.50.

2.) 254: 1991 – 92. *Hawk.* Matte, black; socks, reverse "C" shaped star. $15.40.

3.) 260: 1993 – 94. *Prince.* Matte, light gray; gray points, very light body color, socks/stockings, natural hooves. $14.70.

bottom row

1.) 266: 1995 – 96. *Cloud.* Matte, gray; bald face, socks, large resist blotches, pink hooves and pink shaded muzzle; color often had a rosy cast to it. Included neck ribbon. $11.30.

2.) 3350: 1996 – current. *Misty II, Black Mist, and Twister.* Matte, black pinto; white legs, blaze, natural hooves. Set included Mesteno the Foal and Ruffian #3350. $9.70.

3.) S 1988: Hobby Center Toys. *Triple Crown Winners Set II.* Matte, brown; darker mane and tail, narrow blaze. "Seattle Slew"; set included Man O'War and Terrang S 1988. $27.30.

New for 1997:
290: 1997 – current. *Black Silk.* Matte/semi-gloss, black; apron face, vague socks. B-Ranch series; included ribbon. $7.00.

Terrang

Mold #605; introduced in 1975.

Terrang

top row

1.) 605: 1975 – 90. *Terrang.* Matte, dark brown; no markings. The 1985 and 86 dealer catalogs have Man O'War and Terrang labels switched. $17.50.

2.) 255: 1991 – 92. *Gaucho.* Matte, red roan; light chestnut mane and tail, grayish-red knees and hocks, pink hooves. $15.40.

3.) 261: 1993 – 94. *Ten Gallon.* Matte, dun; dark grayish-brown points, left hind sock, pale midsection, shaded muzzle. $13.30.

bottom row

1.) 267: 1995 – 96. *Azul.* Matte, blue roan/gray; gray base color, black points, dark chestnut shaded face, with gray speckles, hind socks, front hooves are striped, included neck ribbon. $11.30.

2.) S 1987: Hobby Center Toys. *Triple Crown Winners Set I.* Matte, dark bay/chestnut; darker mane and tail, left hind sock. "Count Fleet"; set included Kelso and Silky Sullivan S 1987. $14.20.

3.) S 1988: Hobby Center Toys. *Triple Crown Winners Set II.* Matte, chestnut; darker mane and tail, narrow blaze, three socks (not left fore). "Secretariat"; set included Man O'War and Swaps S 1988. $27.30.

New for 1997:
291: 1997 – current. Ambrosia. Matte, palomino; shaded, white mane, tail, blaze, and socks/stockings, gray shaded knees, hocks, hooves, and muzzle. B-Ranch series; included ribbon. $7.00.

≋ Little Bits Scale Molds and Models ≋

Introduced in the 1983 catalogs, these models average between 4½" and 5" tall, making them the second smallest of the horse molds. There are currently seven molds. Breyer's only exclusively "fantasy" creation, a unicorn, is in this scale (all other fantasy animals were adapted from existing molds).

Like the other scales, Little Bits can be repainted and remade.

American Saddlebred
Mold #9030; introduced in 1985.

Regular Run American Saddlebred Models
top row
1.) 9030: 1985 – 88. *American Saddlebred.* Matte, bay; black points, white 5-point star. $10.80.
2.) 9030: 1985 – 88. *American Saddlebred.* Matte, red chestnut; darker mane and tail, white 5-point star. $10.80.
3.) 9030: 1985 – 88. *American Saddlebred.* Matte, palomino; socks, gray hooves, white mane and tail. $10.80.

bottom row
1.) 9070: 1990 – 94. *American Saddlebred.* Matte, black pinto; narrow stripe, white legs, pink hooves. $10.20.
2.) 1021: 1995 – current. *Belle.* Matte, bay; socks, natural hooves, black points, two stars. Saddle Club Collection. $6.70.

Special Run American Saddlebred Models
top row
1.) S 1985, 90: Reeves acquisition of Breyer, and Breakfast with Peter Stone events. Matte, sorrel; flaxen mane and tail, three socks (not right fore). Came with a hang tag that said "a special edition for a special year!" $39.90.
2.) S 1988: JC Penney. *Breyer Parade of Breeds.* Matte, brown pinto; narrow blaze, white legs, pink hooves. $12.70.

bottom row
1.) S 1989: JC Penney. *Breyer Parade of Breeds Collector's Assortment — 2nd Edition.* Matte, dark bay; black points, three socks (not right fore). $12.70.
2.) S 1990: JC Penney. *Breyer Parade of Breeds Collector's Assortment — 3rd Edition.* Matte, palomino pinto; narrow stripe, white legs, pink hooves. $12.70.

Arabian Stallion
Mold #1001; introduced in 1984.

Regular Run Arabian Stallion Models (Little Bits)
top row
1.) 9001: 1984 – 88. *Arabian Stallion.* Matte, bay; black points. $10.80.
2.) 9001: 1984 – 88. *Arabian Stallion.* Matte, chestnut; darker mane and tail. $10.80.
3.) 9001: 1984 – 88. *Arabian Stallion.* Matte, gray; black/dark gray points. $10.80.
also 1001: 1984 – 85. *Bitsy Breyer and Arabian Stallion Beach Set.* Matte, bay, chestnut, or gray; same models as #9001. Included plastic jointed Bitsy doll, plastic bridle, surf board, and comb. $18.20 ($25.20 complete).

bottom row
1.) 9045: 1989 – 94. *Arabian Stallion.* Matte, alabaster; gray mane, tail, and hooves. $9.00.
2.) 1016: 1994 – current. *Starlight and Carole (Saddle Club Series).* Matte, black; distinct 5-pointed star. Includes plastic jointed doll, plastic English tack, helmet, competitor's number, and comb. $9.00 ($11.00 complete).

Special Run Arabian Stallion Models (Little Bits)
top row
1.) S 1988: JC Penney. *Breyer Parade of Breeds.* Matte, alabaster; light gray mane and tail. Essentially the same as #9045. $10.40.
2.) S 1989: JC Penney. *Breyer Parade of Breeds Collector's Assortment — 2nd Edition.* Matte, black; gray hooves. $12.30.

bottom row
1, 2.) S 1990: JC Penney. *Breyer Parade of Breeds Collector's Assortment — 3rd Edition.* Matte, dapple gray; darker gray or black points, socks. Darker variation shown. $12.30.
3.) S 1996: JC Penney. *Young Equestrian Team.* Matte, chestnut; darker mane and tail, slightly darker knees and hocks, shaded muzzle, socks. Included Bitsy English rider, and Little Bit Quarter Horse and Thoroughbred Stallions S 1996 with riders. $13.00.

Morgan Stallion

Mold #1005; introduced in 1984.

Regular Run Morgan Stallion Models (Little Bits)
top row
1.) 9005: 1984 – 88. *Morgan Horse Stallion.* Matte, bay; black points. $10.80.
2.) 9005: 1984 – 88. *Morgan Horse Stallion.* Matte, chestnut; darker mane and tail. $10.80.
3.) 9005: 1984 – 88. *Morgan Horse Stallion.* Matte, black; left hind stocking. $10.80.
also 9950: 1986 – 87. *Bitsy Breyer Riding Academy.* Matte, bay; black points. Included carrying case that folded open to form a paddock and barn, Bitsy doll, plastic tack, comb, helmet, and 3 sections of fence. $13.70 ($32.90 complete).
also 1005: 1984 – 87. *Bitsy Breyer and Morgan English Set.* Matte, bay, black, or chestnut; same as respective #9005s. Included jointed Bitsy doll, plastic saddle, bridle, hunt cap, and comb. $16.90 ($26.50 complete).

bottom row
1.) 9050: 1989 – 94. *Morgan Stallion.* Matte, sorrel/palomino; flaxen mane and tail, socks, gray hooves. $9.10.
2.) 1018: 1994 – current. *Pepper and Lisa (Saddle Club Series).* Matte, dapple gray; black points. Included jointed Bitsy doll, plastic English tack, hunt cap, and comb. $6.70 ($8.50 complete).
3.) 1024: 1995 – current. *Delilah.* Matte, palomino; white mane and tail, socks/stockings, natural hooves. Saddle Club Collection. $6.70.

Clydesdale

Mold #1025; introduced in 1984.

Clydesdale (Little Bits)
top row
1.) 9025: 1984 – 88. *Clydesdale.* Matte, chestnut; stockings, black mane and tail, gray hooves, bald or solid face. $11.50.
2.) 9065: 1990 – 94. *Shire.* Matte, black; stockings, natural hooves. $10.50.
3.) 3170: 1994 – 95. *Circus Extravaganza.* Matte, bay; rich bay, black points, darker shading; some have right fore sock. Set included Traditional Clydesdale Stallion #3170. $8.70.
4.) 3175: 1994 – 95. *Action Drafters, Big and Small.* Matte, roan; basically gray with chestnut shading, black points. Set included Traditional Friesian #3175. $9.50.

bottom row
1.) S 1989: JC Penney. *Breyer Parade of Breeds Collector's Assortment — 2nd Edition.* Matte, sorrel; flaxen mane and tail, stockings. $12.70.
2.) S 1989: Hobby Center Toys. Semi-gloss, dapple gray; sparsely dappled, stockings, medium gray mane and tail. $23.10.
3.) S 1990: JC Penney. *Breyer Parade of Breeds Collector's Assortment — 3rd Edition.* Matte, dapple gray; medium dappling, stockings, dark gray mane and tail. $12.70.

Special Run Morgan Stallion Models (Little Bits)
top row
1.) S 1985: JC Penney. *Merry-Go-Round Horse.* Matte, light purple; pink mane and tail, wood base, brass pole. $32.20.
2.) S 1985: Riegseckers. Matte, light purple; pink mane and tail. $32.20.
3.) S 1988: JC Penney. *Breyer Parade of Breeds.* Matte, bay; black points, gray or black hooves. $12.00.

bottom row
1.) S 1989: JC Penney. *Breyer Parade of Breeds Collector's Assortment — 2nd Edition.* Matte, chestnut; socks, darker mane and tail, gray hooves. $12.00.
2.) S 1990: JC Penney. *Breyer Parade of Breeds Collector's Assortment — 3rd Edition.* Matte, bay; black points, hind socks. $11.60.
3.) S 1993: Breakfast with Peter Stone. Matte, light bay/buckskin; black points, hind socks. $35.00.

Quarter Horse Stallion

Mold #1015; introduced in 1984.

Quarter Horse Stallion (Little Bits)
top row
1, 2.) 9015: 1984 – 88. *Quarter Horse Stallion.* Matte, bay; right hind stocking, black points. Variations shown with black legs, and with socks. $10.80.
3, 4.) 9015: 1984 – 88. *Quarter Horse Stallion.* Matte, buckskin; socks, gray hooves, black points, no dorsal stripe. Variations shown with black legs, and with socks. $10.80.
also 1015: 1984 – 87. *Bitsy Breyer and Quarter Horse Western Set.* Matte, bay, buckskin, or palomino; same as respective #9015s. Included plastic, jointed Bitsy, plastic saddle, bridle, hat, and comb. $13.00 ($30.00 complete).

bottom row
1.) 9015: 1984 – 88. *Quarter Horse Stallion.* Matte, palomino; socks, gray hooves, white mane and tail. $10.80.
2, 3.) 9035: 1985 – 88. *Bay Pinto.* Matte, bay pinto; black points. Variations shown with black legs, and with socks. $10.80.

Quarter Horse Stallion (Little Bits)
top row
1.) 9040: 1985 – 88. *Appaloosa.* Matte, black appaloosa; hind socks, blanket pattern over hindquarters only. $10.80.
2.) 9060: 1989 – 94. *Quarter Horse Stallion.* Matte, black leopard appaloosa; black points, black speckles and spots on white or cream base color. $9.70.
3.) 9075: 1989 – 94. *Paint.* Matte, black pinto; socks, gray hooves. $9.70.
4, 5.) 9080: 1989 – 94. *Appaloosa.* Matte, chestnut appaloosa; blanket pattern over hindquarters, socks, gray hooves. $9.90.

bottom row
1.) 1019: 1994 – current. *Spot and Kate (Saddle Club Series).* Matte, black appaloosa; socks, blanket pattern over most of barrel, stripe. Included plastic, jointed Bitsy, Western tack, hat, and comb. $8.60 ($11.00 complete).
2.) 1023: 1995 – current. *Moonglow.* Matte, chestnut; stockings, bald face, darker mane and tail. Saddle Club Collection. $6.70.
3.) 1026: 1996 – current. *Chocolate and Jeannie.* Semi-gloss, dark bay; black points, blaze, right hind sock. Saddle Club Collection. $6.70.

Quarter Horse Stallion (Little Bits)
top row
1.) S 1988: JC Penney. *Breyer Parade of Breeds.* Matte, leopard appaloosa; black points, socks, spots are chestnut and dark brown. $12.00.
2.) S 1988: JC Penney. *Breyer Parade of Breeds.* Matte, gray; black points, socks. $12.00.
3.) S 1989: JC Penney. *Breyer Parade of Breeds Collector's Assortment — 2nd Edition.* Matte, black; socks, gray hooves. $12.00.

bottom row
1.) S 1990: JC Penney. *Breyer Parade of Breeds Collector's Assortment — 3rd Edition.* Matte, black leopard appaloosa; black points, socks, relatively large spots. $12.00.
2.) S 1996: JC Penney. *Young Equestrian Team.* Matte, dark bay pinto; black points, striped front hooves. Included Bitsy western rider, and Little Bit Arabian and Thoroughbred Stallions S 96. $13.00.

Thoroughbred Stallion

Mold #1010; introduced in 1984.

Regular Run Thoroughbred Stallion Models
top row
1.) 9010: 1984 – 88. *Thoroughbred Stallion.* Matte, red bay; black points. $10.80.
2.) 9010: 1984 – 88. *Thoroughbred Stallion.* Matte, chestnut; darker mane and tail, gray hooves. $10.80.
3.) 9010: 1984 – 88. *Thoroughbred Stallion.* Matte, black; natural hooves, right hind sock. $10.80.
also 1010: 1984 – 87. *Bitsy Breyer and Thoroughbred Jockey Set.* Matte, bay, chestnut, or black models; Models same as respective #9010s. Included jointed Bitsy doll, plastic saddle, bridle, helmet, and comb. $17.50 ($21.70 complete).
also S 1986: JC Penney. *"Little Bits" Horse Assortment.* Matte, bay, black, and chestnut; models same as respective #9010s. Included all three models. $31.50.
4.) 9055: 1989 – 94. *Thoroughbred Stallion.* Matte, dark gray; black points, hind socks. $9.50.

bottom row
1.) 1017: 1994 – current. *Topside and Stevie (Saddle Club Series).* Matte, bright bay/buckskin; black points. Includes plastic, jointed Bitsy, English tack, helmet, and comb, and competitor's number. $8.60 ($12.00 complete).
2.) 1017: 1995 – current. *Cobalt and Veronica (Saddle Club Series).* Matte, black; no markings. Includes plastic, jointed doll, plastic English tack, helmet, and comb. $8.60 ($12.00 complete).
3.) 1022: 1995 – current. *Prancer.* Matte, bay; black points, socks, star. Saddle Club Collection. $6.70.

Special Run Thoroughbred Stallion Models
top row
1.) S 1988: JC Penney. *Breyer Parade of Breeds.* Matte, bay; darker bay, right hind sock, bald face. $14.00.
2.) S 1989: JC Penney. *Breyer Parade of Breeds Collector's Assortment — 2nd Edition.* Matte, bay; red bay, hind socks. $14.00.

bottom row
1.) S 1990: JC Penney. *Breyer Parade of Breeds Collector's Assortment — 3rd Edition.* Matte, rose gray; resist dappled, socks, reddish gray points, gray hooves. $13.70.
2.) S 1996: JC Penney. *Young Equestrian Team.* Matte, alabaster; painted white base coat, gray shaded knees, hocks, muzzle, and mane and tail. Included Bitsy race/endurance rider, and Little Bit Arabian and Quarter Horse Stallions S 96. $13.00.

Unicorn

Mold #1020; introduced in 1984.

Unicorn
top
9020: 1984 – 94. *Unicorn.* Matte, alabaster; gold on horn, gray shading on mane, tail, beard, and hooves. $9.40.

bottom
S 1985: Montgomery Wards. Matte, white; blue mane, tail, beard, and feathers. Some were done as carousels. $31.50 (carousel $41.10).

☙ Stablemate Scale Horse Molds and Models ❧

Introduced in 1975, Stablemates are the smallest of Breyer's models, averaging about 2" high and 3" long. There are currently 16 molds in this series, and most molds have stayed in production since 1976, simply changing colors and names. A few molds are rarer than the rest, such as the Quarter Horse Mare and the Saddlebred. Breyer plans to introduce its first new Stablemate mold in more than two decades in 1997 or 1998.

Until 1992 Stablemates were made of the same cellulose acetate as Breyer's other models; but in 1992, Breyer switched to a lighter, less expensive plastic and started having the models manufactured in China. The new plastic makes a more "brittle," china-like sound if you tap the model's feet on a solid surface. On unpainted areas of a model, the plastic can appear slightly more translucent. All Stablemates to date have either a matte or semi-gloss finish, depending on how glossy the paint itself was. Remember, batch variations in color and variations in markings (stockings versus solid legged versions) are fairly common.

Like the larger models, Stablemates are shown in live and photo shows, and can be repainted, reshaped, and have hair manes and tails added.

The Riding Stable Set is the exception to most statements here. This set is made from a rubbery type of plastic, and is only roughly in scale with the other molds shown here. Because it is close to this scale it is included in this section, but keep in mind that the horses included in that set are not considered to be true Stablemates.

Except for the new Saddlebred Mare mold, the Stablemate molds illustrated here were originally produced by the Hagen-Renaker Company as porcelain figurines.

Arabian Mare

Mold #5011; introduced in 1975.

Regular Run Arabian Mare Models (Stablemate)
top row
1.) 5011: 1975 – 76. *Arabian Mare.* Matte, dapple gray; stockings, gray hooves, darker mane and tail. $19.90.
2.) 5017: 1975 – 88. *Arabian Mare.* Matte, alabaster; light gray mane and tail, shaded hooves. $6.90.
3.) 5014: 1975 – 88. *Arabian Mare.* Matte, bay; darker points, socks/stockings. $7.00.
4.) 5130: 1989 – 94. *Arabian Mare.* Matte, alabaster; gray hooves, mane, and tail. $6.70.

bottom row
1.) 5650: 1994 – 95. *Saddle Club Collection.* Matte, dapple gray; darker gray points, socks. $2.40.
2.) 5182: 1995 – current. *Arabian Mare.* Matte, palomino; gray hooves, white/lighter mane, tail, and face, socks. $2.30.
3.) 5650: 1996 – current. *Saddle Club Stablemates Collection.* Matte, gray; darker gray points. $2.30.

Special Run Arabian Mare Models (Stablemate)

top row

1.) S 1989: Sears. *Stablemate Set*. Matte, alabaster; gray hooves, mane, and tail. Same as #5130. $7.10.
2.) S 1990: Sears. *Stablemate Assortment II*. Matte, black; hind socks/stockings. $8.00.
3.) S 1991: Sears. *Stablemate Assortment III*. Matte, red chestnut; hind socks, darker mane and tail. $8.00.
4.) S 1993: Sears. *Stablemate Assortment IV*. Matte, medium gray; black mane and tail, stockings, gray hooves. $6.20.
also S 1994: JC Penney. *12-Piece Stablemates Set*. Matte, medium gray; black mane and tail, stockings, gray hooves. Same as S 1993. $5.90.

bottom row

1.) S 1995: JC Penney. *Set of 12 Miniatures*. Matte, roan leopard appaloosa; gray points, gray shaded face, chestnut spots. $4.30.
2.) S 1996: Götz. *Butterscotch*. Matte, roan appaloosa; gray shaded face, mane, and tail. $8.30.
3.) S 1996: JC Penney. *12-Piece Stablemate Set*. Matte, gray/black roan; black points, dark face, black hooves, vague sock on left hind. $3.50.

New for 1997:

59972: 1997 – current. *Pinto Mare and Foal*. Matte, chestnut pinto; left hind sock, blaze. Set included Stablemate Lying Foal #59972. $2.00.

Arabian Stallion

Mold #5010; introduced in 1975.

Regular Run Arabian Stallion Models (Stablemate)

top row

1.) 5010: 1975 – 76. *Arabian Stallion*. Matte, dapple gray; darker mane and tail, stockings. $32.90.
2.) 5016: 1975 – 88. *Arabian Stallion*. Matte, alabaster; light gray hooves, mane, and tail. $9.10.
3.) 5013: 1975 – 88. *Arabian Stallion*. Matte, bay; hind stockings (or all four), black points (or just mane and tail), gray hooves. $8.70.

bottom row

1.) 5120: 1989 – 94. *Arabian Stallion*. Matte, dark gray; gray hooves, socks, black points. $6.30.
2.) 5181: 1995 – current. *Arabian Stallion*. Matte, chestnut; darker hooves, mane, and tail. $2.30.

Special Run Arabian Stallion Models (Stablemate)

top row

1.) S 1989: Sears. *Stablemate Set*. Matte, gray; black mane and tail, gray hooves, socks. Essentially the same as #5120. $7.00.
2.) S 1990: Sears. *Stablemate Assortment II*. Matte, buckskin; black points, no dorsal stripe. $7.70.
3.) S 1991: Sears. *Stablemate Assortment III*. Matte, black; hind socks. $7.40.

bottom row

1.) S 1993: Sears. *Stablemate Assortment IV*. Matte, chestnut; dappled, darker mane and tail. $6.00.
2.) S 1994: JC Penney. *12-Piece Stablemates Set*. Matte, chestnut; left hind sock, gray or black hooves. Same as S 1993. $6.00.
also S 1995: JC Penney. *Set of 12 Miniatures*. Matte, chestnut; lighter on belly and legs, black mane and tail. $4.30.
3.) S 1996: JC Penney. *12-Piece Stablemate Set*. Matte, dark rose gray; hind socks, black front hooves, grey back hooves. $3.50.

New for 1997:

59974: 1997 – current. *Arabian and Foal*. Matte, chestnut; darker points. Set included Stablemate Standing Foal #59974. $2.00.

Citation

Mold #5020; introduced in 1975.

Citation
top row
1.) 5020: 1975 – 90. *Citation*. Matte, bay; left hind sock, dark points, red-brown overall. $7.00.
2.) 5019: 1991 – 94. *Standing Thoroughbred*. Matte, bay; light bay, hind socks, later models do not have black on legs. $6.40.
3.) 5175: 1995 – current. *Standing Thoroughbred*. Matte, alabaster; light gray mane and tail. $2.30.

bottom row
1.) 5650: 1996 – current. *Saddle Club Stablemates Collection*. Matte, sandy bay; black points, natural hooves. $2.30.
2.) S 1989: Sears. *Stablemate Set*. Matte, red leopard appaloosa; cream base color, chestnut spots and points. $7.80.
3.) S 1990: Sears. *Stablemate Assortment II*. Matte, chestnut; brown chestnut, darker mane and tail, socks. $7.60.

Citation
top row
1.) S 1991: Sears. *Stablemate Assortment III*. Matte, dark gray; black points. $7.30.
2.) S 1993: Sears. *Stablemate Assortment IV*. Matte, dapple gray; "bubble" dappling, darker/black points. $5.90.
also S 1994: JC Penney. *12-Piece Stablemates Set*. Matte, dapple gray; "bubble" dappling, darker/black points. Same as S 1993. $5.90.
3.) S 1995: JC Penney. *Set of 12 Miniatures*. Matte, gray; light resist dappling on shoulders and quarters, darker/black points, hind socks. $4.30.

bottom row
1.) S 1995: JC Penney. *Set of 12 Miniatures*. Matte, liver chestnut or gray blanket appaloosa; blanket over most of barrel, dark brown or black spots; horse can be either liver chestnut or gray. $4.30.
2.) S 1996: JC Penney. *12-Piece Stablemate Set*. Matte, bay appaloosa; black points, right hind sock, blanket over hindquarters with brown spots. $3.50.

Draft Horse

Mold #5055; introduced in 1976.

Regular Run Draft Horse Models
top row
1.) 5055: 1976 – 87. *Draft Horse*. Matte, dark or light sorrel/chestnut; various socks, gray hooves. $8.70.
2, 3.) 5180: 1989 – 94. *Draft Horse*. Matte, dapple gray; darker gray/black points, socks, gray hooves. Early models used regular dappling, later ones (1992 and later) used bubble dappling (both shown). $7.70.

bottom row
1.) 5650: 1994 – 95. *Saddle Club Collection*. Matte, alabaster; light gray hooves, mane, and tail. $2.40.
2.) 5187: 1995 – current. *Draft Horse*. Matte, bay; brown (gray tone) bay, stockings/socks, natural hooves. $2.30.

Riegsecker Special Run Draft Horse Models
top row
1.) S 1985: Riegseckers of Indiana (200). Matte, gray; hind socks, lighter face, darker mane and tail. $37.10.
2.) S 1985: Riegseckers of Indiana (200). Matte, black; right hind sock. $37.10.
3.) S 1985: Riegseckers of Indiana (200). Matte, palomino; lighter mane and tail, bald face, socks, gray hooves. $37.10.
4.) S 1985: Riegseckers of Indiana (200). Matte, chestnut; socks, gray hooves, darker mane and tail. $37.10.

bottom row
1.) S 1985: Riegseckers of Indiana (200). Matte, red sorrel; flaxen mane and tail, right hind sock. $37.10.
2.) S 1985: Riegseckers of Indiana (200). Matte, red roan; chestnut points, socks, gray hooves. $37.10.
3.) S 1985: Riegseckers of Indiana (200). Unpainted. $37.10.

Other Special Run Draft Horse Models
top row
1.) S 1989: Sears. *Stablemate Set*. Matte, dapple gray; "bubble" dapple, socks, gray hooves. $8.30.
2.) S 1990: Sears. *Stablemate Assortment II*. Matte, black; no markings. $8.30.
3.) S 1991: Sears. *Stablemate Assortment III*. Matte, bay; black points. $8.30.

bottom row
1.) S 1991: Sears. *Stablemate Assortment III*. Matte, (khaki) dun; black points, dorsal stripe, greenish shadings. $8.30.
2.) S 1993: Sears. *Stablemate Assortment IV*. Matte, (creamy) dun; black points, hooves can be black, cream, or gray. $6.60.
also S 1994: JC Penney. *12-piece Stablemates Set*. Matte, (creamy) dun; black points, hooves can be black, cream, or gray. Same as S 1993. $6.60.
3.) S 1996: JC Penney. *12-piece Stablemate Set*. Matte, black pinto; (spash overo) white legs, belly, and chest, blaze, pink muzzle and hooves. $3.50.

Lying Foal

Mold #5700LF; introduced in 1975.
The Lying and Standing Foals were almost always sold in sets. Recently, these molds have been sold separately, or as part of a set with other Stablemates.

Regular Run Lying Foal Models
top row
1.) 5701: 1975 – 76. *Thoroughbred Lying and Standing Foals*. Matte, black; some have hind stockings, some do not. $11.50.
2.) 5700: 1975 – 76. *Thoroughbred Lying and Standing Foals*. Matte, bay; darker mane and tail, some have hind stockings, some do not. $11.50.

bottom row
1.) 5702: 1975 – 76. *Thoroughbred Lying and Standing Foals*. Matte, chestnut; stockings, darker or lighter mane and tail. $11.50.
2.) 3085: 1976 – 80. *Stable Set*. Matte, dark bay; some with hind stockings, black mane and tail. $12.90.

Special Run Lying Foal Keychains
1.) S 1994: BreyerFest '94 Special (500). *Stablemate Foal Keychain*. Amber plastic; with gold keychain and Breyer tag. $15.00.
2.) S 1994: BreyerFest '94 Special (500). *Stablemate Foal Keychain*. Black plastic; with gold keychain and Breyer tag. $15.00.
3.) S 1996: BreyerFest '96 Special (500). *Stablemate Foal Keychain*. Clear plastic; with gold keychain and Breyer tag. $12.00.
4.) S 1996: BreyerFest '96 Special (500). *Stablemate Foal Keychain*. Blue plastic; with gold keychain and Breyer tag. $12.00.

New for 1997:
59971: 1997 – current. *Morgan and Foal*. Matte, buckskin; black points. Set included Stablemate Morgan Stallion #59971. $1.50.
59972: 1997 – current. *Pinto Mare and Foal*. Matte, chestnut pinto; hind socks, blaze. Set included Stablemate Arabian Mare #59972. $1.50.

Standing Foal

Mold #5700SF; introduced in 1975.

Regular Run Standing Foal Models
top row
1.) 5701: 1975 – 76. *Thoroughbred Lying and Standing Foals*. Matte, black; some have hind stockings, some do not. $11.50.
2, 3.) 5700: 1975 – 76. *Thoroughbred Lying and Standing Foals*. Matte, bay; darker mane and tail, some have hind stockings, some do not. $11.50.

bottom row
1.) 5702: 1975 – 76. *Thoroughbred Lying and Standing Foals*. Matte, chestnut; stockings, darker or lighter mane and tail. $11.50.
2.) 3085: 1976 – 80. *Stable Set*. Matte, dark bay; some with darker legs and stockings, black mane and tail. Included cardboard stable and either the bay Quarter Horse Stallion or Seabiscuit. $13.20.

Special Run Standing Foal Keychains
1.) S 1994: BreyerFest '94 Special (500). *Stablemate Foal Keychain*. Amber plastic; with gold keychain and Breyer tag. $15.00.
2.) S 1994: BreyerFest '94 Special (500). *Stablemate Foal Keychain*. Black plastic; with gold keychain and Breyer tag. $15.00.
3.) S 1996: BreyerFest '96 Special (500). *Stablemate Foal Keychain*. Clear plastic; with gold keychain and Breyer tag. $12.00.
4.) S 1996: BreyerFest '96 Special (500). *Stablemate Foal Keychain*. Blue plastic; with gold keychain and Breyer tag. $12.00.

New for 1997:
59973: 1997 – current. *Appaloosa and Foal*. Matte, black appaloosa; blanket pattern, stockings. Set included Stablemate Quarter Horse Stallion #59973. $1.50.
59974: 1997 – current. *Arabian and Foal*. Matte, light chestnut; pale lower legs (maybe socks). Set included Stablemate Arabian Stallion #59974. $2.00.

Morgan Mare

Mold #5038; introduced in 1976.

Morgan Mare
top row
1.) 5040: 1976. *Morgan Mare*. Matte, chestnut; hind stockings, lighter lower forelegs, gray hooves. $29.80.
2.) 5038: 1976 – 88. *Morgan Mare*. Matte, bay; socks, black points. $8.30.
3.) 5039: 1976 – 88. *Morgan Mare*. Matte, black; three or four socks, gray or black hooves. $8.30.

bottom row
1.) 5160: 1989 – 94. *Morgan Mare*. Matte, palomino; socks, white or lighter mane and tail, gray shaded muzzle, gray hooves. $6.30.
2.) 5185: 1995 – current. *Morgan Mare*. Matte, red chestnut; left hind sock, slightly darker mane and tail, gray hooves, shaded muzzle. $2.30.
3.) S 1989: Sears. *Stablemate Set*. Matte, palomino; socks, white or lighter mane and tail, gray shaded muzzle, gray hooves. $7.80.

Morgan Mare
top row
1.) S 1990: Sears. *Stablemate Assortment II*. Matte, chestnut; socks. $7.60.
2.) S 1991: Sears. *Stablemate Assortment III*. Matte, bay; black points, socks. $7.30.
3.) S 1993: Sears. *Stablemate Assortment IV*. Matte, chocolate sorrel; left hind sock, dark gray/black hooves, flaxen mane and tail. $6.00.
also S 1994: JC Penney. *12-piece Stablemates Set*. Matte, chocolate sorrel; left hind sock, dark gray/black hooves, flaxen mane and tail. Same as S 1993. $6.00.

bottom row
1.) S 1995: JC Penney. *Set of 12 Miniatures*. Matte, sorrel; socks, flaxen mane and tail. $4.30.
2.) S 1996: JC Penney. *12-piece Stablemate Set*. Matte, light red dun; darker mane and tail, slightly darker knees, hocks, and ankles, gray hooves. $3.50.

Morgan Stallion

Mold #5035; introduced in 1975.

Morgan Stallion (Stablemate)
top row
1.) 5016: 1975. *Arabian Stallion*. Matte, alabaster; light gray mane and tail. $21.30.
2.) 5010: 1975. *Arabian Stallion*. Matte, dapple gray; darker mane and tail, left hind sock. $24.90.
3.) 5013: 1975. *Arabian Stallion*. Matte, bay; black mane, tail, knees, and hocks, left hind sock (other ankles reddish), black or dark gray hooves. $14.70.
4.) 5037: 76. *Morgan Stallion*. Matte, chestnut; socks, gray hooves, darker mane and tail. $24.80.

bottom row
1.) 5036: 1976 – 88. *Morgan Stallion*. Matte, black; left hind sock. $7.80.
2.) 5035: 1976 – 88. *Morgan Stallion*. Matte, bay; black mane, tail, knees, and hocks, left hind sock (other ankles reddish), black or dark gray hooves. Essentially same as #5013. $7.80.
3.) 5150: 1989 – 94. *Morgan Stallion*. Matte, chestnut; socks, gray hooves. $6.40.
4.) 5650: 1994 – 95. *Saddle Club Collection*. Matte, bay; left hind sock, black points. $2.40.

Native Dancer

Mold #5023; introduced in 1976.

Native Dancer
top row

1.) 5023: 1976 – 94. *Native Dancer*. Matte, gray; solid medium gray, black points. $7.60.
2, 3.) 5178: 1995 – current. *Appaloosa*. Matte, bay appaloosa; black points, light brown spots. $2.30.
4.) 5650: 1996 – current. *Saddle Club Stablemate Collection*. Matte, chestnut pinto; blaze, white tail, chestnut and white mane. $2.30.
5.) S 1989: Sears. *Stablemate Set*. Matte, blood bay; black points. $8.10.

bottom row

1.) S 1990: Sears. *Stablemate Assortment II*. Matte, black point alabaster; black points. $7.70.
2.) S 1991: Sears. *Stablemate Assortment III*. Matte, palomino; white/lighter mane and tail. $7.30.
3.) S 1993: Sears. *Stablemate Assortment IV*. Matte, black; left hind sock. $6.90.
also S 1994: JC Penney. *12-Piece Stablemates Set*. Matte, black; left hind sock. Same as S 1993. $6.00.
4.) S 1995: JC Penney. *Set of 12 Miniatures*. Matte, medium bay; vague right socks. $4.30.
5.) S 1996: JC Penney. *12-Piece Stablemate Set*. Matte, red dun; darker chestnut points, gray shaded muzzle. $3.50.

Morgan Stallion (Stablemate)
top row

1.) 5184: 1995 – current. *Morgan Stallion*. Matte, bay; Same as #5650 $2.30.
2.) S 1989: Sears. *Stablemate Set*. Matte, light chestnut; socks. $8.30.
3.) S 1990: Sears. *Stablemate Assortment II*. Matte, dark red chestnut socks. $7.70.
4.) S 1991: Sears. *Stablemate Assortment III*. Matte, palomino; socks white or lighter mane and tail. $7.40.

bottom row

1.) S 1993: Sears. *Stablemate Assortment IV*. Matte, dark bay; brown bay, black points. $6.00.
also S 1994: JC Penney. *12-Piece Stablemates Set*. Matte, dark bay brown bay, black points. Same as S 1993 (bay). $6.00.
2.) S 1993: Sears. *Stablemate Assortment IV*. Matte, black appaloosa blanket over hindquarters and barrel, small "spatter" spots. $6.00.
also S 1994: JC Penney. *12-Piece Stablemates Set*. Matte, black appaloosa; blanket over hindquarters and barrel, small "spatter" spots. Same as S 1993 (black appaloosa). $6.00.
3.) S 1995: JC Penney. *Set of 12 Miniatures*. Matte, black; black and gray or black and white mane and tail. $4.30.
4.) S 1996: JC Penney. *12-Piece Stablemate Set*. Matte, alabaster/light gray; light gray points, pink muzzle and hooves, otherwise white. $3.50.

New for 1997:
59971: 1997 – current. *Morgan and Foal*. Matte, buckskin; black points three socks (not right front). Set included Stablemate Lying Foal #59971 $2.00.

S 1997: Götz. Matte, red roan; speckle roaning, darker chestnut points shaded head, left (or both) hind socks. $7.50.

Quarter Horse Mare

Mold #5048; introduced in 1976.

Quarter Horse Mare (Stablemate)
top row

1.) 5049: 1976. *Quarter Horse Mare*. Matte, chestnut; darker mane and tail, stockings, black hooves. $27.00.
2.) 3085: 1976 – 80. *Stable Set*. Matte, dark bay; black points. $24.20.

bottom row

1.) 5048: 1976 – 87. *Quarter Horse Mare*. Matte, palomino; stockings, white mane and tail, gray hooves. $10.50.
2.) 5050: 1976 – 88. *Quarter Horse Mare*. Matte, buckskin; no dorsal stripe, black points, socks, gray hooves. Some models do not have black legs. $10.50.

Quarter Horse Stallion

Mold #5045; introduced in 1976.

Quarter Horse Stallion (Stablemate)
top row
1.) 5046: 1976. *Quarter Horse Stallion*. Matte/semi-gloss, chestnut; darker mane and tail, socks/stockings, gray hooves. $28.00.
2.) 3085: 1976 – 80. *Stable Set*. Matte, dark bay; black points. $24.20.
3.) 5047: 1976 – 87. *Quarter Horse Stallion*. Matte, buckskin; black points, no dorsal stripe. $10.50.
4.) 5045: 1976 – 88. *Quarter Horse Stallion*. Matte, palomino; stockings, lighter mane and tail. $9.70.

bottom row
1.) 5186: 1995 – current. *Quarter Horse Stallion*. Matte, buckskin; black points. $2.30.
2.) S 1993: Sears. *Stablemate Assortment IV*. Matte, red leopard appaloosa; chestnut mane, tail, and spots, gray hooves and muzzle. $7.40.
also S 1994: JC Penney. *12-piece Stablemates Set*. Matte, red leopard appaloosa; chestnut mane, tail, and spots, gray hooves and muzzle. Same as S 1993. $7.40.
3.) S 1995: JC Penney. *Set of 12 Miniatures*. Matte, red chestnut; socks, natural hooves. $4.30.
4.) S 1996: JC Penney. *12-piece Stablemate* Set. Matte, buckskin/golden bay; black points, hind socks. $3.50.

New for 1997:
59973: 1997 – current. *Appaloosa and Foal*. Matte, black leopard appaloosa; black points. Set included Stablemate Standing Foal #59973.

Riding Stable Set

These models are significantly different from Breyer's "real" Stablemates, being comparable only in their size. They were made from a rubbery plastic instead of cellulose acetate.

The Riding Stable Set
9900: 1986 – 92. *Riding Stable Set*. various. Included five horses in various action positions, two foals, two ponies, four adult riders, two child riders, other accessories, and a plastic four-stall stable called "Pine Lodge Riding School." Actual models apparently varied with year of production. Still available from many retailers. Made in the United Kingdom by Britains Ltd. $63.00.

Saddlebred

Mold #5001; introduced in 1975.

Saddlebred (Stablemate)
top row
1.) 5001: 1975 – 76. *Saddlebred*. Matte, dapple gray; socks, darker points, gray hooves, bald face. $25.20.
2.) 5002: 1975 – 88. *Saddlebred*. Matte, bay; three or four socks, natural/gray hooves; more chestnut than bay. $9.70.

bottom row
1.) 5110: 1989 – 90. *Saddlebred*. Matte, black; gray hooves. $9.70.
also S 1989: Sears. *Stablemate Set*. Matte, black; gray hooves. Same as #5110. $9.40.
2.) S 1996: JC Penney. *12-Piece Stablemate Set*. Matte, dapple gray; black points, right hind sock, red on white ribbons. $3.50.

Saddlebred Mare (not shown)

Mold number to be determined; will be introduced in 1997 or 1998.
Saddlebred Mare. Matte, chestnut; flaxen mane and tail, socks, blaze. $2.00.

Seabiscuit

Mold #5024; introduced in 1976.

Seabiscuit
top row
1.) 5024: 1976 – 90. *Seabiscuit*. Matte, bay; stockings on some, others without, black points. $8.30.
2.) 5025: 1991 – 94. *Running Thoroughbred*. Matte, black; gray hooves. $6.70.
3.) 5650: 1994 – 95. *Saddle Club Collection*. Matte, chestnut; socks/stockings, gray hooves, slightly darker mane and tail. $2.40.

bottom row
1.) 5179: 1995 – current. *Running Paint*. Matte, chestnut pinto; socks/stockings, slightly darker mane and tail. $2.30.
2.) S 1989: Sears. *Stablemate Set*. Matte, chestnut; red chestnut; darker mane and tail, gray hooves. $8.40.

Seabiscuit
top row
1.) S 1990: Sears. *Stablemate Assortment II*. Matte, palomino; lighter or white mane and tail. $7.70.
2.) S 1991: Sears. *Stablemate Assortment III*. Matte, dapple gray; black points, medium gray. $7.40.

bottom row
1.) S 1993: Sears. *Stablemate Assortment IV*. Matte, light gray; slightly darker gray points. $6.00.
also S 1994: JC Penney. *12-Piece Stablemates Set*. Matte, light gray; slightly darker gray points. Same as S 1993. $6.00.
2.) S 1996: JC Penney. *12-Piece Stablemate Set*. Matte, bay; medium red bay, black points, right hind sock. $3.50.

Silky Sullivan

Mold #5022; introduced in 1976.

Silky Sullivan (Stablemate)
top row
1, 2.) 5022: 1976 – 94. *Silky Sullivan*. Matte, dark chestnut; right hind stocking, gray/black hooves; darker mane and tail, some had socks. $7.00.
3.) 5177: 1995 – current. *Thoroughbred Racehorse*. Matte, black; gray or black hooves. $2.30.

bottom row
1.) 5650: 1996 – current. *Saddle Club Stablemate Collection*. Matte, mahogany bay; black points, hind socks, blaze. $2.30.
2.) S 1989: Sears. *Stablemate Set*. Matte, buckskin; black points, no dorsal stripe. $8.30.
3.) S 1990: Sears. *Stablemate Assortment II*. Matte, light bay; socks/stockings, black points (or black mane, tail, and knees with high hind stockings and fore socks). $7.70.

Silky Sullivan (Stablemate)
top row
1.) S 1991: Sears. *Stablemate Assortment III*. Matte, red bay; hind socks. $7.40.
2.) S 1993: Sears. *Stablemate Assortment IV*. Matte, grulla/dun; black points, left hind sock. $6.00.
also S 1994: JC Penney. *12-Piece Stablemates Set*. Matte, grulla/dun; black points, left hind sock. Same as S 1993. $6.00.
3.) S 1995: JC Penney. *Set of 12 Miniatures*. Matte, roan; gray body with black points, chestnut shaded face. $4.30.

bottom row
1.) S 1995: JC Penney. *Set of 12 Miniatures*. Matte, light rose gray; rosy gray shadings on mane, knees, hocks, and hooves. $4.30.
2.) S 1996: JC Penney. *12-Piece Stablemate Set*. Matte, black leopard appaloosa; black points, black spots on body, neck, and face. $3.50.

Swaps

Mold #5021; introduced in 1976.

Swaps (Stablemate)
top row
1.) 5021: 1976 – 94. *Swaps*. Matte, chestnut; darker mane and tail, right hind sock. $7.00.
2.) 5176: 1995 – current. *Thoroughbred Racehorse*. Matte, red chestnut; dark gray/black hooves. $2.30.
3.) 5650: 1996 – current. *Saddle Club Stablemate Collection*. Matte, chestnut leopard appaloosa; chestnut mane, tail, and spots, chestnut and gray shaded legs. $2.30.

bottom row
1.) S 1989: Sears. *Stablemate Set*. Matte, black leopard appaloosa; black points, small spots. $8.30.
2.) S 1990: Sears. *Stablemate Assortment II*. Matte, rose gray; grayish mane and tail. $7.70.
3.) S 1990: Sears. *Stablemate Assortment II*. Matte, dark gray; black points. $7.60.

Swaps (Stablemate)
top row
1.) S 1991: Sears. *Stablemate Assortment III*. Matte, dark bay; front socks, darker points. $6.90.
2.) S 1993: JC Penney. *Stablemate Assortment IV*. Matte, buckskin; black points, no dorsal stripe. $6.00.
also S 1994: JC Penney. 12-Piece *Stablemates Set*. Matte, buckskin; black points, no dorsal stripe. Same as S 1993. $5.20.

bottom row
1.) S 1995: JC Penney. *Set of 12 Miniatures*. Matte, roan; gray body, darker points with chestnut shadings. $4.30.
2.) S 1996: JC Penney. *12-Piece Stablemate Set*. Matte, bay; black points. $3.50.

Stablemate Swaps model not shown:
S 1996: Inroads Interactive. Matte, peachy dun; gray points, dorsal stripe, bald face. Came with Multimedia Horses CD ROM. $12.00.

Thoroughbred Mare

Mold #5026; introduced in 1975.

Thoroughbred Mare (Stablemate)
top row
1.) 5026: 1975 – 87. *Thoroughbred Mare*. Matte, chestnut; socks/stockings, darker mane and tail, gray hooves. $7.60.
2, 3, and 4.) 5028: 1975 – 88. *Thoroughbred Mare*. Matte, black; socks/stockings, gray hooves. Three variations shown (differences in gloss and stockings). $7.60.

bottom row
1.) 5030: 1975 – 88. *Thoroughbred Mare*. Matte, bay; red bay, socks/stockings, black points. Variations in stockings known. $7.60.
2.) 5140: 1989 – 90. *Thoroughbred Mare*. Matte, dark bay; black points, left hind stocking, gray hooves. $8.30.
3.) 5141: 1991 – 94. *Thoroughbred Mare*. Matte, red chestnut; darker points, left hind sock. $6.60.

Thoroughbred Mare (Stablemate)
top row
1.) 5183: 1995 – current. *Thoroughbred Mare*. Matte, dark gray; socks/stockings, darker points. $2.30.
2.) 5650: 1995 – current. *Thoroughbred Mare*. Matte, black; no markings. $2.40.
3.) S 1989: Sears. *Stablemate Set*. Matte, dark bay; black points, left hind stocking, gray hooves. Same as #5140. $8.30.

bottom row
1.) S 1990: Sears. *Stablemate Assortment II*. Matte, blood bay; black points. $7.70.
2.) S 1991: Sears. *Stablemate Assortment III*. Matte, alabaster; light gray points. $7.40.
3.) S 1995: JC Penney. *Set of 12 Miniatures*. Matte, dark brown/bay; vague hind socks, black points. $4.30.

❧ Other Animal Molds and Models ❧

Most of these models originated in the early to mid '60s. Many of the older models (pre-1975) have a glossy finish, while most of the recent ones have a matte finish. Breyer has recently begun bringing in new versions of the older molds (like the Texas Longhorn Bull and the Boxer).

This section lists the molds by general subject: Dogs and cats are first, followed by the cattle molds, then the wildlife.

Basset Hound

Mold #325; introduced in 1966.

Basset Hound
top row
1.) 325: 1966 – 68. *Bloodhound*. Matte, dark brown; eye whites, red rimmed below, whisker dots on muzzle. This color is fondly called "woodgrain" (but has no grain). $67.20.
2.) 326: 1969 – 85. *Jolly Cholly Basset Hound*. Matte/semi-gloss, tri-color; generally brown, dark brown/black saddle, whitish muzzle and belly, eye whites. Some catalogs added "Dog" after breed name. $27.30.

bottom
324: 1994 – 95. *Chaser Hound Dog*. Matte, brown/bi-color; generally brown, lighter muzzle, throat, and belly. Similar to #325, but without the darker saddle. Included a red and green plaid "dog bed." $18.20.

Boxer

Mold #66; introduced in 1958.

Boxer

top row

1, 2.) 66: 1958 – 74. *Boxer*. Matte/semi-gloss/glossy, tan/fawn; darker muzzle, white stripe down face; chain or vinyl stud collar; some catalogs added "Dog" after breed name. In 1972 – 74 the glossy was available; matte (fawn color) and glossy are shown. $38.40.

bottom row

1.) 966: 1959 – 65. *Boxer*. Woodgrain; black muzzle, white face stripe. $287.00.

2.) S late 1950s – 60s: Dog breeder (about 25). *Boxer*. Glossy, white/very light shaded gray; black muzzle and inner ears. No mold marks. $399.00.

Boxer

322: 1995 – 96. *Pug Boxer*. Matte, chocolate brown/brindle; darker muzzle and face, white feet, belly. $19.10.

Poodle

Mold #67; introduced in 1958.

Poodle

top row

1.) 967: 1961 – 64. *Poodle*. Woodgrain; red tongue, black collar with gold painted-on buckle. $294.00.

2.) 67: 1958 – 68. *Poodle*. Glossy, black; red, blue, or other color collar, red or pink tongue. Some included a sewing kit. $54.60 ($82.30 with sewing kit).

bottom row

1.) 68: 1958 – 68. *Poodle*. Glossy, white; blue (1958 – 60), red, or other color collar, red or pink tongue. Some were used on lamps (1960s), and some included a sewing kit. $54.60 ($82.30 with sewing kit).

2.) 69: 1968 – 73. *Poodle*. Matte, silver gray; red or gold collar, red tongue, darker paws. $57.40.

Famous Dogs

Rin Tin Tin
Mold #64; introduced in 1958.
top row
1.) 64: 1958 – 66. *Rin Tin Tin.* Matte/semi-gloss, brown; darker back, lighter face and legs. $57.40.
2.) 327: 1972 – 73. *German Shepherd.* Matte/semi-gloss, charcoal gray; lighter face and legs, shaded body. Light and dark variations are known. $56.00.

Benji
Mold #3090B; introduced in 1977.
3.) 7701: 1978 – 79. *Benji.* Matte/semi-gloss, tan; shaded. $32.20.
also 3090: 1977-78. *Benji and Tiffany Set.* Matte/semi-gloss, tan shaded. Same as #7701. $55.30 if in original packaging.

Lassie
Mold #65; introduced in 1958.
bottom row
1.) 65: 1958 – 65. *Lassie.* Semi-gloss, bi-color; chestnut and white, red or dark pink tongue. $70.00.
2.) 323: 1995 – 96. *Honey Collie.* Matte, golden bi color; darker shading from eye to foreleg, black nose, light pink tongue $17.80.

Tiffany
Mold #3090T; introduced in 1977.
3.) 3090: 1977 – 78. *Benji and Tiffany Set.* Matte/semi-gloss, white; black nose and eyes. Came in set with Benji. $26.60.

St. Bernard

Mold #328; introduced in 1972.

St. Bernard
top
328: 1972 – 81. *St. Bernard.* Semi-gloss/matte, bi-color; brown back, shoulders, haunches, and ears, white ruff, muzzle, tail, legs, throat, black lip line, red tongue and lower eyelids, black nose and gray shaded muzzle. $39.20.

bottom
321: 1995 – 96. *Brandy St. Bernard.* Matte, golden bi-color; markings same as #328, but base body color is golden instead of reddish-brown. $18.70.

Kitten

Mold #335; introduced in 1966.

Kitten
top row
1.) 335: 1966 – 71. *Siamese Kitten.* Matte, gray or seal point; cream body color; points vary from brownish to gray, blue eyes, whisker spots and dark nose. Some have green eyes. $98.70.
2.) 336: 1966 – 73. *Calico Kitten.* Matte, orange tabby; orangish base color with gray striping, shaded ears, green eyes, whisker spots and pink nose. Some may have blue eyes. $92.40.

bottom row
1.) 337: 1994 – 95. *Cleopatra, Kitten.* Matte, orange tabby; cream base color with orangish stripes, white paws, light blue eyes, whisker spots and pink nose. $21.00.
2.) 338: 1994 – 95. *Leonardo, Kitten.* Matte, gray tabby; white paws, gold eyes, whisker spots and pink nose. $21.00.

Kitten

383: 1995 – 96. *Socks, Kitten.* Matte/Semi-gloss, black and white; half white face, white belly and legs, golden yellow eyes, and black nose. $18.50.

Cows and Calves

Cow mold #341; introduced in 1972. Calf mold #347; introduced in 1972.

Cows and Calves
top row
1.) 342: 1972 – 73. *Guernsey Cow.* Matte, tan and white pinto pattern; horns are forward. $62.30.
2.) 348: 1972 – 73. *Guernsey Calf.* Matte, tan and white pinto pattern. $39.90.
3.) 343: 1972 – 73. *Jersey Cow.* Matte, dark tan; solid color, lighter lower legs, horns are semi-upright. $62.30.
4.) 349: 1972 – 73. *Jersey Calf.* Matte, tan; solid. $39.90.

bottom row
1.) 344: 1972 – 73. *Ayrshire Cow.* Matte, dark red and white pinto pattern; horns are very upright. $83.30.
2.) 350: 1972 – 73. *Ayrshire Calf.* Matte, dark red and white pinto pattern. $43.40.
3.) 345: 1972 – 73. *Brown Swiss Cow.* Matte, cocoa brown; solid color with lighter legs, horns are forward. $62.30.
4.) 351: 1972 – 73. *Brown Swiss Calf.* Matte, cocoa brown; solid. $39.90.

Cows and Calves
top row
1.) 3447: 1974 – 89. *Cow Family.* (Cow) Matte, black and white pinto pattern; horns point forward and slightly down. $33.60.
also 341: 1972 – 73. *Holstein Cow.* Matte, black and white pinto pattern; Same as #3447. $34.30.
2.) 3447: 1974 – 91. *Cow Family.* (Calf) Matte, black and white pinto pattern. $23.80.
also 347: 1972 – 73. *Holstein Calf.* Matte, black and white pinto pattern. $21.00.
3.) S 1988: Mail order sources (Black Horse Ranch, Small World). *Crooked Horned Holstein Cow.* Matte, black and white pinto pattern; apparently this model was assembled using one horn from another cow, although this is hard to see. $64.40.

bottom row
1.) 3448: 1992 – 95. *Jersey Cow Family Gift Set.* Matte, tan; solid tan, lighter belly, gray hooves and tail tip, star, pink/white muzzle, no horns (polled). $24.50.
2.) 3448: 1992 – 95. *Jersey Cow Family Gift Set.* Matte, tan; solid body, lighter underbelly, star, pink muzzle, gray hooves. Included Jersey Cow #3448. $12.60.

Another Holstein Cow
382: 1996. *Holstein Cow.* Matte, black and white pinto pattern; white stockings, white triangle star, no horns. $18.40.

Cows and Calves

The 1988 versions of these five Cows are shown here. The 1993 versions are very similar, and minor variations might exist.

top row

1.) S 1988, 1993: Mail order sources (about 200). *Polled Holstein Cow.* Matte, black and white pinto pattern. $60.20.
2.) S 1988, 1993: Mail order sources (about 200). *Polled Guernsey Cow.* Matte, tan and white pinto pattern. $60.20.
3.) S 1988, 1993: Mail order sources (about 200). *Polled Jersey Cow.* Matte, dark tan; solid color. $60.20.

bottom row

1.) S 1988, 1993: Mail order sources. *Polled Ayrshire Cow.* Matte, red and white pinto pattern. $60.20.
2.) S 1988, 1993: Mail order sources (about 200). *Polled Brown Swiss Cow.* Matte, cocoa brown. $60.20.
3.) S 1974: Bentley Sales (about 100). *Black Angus Calf.* Matte, black; no markings. $56.00.

Cow models not shown:
S 1984: Bentley Sales Co. *Jersey Cow.* Semi-gloss, dark tan. $103.60.
S 1984: Bentley Sales Co. *Guernsey Cow.* Semi-gloss, brown and white. $103.60.

New Cow for 1997:
394: 1997 – current. *Holstein Cow.* Matte, black pinto pattern; mostly black head with elongated star/stripe, then mostly white body with small black patches all over, black hooves. $11.00.

Calf model not shown:
S 1980: Mail order sources. *Calf.* Unpainted. $31.50.

Brahma Bull

Mold #70; introduced in 1958.

Brahma Bull
top
70: 1958 – 67, 1968 – 95. *Brahma Bull.* Glossy, semi-gloss, or matte, gray; light gray on barrel, shaded quarters, darker neck, horns light with dark tips. $23.10 ($37.80 Glossy).

bottom row
1.) 970: 1961 – 63. *Brahma Bull.* Woodgrain; white horns. $157.50
2.) 385: 1996 – current. *Brahma Bull.* Matte, shaded red; darker on neck, hindquarters, and legs, lighter on barrel and shoulders, horns light with dark tips. $21.40.

Charolais Bull

Mold #360; introduced in 1975.

Charolais Bull
top
360: 1975 – 95. *Charolais Bull.* Matte, alabaster; pink/natural hooves; early ones have brown shadings on legs and face. $23.80.

bottom
S 1985: Simmental Breeders Association. *Polled Simmental Bull.* Matte, brown and white; reddish brown with white cape. Markings variations known (air brushed versus stenciled). $175.00.

Charolais Bull
386: 1996 – current. *Charolais Bull.* Matte, chestnut and white pinto pattern; pink/natural hooves; white face and legs, chestnut neck, etc. $21.80.

Charolais Bull model not shown:
S 1985: Shorthorn Breeders Association. *Polled Shorthorn Bull.* Matte, dark brown. $175.00.

Polled Hereford and Black Angus Bulls

Polled Hereford Bull
Mold #74; introduced in 1968.
top row
1.) 74: 1968 – current. *Polled Hereford Bull.* Matte, red-brown and white; white nape, face, lower neck, belly, tail tip. This model is done in the larger scale like the recent Black Angus Bull. $21.20.

Black Angus Bull
Mold #365; introduced in 1978.
2.) 365: 1978 – current. *Black Angus Bull.* Matte, black; standing. $21.10.

bottom
S 1984: Red Angus Association (about 300). *Red Angus Bull.* Matte, red-brown, some have pink muzzles, and some have darker muzzles. Came with "Big Red One" certificate. $168.00.

Walking Black Angus and Walking Hereford Bulls

Walking Black Angus Bull
Mold #72; introduced in 1960.
top row
1, 2.) 72: 1960 – 62, 1963 – 78. *Black Angus Bull.* Matte/glossy, black; fully rough-sided and smooth barreled (known as poodle cut), red halter, eye whites. Matte had red or brown halter, glossy had gold halter, poodle cut was apparently only done in glossy; all glossies have eye-whites. Detailing varies. $77.00 ($111.30 Poodle cut).

bottom row
1.) 72: As #72 above, but matte finish with rough sides
2.) 73: 1961 – 63. *Hornless Hereford.* Glossy, red-brown and white; white nape, neck, face, and belly, reddish-brown halter, eye whites. Also came in poodle cut. $100.80 ($126.90 Poodle Cut).

Walking Hereford Bull
Mold #71; introduced in 1958.
top row
3.) 71: 1958 – 81. *Hereford Bull.* Matte/glossy, dark brown; white face, nape, neck, belly, and tail tip, pinkish horns (no halter). $45.50.

bottom row
3.) 971: 1963 – 65. *Hereford Bull.* Woodgrain; no markings, white horns (no halter). $315.00.

Walking Blank Angus Bull model not shown:
Unknown number: unknown dates. *Black Angus Bull.* Woodgrain. $371.70.

Spanish Fighting Bull

Mold #73; introduced in 1970.

Spanish Fighting Bull
73: 1970 – 85. *Spanish Fighting Bull.* Matte, black; horns light with dark tips. In 1972 – 74, this model was also in the Presentation collection, mounted on a wooden base. $73.50 ($168.00 Presentation).

New for 1997:
395: 1997 – current. *Spanish Fighting Bull.* Matte, steel gray; shaded, with white horns. $15.00.

Texas Longhorn Bull

Mold #75; introduced in 1961.

Texas Longhorn Bull
top
975: 1963 – 66. *Texas Longhorn Bull.* Woodgrain; no markings, gray striped horns. Also used on lamps in the mid 1960s (shown). $192.00 ($255.00 on lamp).

bottom row
1.) 75: 1961 – 89. *Texas Longhorn Bull.* Matte, light brown/tan; stockings, gray hooves, horns are light with gray shadings and dark tips, bald face. In 1972 – 74, this model was also in the Presentation collection, mounted on a wooden base; also used on lamps in mid to late 1960s (lamp shown). $28.00 ($65.00 on lamp, $105.00 Presentation).
2.) 370: 1990 – 95. *Texas Longhorn Bull.* Matte, dark chestnut pinto pattern; gray hooves, gray horns with dark tips, broad blaze. $24.50.

Texas Longhorn Bull
384: 1996 – current. *Texas Longhorn Bull.* Matte, chestnut pinto pattern with speckles; chestnut legs, chestnut patch on neck to shoulders, speckles on body, white between horns. $22.50.

Jasper the Market Hog
Mold #355; introduced in 1974.

Jasper the Market Hog
top
355: 1974 – current. *Jasper the Market Hog.* Matte, white and gray; gray marking on lower back and hindquarters, pink hooves, nose. $12.20.

bottom
S 1980: Hog Breeders Association. *Hampshire Hog.* Matte, black and white. $112.00.

Jasper models not shown:
S 1980: Hog Breeders Association. *Duroc Hog.* Matte, red and brown; bald face and gray hooves. $112.00.
S 1980: Hog Breeders Association. *Hog.* Matte, tan; gray hooves. $112.00.
S 1980: Hog Breeders Association. *Hog.* Matte, black; blaze and stockings. Might have bent ears. $112.00.
S 1980: Hog Breeders Association. *Yorkshire Hog.* Matte, white; might have pink shading on nose. $112.00.
S 1980: Hog Breeders Association. *Poland China Hog.* Matte, white with black spots; same pattern as #355, with additional airbrushed spots, and shaded face. $112.00.

Buffalo
Mold #76; introduced in 1965.

Buffalo
top row
1.) 76: 1965 – 91. *Buffalo.* Matte, brown; medium brown lower barrel and hindquarters, dark brown elsewhere, horns white with dark tips. In 1972 – 74, this model was also in the Presentation collection, mounted on a wooden base; some models were used on lamps (mid 1960s). $33.60 ($65.00 on lamp, $105.00 Presentation).
2.) 380: 1992 – 93. *Tatanka.* Matte, alabaster; slight shading. $43.40.

bottom
381: 1994 – 96. *American Bison.* Matte, brown; dark head, forelegs, lighter hump, medium barrel and hindquarters. $22.10.

AMERICAN BISON

Presentation Collection Buffalo
1965 – 91. *Presentation Collection Buffalo.*

Buffalo models not shown:
Unknown number: ca. 1965. *Buffalo.* Bronze/Antique Bronze; shaded. $385.00.
S 1974?: Movie company (about 10). Matte, light smoke gray; Rumored to have been movie props for the movie *The White Buffalo.* $441.00.
Unknown number: Unknown dates. *Buffalo.* Woodgrain. $507.50.

New for 1997:
388: 1997 – current. *American Bison.* Matte, "muddy" brown; shaded darker over nape, head, and lower legs. This one is overall grayer than the older #76. $15.00.

Bear

Mold #306; introduced in 1967.

Bear
top row
1.) 307: 1967 – 71. *Bear.* Matte, brown; paler face with dark nose. $45.50.
2.) 306: 1967 – 73. *Bear.* Matte, black; paler face with dark nose. $43.40.
also 3068: 1974-76. *Bear Family.* Matte, black; same as #306. $48.30.

bottom row
1.) 3069: 1987 – 89. *Cinnamon Bear and Cub.* Matte, reddish-brown; paler face with dark nose. $39.20.
2.) 3071: 1992 – 95. *Bear Family Gift Set.* Matte, white; no markings, reddish eyes. $26.60.

New for 1997:
392: 1997 – current. *Bear.* Matte, brown; shaded, lighter or white muzzle, lighter brown overall than the previous brown Bear. $15.00.

Bear Cub

Mold #308; introduced in 1967.

Bear Cub
top row
1.) 309: 1967 – 71. *Bear Cub.* Matte, brown; paler face with dark nose. $25.90.
2.) 308: 1967 – 73. *Bear Cub.* Matte, black; paler face with dark nose. $23.10.
also 3068: 1974 – 76. *Bear Family.* Matte, black; same as #308. $35.00.

bottom row
1.) 3069: 1987 – 89. *Cinnamon Bear and Cub.* Matte, reddish-brown; paler face with dark nose. $25.90.
2.) 3071: 1992 – 95. *Bear Family Gift Set.* Matte, white; no markings, reddish eyes. $16.10.

Modernistic Buck and Doe

Modernistic Buck, mold #101, and the Modernistic Doe, mold #102; both introduced in 1961.

top
101: 1961 – 63. *Modernistic Buck.* Semi-gloss, metallic gold; called a decorator by some, solid color, black eyes; also known as the Golden Buck. This buck actually looks more like a stylized antelope because of the horns (instead of antlers). $98.00.

bottom
102: 1961 – 63. *Modernistic Doe.* Semi-gloss, metallic gold; called a decorator by some, solid color, black eyes. Also known as the Golden Doe. $98.00.

Deer Family

Buck (Mold #301), Doe (Mold #302), and Fawn (Mold #303) were all introduced in 1974.

3123: 1974 – current. *Deer Family.* Matte, tan; Included Doe and Fawn #-3123 and carrying case. $21.90.

The same models included in the set were also available individually.
301: 1965 – 73. *Buck Deer.* Matte, tan. $9.50.
302: 1965 – 73. *Doe Deer.* Matte, tan; Might have been used for night lights. $9.50.
303: 1965 – 73. *Fawn Deer.* Matte, tan; white spots on sides, black hooves. $5.90.

Moose and Elk

Moose — Mold #79; introduced in 1966. Elk — Mold #77; introduced in 1968.

Moose
top
79: 1966 – 96. *Moose.* Matte, dark brown; darker neck, lighter antlers, body color can range from reddish-brown to chocolate-brown. In 1972 – 74, this model was also in the Presentation collection, mounted on a wooden base. $21.80. ($108.50 Presentation).

New for 1997:
387: 1997 – current. *Moose.* Matte, light brown; shaded over shoulders and neck, gray hooves, muzzle, tips of antlers. $15.00.

Elk
bottom
77: 1968 – current. *Elk.* Matte, brown; lighter rump, darker neck. Color variations exist. $20.80.

Bighorn Ram

Mold #78; introduced in 1969.

Bighorn Ram
top
78: 1969 – 80. *Bighorn Ram.* Matte, tan; white rump, paler around muzzle, ears, and eyes, gray hooves. Color variations are shown. $82.60.

bottom
85: 1970 – 73. *Dall Sheep.* Matte, tan; white rump, paler around muzzle, ears, and eyes, gray hooves. Tan and gray-horned variations exist (both are shown). $108.50.

New for 1997:
393: 1997 – current. *Ram.* Matte, brown and tan; lighter head, horns, and lower legs. $15.00.

Mountain Goat

Mold #312; introduced in 1973.

Mountain Goat
312: 1973 – 76, 1989. *Montana Mountain Goat.* Matte, alabaster; shaded body, horns, and muzzle, gray hooves, brownish gray horns. This was called Rocky Mountain Goat in 1973; earlier models were made of yellowish plastic (oil-crisis years). The 1989 models were reissues. $44.80.

Pronghorn Antelope

Mold #310; introduced in 1971. The Pronghorn Antelope is really a goat, despite the name, and roams the western plains of the United States.

Pronghorn Antelope
310: 1971 – 76. *Pronghorn Antelope.* Matte, brown and white; white sides, rear, white throat with brown bars. A color variation (top) and a test color is shown (alabaster) on the bottom. $115.50.

New for 1997:
389: 1997 – current. *Pronghorn Antelope.* Matte, chestnut and white; red-gold body color including legs, white belly, striped front of neck, shaded muzzle, and gray antlers/horns. $15.00.

Elephant

Mold #91; introduced in 1958.

Elephant

top row

1.) 601: 1958 – 60. *Corky and Bimbo.* Matte/semi-gloss, battleship gray; solid, dense color, white tusks. Set included plastic boy and hang tag (shown). $141.40 ($364.00).

2.) 991: 1958 – 60. *Elephant.* Woodgrain; white tusks. $434.00.

3.) 92: 1958 – 60. *Elephant.* Semi-gloss, pale pink; solid pink plastic. $441.00.

bottom row

1.) Unknown number: unknown date. *Elephant.* Unpainted. $78.40.

2.) 391: 1992. *Elephant.* Matte, light gray; white tusks. Made for the election year, had a American flag in the box. $23.10 with box.

also 91: 1958-74. *Elephant.* Matte, gray; white tusks. Essentially the same as #391. $21.00.

Elephant models not shown:

94: 1958-59. *Elephant.* Matte/semi-gloss, gray; white tusks. Included red howdah. $56.00 ($371.00 with howdah).

Unknown number: unknown dates. *Elephant.* Semi-gloss/glossy, gold; antiqued appearance. Possibly only two exist. $350.00.

✖ Clocks and More ✖

None of the many lamps, clocks, nightlights, or music boxes that are known to exist were actually made by Breyer. The models were bought by other companies or by craftsmen and modified to mount on lamp bases, on or over clocks, or to fit a music box or nightlight inside.

Most of these creations were made in the 1960s and 1970s. Recently, however, one mail-order catalog had a Texas Longhorn Bull lamp for sale. The bull was the model in production in 1995, and was mounted on a wooden base with a lamp. So potentially, more lamps will show up in the future as well.

The Westen Horse #57 was the first horse model made by Breyer, and its creation was actually the catalyst for the start of Breyer Animal Creations. The Mastercrafter Clock Company mounted this model over or next to a mantel clock for a short period of time around 1950.

More complete descriptions of the models can be found in the appropriate chapters.

Clocks

Alabaster Western Horse Over Clock

1950. Western Horse over clock (Alabaster). Mastercrafter Clock. $155.00.

1950. Western Horse over clock (Palomino). Mastercrafter Clock. $165.00.

1950/51. Western Horse beside clock (Alabaster). Mastercrafter Clock. $150.00.

Palomino Western Horse Beside Clock
1950/51. Western Horse beside clock (Palomino). Mastercrafter
    Clock. $165.00.
1950s. Davy Crockett on Fury Prancer (Dark brown or black);
    shown at the bottom of page 141. Mastercrafter Clock.
    $180.00.

Music Boxes

Years produced correspond with years models
were made. No information was available on who
made these.

Fury Prancer with Clock and as a Music Box
Fury Prancer (Alabaster) with William Tell; music box, plays
    William Tell Overture. $85.00.

Indian Brave and Pinto Fury Prancer Music Box
Fury Prancer (Black pinto) alone, or with Indian; music box,
    unknown tune. $85.00.
Fury Prancer (Palomino) with Lucky Ranger; music box, plays
    Home on the Range. $95.00.

Lamps

The years these were produced correspond to the years the models were available; be careful, though, not all are older and many were made from relatively common models!

Belgian (Glossy, Smoke). $155.00.

Woodgrain Family Arabian Foal Lamp (shown)
Family Arabian Foal (Woodgrain). $40.00.
Fighting Stallion (Bay). $45.00.

Woodgrain Fighting Stallion Lamp (shown)
Fighting Stallion (Woodgrain). $105.00.
Fury Prancer (Palomino) with Davy Crockett on plaster base. $120.00.

Davy Crockett and Palomino Fury Prancer Lamp (shown)
Fury Prancer (Polomino) with Davy Crockett. $115.00.
Fury Prancer (Palomino) with Lucky Ranger. $115.00.
Rearing Stallion (bay). $45.00.
Running Foal (Matte, Smoke), pink base. $85.00.

Woodgrain Running Foal Wall Lamp
Running Foal (Woodgrain), wall mount. $97.10.

Running Mare and Foal (Bay) Lamp (shown)
Running Mare and Foal (Bay). $45.00.
Running Mare and Foal (Smoke and Alabaster, respectively). $55.00.
Running Mare and Foal (Woodgrain). $195.00.
Stud Spider (Bay Appaloosa). Fedco. $55.00.
Western Horse (Palomino). $55.00.
Buffalo (Brown). $65.00.
Texas Longhorn (Brown). $65.00.
Texas Longhorn (Red brown pinto pattern). Expressions of Pot-
    pourri. $55.00.

Woodgrain Texas Longhorn Lamp
Texas Longhorn (Woodgrain). $255.00.

One hobby magazine (now out of print) mounted several models onto lamp bases. These were fairly common models (and usually the current ones). They did these lamps in the late 1980s or early 1990s.

Nightlights

Years produced correspond with years models were made. No information was available on who made these.

Family Arabian Mare (Palomino), switch on base instead of model. $55.00.
Family Arabian Mare and Foal (Glossy, Alabaster), bulb in mare. $65.00.
Family Arabian Mare and Foal (Glossy, Bay), bulb in mare. $65.00.
Fury Prancer (Brown Pinto). $75.00.

Old Mold Alabaster Proud Arabian Mare Night Light (shown)
Proud Arabian Mare (Alabaster). $75.00.
Proud Arabian Mare (Glossy, Bay). $65.00.
Proud Arabian Mare and Foal (Glossy Bay), bulb in mare. $75.00.
Quarter Horse Gelding (Glossy, Bay). $75.00.

Alabaster Western Horse Night Light (shown)
Western Horse (Alabaster), free standing. $75.00.
Western Horse (Black Pinto). $40.00.
Western Horse (Brown Pinto). $75.00.

❧ Repaints, Remakes, and Test Colors ❧

Repaints

Repainting is not as simple as it sounds. Actually, you *can* repaint a model with only a can of spray paint, but most high-quality repaints are done meticulously, using techniques garnered from trial and error, observing skilled artists, and from the numerous magazine and newsletter articles on the subject.

A variety of tools and media can be used to make a good repainted model. Almost anything goes, from expensive airbrushes to ordinary colored pencils (for highlighting). Most amateur repainters use either acrylic or oil paints applied by brush for the body color and markings. Many also use an airbrush (airbrushes are fairly expensive and can be difficult to use well).

143

Remakes

Like repainting, remaking is an art. Remaking colors are literally the company's way of testing new combinations of colors, different painting techniques, and different markings on models, all to see if the model is attractive. Often, you will find a test color model available at auction (at BreyerFest) one year, then see a similar version of that color as a regular or special run sometime in the next few years.

Test color models are highly prized by collectors. In general, the factory painters seem to use more care when painting test colors, so the models are usually very good for live and photo shows.

Test color Lady Phase models

Test color Smoky models

Test color Clydesdale Mare and Proud Arabian Stallion models

Test color Pony of the Americas, Galiceno, Saddlebred Weanling, and Mustang Foal models

Test color Hanoverian models

Test color Stock Horse Stallion and Hanoverian models

Test color Action Stock Horse Foal and (Standing) Stock Horse
Foal models

Test color San Domingo, El Pastor, and Legionario models

These lists will help you find the mold and model when you know only part of the information you need.

Model List by Name

This reference list gives the models by name. In many cases, different models and even different molds were given the same name at different times in Breyer's history. This means of sorting the models should help you find a model that you know only by a name. You should use this list then to locate the mold you need, then refer to the appropriate section for more information.

The following conventions apply to this list:
1.) each name is listed only once;
2.) if the same name was used to designate more than one model or set, each is separated by a number;
3.) if a name designated a set of models, the models in each set are separated by commas;
4.) mold names are shown in **bold italics**;
5.) model color is given in parenthesis following the mold name;
6.) when no finish is given (matte, semi-gloss, etc.), assume the model has a matte finish.

The abbreviations used in the following list are:

T = Traditional scale	O = Other Animal	Sg = Semi-gloss
C = Classic scale	LE = Limited Edition	Fl = Flocked
L = Little Bits scale	CE = Commemorative Edition	M = Matte
S = Stablemate scale	Gl = Glossy	

12 Piece Stablemates Set — 1: (SR 94) (S) *Arabian Mare* (Medium gray), (S) *Arabian Stallion* (Chestnut), (S) *Citation* (Dapple gray), (S) *Draft Horse* (Creamy dun), (S) *Morgan Mare* (Chocolate sorrel), (S) *Morgan Stallion* (Black blanket appaloosa), (S) *Morgan Stallion* (Dark bay), (S) *Native Dancer* (Black), (S) *Quarter Horse Stallion* (Red leopard appaloosa), (S) *Seabiscuit* (Light gray), (S) *Silky Sullivan* (Grulla/dun), (S) *Swaps* (Buckskin); 2: (SR 96) (S) *Arabian Mare* (gray roan), (S) *Arabian Stallion* (dark rose gray), (S) *Citation* (bay appaloosa), (S) *Draft Horse* (black pinto), (S) *Morgan Mare* (light red dun), (S) *Morgan Stallion* (alabaster), (S) *Native Dancer* (red dun), (S) *Quarter Horse Stallion* (buckskin), (S) *Saddlebred* (dapple gray), (S) *Seabiscuit* (medium red bay), (S) *Silky Sullivan* (black leopard appaloosa), (S) *Swaps* (bay).

A Pony For Keeps — (C) *Ginger* (Alabaster), (C) *Merrylegs* (Alabaster), (C) *Might Tango* (Light dapple gray), (C) *Mustang Stallion* (Chestnut, gray lower legs)

Abdullah Champion Trakehner — (T) *Trakehner* (Light dapple gray, LE)

Action American Buckskin Stock Horse Foal — (T) *Action Stock Horse Foal* (Buckskin)

Action Appaloosa Foal — (T) *Action Stock Horse Foal* (Chestnut leopard appaloosa)

Action Drafters, Big and Small — (T) *Friesian* (Dark bay), (L) *Clydesdale* (Grulla/roan)

Adios — (T) *Adios* (Unpainted)

Adios Famous Standardbred — (T) *Adios* (Bay)

Adorable Horse Foal Set — (T) *Grazing Foal* (Bay blanket appaloosa), (T) *Lying Foal* (Sorrel), (T) *Running Foal* (Rose gray), (T) *Scratching Foal* (Alabaster)

All American Saddlebred in Parade Costume — (T) *All American Saddlebred In Parade Costume* (Palomino)

Ambrosia — (C) *Terrang* (Palomino)

Amber and Ashley, Twin Morgan Foals — (T) *Amber* (Chestnut), (T) *Ashley* (Chestnut)

American Bison — 1: (O) *Buffalo* (Dark brown); 2: (O) *Buffalo* (Muddy brown)

American Buckskin Stock Horse Foal — (T) *Stock Horse Foal* (Buckskin)

American Buckskin Stock Horse Mare — (T) *Stock Horse Mare* (Buckskin)

American Buckskin Stock Horse Stallion — (T) *Stock Horse Stallion* (Buckskin)

American Indian Pony — (T) *Foundation Stallion* (Red roan/flea bit gray)

American Mustang — (T) *Mustang* (Sorrel)

American Saddlebred — 1: (T) *Five Gaiter* (Dapple gray, black on red ribbons); 2: (L) *American Saddlebred* (Bay); 3: (L) *American Saddlebred* (Red chestnut); 4: (L) *American Saddlebred* (Palomino); 5: (L) *American Saddlebred* (Black pinto)

Amerigo — (T) *Mustang* (Palomino pinto)

Andrew — (C) *Silky Sullivan* (Gray)

Apache — (C) *Man O'War* (Gray)

Appaloosa — 1: (L) *Quarter Horse Stallion* (Black blanket appaloosa); 2: (L) *Quarter Horse Stallion* (Chestnut appaloosa); 3: (S) *Native Dancer* (Bay appaloosa)

Appaloosa and Foal — (S) *Quarter Horse Stallion* (black leopard appaloosa), (S) *Standing Foal* (black blanket appaloosa)

Appaloosa American Classic Set — (T) *Appaloosa Performance Horse* (Black blanket appaloosa), (T) *Running Stallion* (Palomino blanket appaloosa), (T) *Stud Spider* (Blue roan leopard appaloosa)

Appaloosa Champion — (T) *Foundation Stallion* (Red roan appaloosa)

Appaloosa Family — (C) *Quarter Horse Foal* (Black blanket appaloosa), (C) *Quarter Horse Mare* (Black blanket appaloosa), (C) *Quarter Horse Stallion* (Black blanket appaloosa)

Appaloosa Gelding — (T) *Quarter Horse Gelding* (Chestnut blanket appaloosa)

Appaloosa Mustang Family Gift Set — (C) *Mustang Foal* (Bay appaloosa), (C) *Mustang Mare* (Black blanket appaloosa), (C) *Mustang Stallion* (Dun appaloosa)

Appaloosa Performance Champion — (T) *Haflinger* (Palomino appaloosa)

Appaloosa Performance Horse — (T) *Appaloosa Performance Horse* (Chestnut roan appaloosa)

Appaloosa Sport Horse — (T) *Morganglanz* (Leopard appaloosa)

Appaloosa Stallion — (T) *Appaloosa Performance Horse* (Gray blanket appaloosa)

Appaloosa Stock Horse Foal — 1: (T) *Action Stock Horse Foal* (Gray blanket appaloosa); 2: (T) *Stock Horse Foal* (Gray blanket appaloosa)

Appaloosa Stock Horse Mare — 1: (T) *Stock Horse Mare* (Black appaloosa); 2: (T) *Stock Horse Mare* (Black appaloosa, leg up)

Appaloosa Stock Horse Stallion — (T) *Stock Horse Stallion* (Light bay blanket appaloosa)

Appaloosa Yearling — (T) *Quarter Horse Yearling* (Sandy bay blanket appaloosa)

Appy Mare — (T) *Stock Horse Mare* (Red roan/leopard appaloosa)

AQHA Ideal American Quarter Horse — 1: (T) *Ideal American Quarter Horse* (Dark red chestnut, mistake version); 2: (T) *Ideal American Quarter Horse* (Chestnut)

AQHA Offspring of King P-234 — (T) *Ideal American Quarter Horse* (Bay)

Ara-Appaloosa Foal — (T) *Family Arabian Foal* (Leopard appaloosa)

Ara-Appaloosa Mare — (T) *Family Arabian Mare* (Leopard appaloosa)

Ara-Appaloosa Stallion — (T) *Family Arabian Stallion* (Leopard appaloosa)

Arabian and Foal — (S) *Arabian Stallion* (Chestnut), (S) *Standing Foal* (Light chestnut)

Arabian Foal — 1: (C) *Arabian Foal* (Alabaster); 2: (C) *Arabian Foal* (Black); 3: (C) *Arabian Foal* (Chestnut); 4: (C) *Arabian Foal* (Gray); 5: (T) *Family Arabian Foal* (Bay); 6: (T) *Family Arabian Foal* (Alabaster); 7: (T) *Family Arabian Foal* (Gl, charcoal); 8: (T) *Family Arabian Foal* (Charcoal); 9: (T) *Family Arabian Foal* (Gl, alabaster); 10: (T) *Family Arabian Foal* (Gl, bay); 11: (T) *Family Arabi-*

an **Foal** (Gl, gray blanket appaloosa); 12: (T) **Family Arabian Foal** (Woodgrain); 13: (T) **Family Arabian Foal** (Gray blanket appaloosa); 14: (T) **Proud Arabian Foal** (Gl, alabaster); 15: (T) **Proud Arabian Foal** (Gl, bay); 16: (T) **Proud Arabian Foal** (Gl, gray blanket appaloosa)

Arabian Horses of the World Set — (T) **Family Arabian Stallion** (Black point alabaster), (T) **Proud Arabian Mare** (Flea bit gray), (T) **Proud Arabian Stallion** (Bay, blaze)

Arabian Mare — 1: (T) **Family Arabian Mare** (Bay); 2: (T) **Family Arabian Mare** (Gl, gray blanket appaloosa); 3: (T) **Family Arabian Mare** (Alabaster); 4: (T) **Family Arabian Mare** (Gl, charcoal); 5: (T) **Family Arabian Mare** (Charcoal); 6: (T) **Family Arabian Mare** (Gl, alabaster); 7: (T) **Family Arabian Mare** (Gl, bay); 8: (T) **Family Arabian Mare** (Gray blanket appaloosa); 9: (T) **Proud Arabian Mare** (Gl, alabaster, old mold); 10: (T) **Proud Arabian Mare** (Gl, bay, old mold); 11: (T) **Proud Arabian Mare** (Woodgrain, old mold); 12: (T) **Proud Arabian Mare** (Gl, gray blanket appaloosa, old mold); 13: (S) **Arabian Mare** (Dapple gray); 14: (S) **Arabian Mare** (Alabaster); 15: (S) **Arabian Mare** (Bay); 16: (S) **Arabian Mare** (Alabaster); 17: (S) **Arabian Mare** (Palomino);

Arabian Mare and Foal — (C) **Arabian Foal** (Dappled bay), (C) **Arabian Mare** (Dappled bay)

Arabian Mare and Foal Set — (T) **Proud Arabian Foal** (Red bay pinto), (T) **Proud Arabian Mare** (Red bay pinto)

Arabian Stallion — 1: (T) **Family Arabian Stallion** (Gl, alabaster); 2: (T) **Family Arabian Stallion** (Gl, bay); 3: (T) **Family Arabian Stallion** (Bay); 4: (T) **Family Arabian Stallion** (Alabaster); 5: (T) **Family Arabian Stallion** (Charcoal); 6: (T) **Family Arabian Stallion** (Gl, gray blanket appaloosa); 7: (T) **Family Arabian Stallion** (Gl, charcoal); 8: (T) **Family Arabian Stallion** (Gray blanket appaloosa); 9: (L) **Arabian Stallion** (Bay); 10: (L) **Arabian Stallion** (Chestnut); 11: (L) **Arabian Stallion** (Gray); 12: (L) **Arabian Stallion** (Alabaster); 13: (S) **Arabian Stallion** (Dapple gray); 14: (S) **Arabian Stallion** (Alabaster); 15: (S) **Arabian Stallion** (Bay); 16: (S) **Arabian Stallion** (Dark gray); 17: (S) **Arabian Stallion** (Bay); 18: (S) **Morgan Stallion** (Alabaster); 19: (S) **Morgan Stallion** (Dapple gray); 20: (S) **Morgan Stallion** (Bay)

Arabian Stallion & Frisky Foal Set — 1: (T) **Sham** (Bay), (C) **Arabian Foal** (Gray); 2: (T) **Sham** (Bay-going-gray), (C) **Arabian Foal** (Light bay)

Arabian Stallion with English Tack Set — (T) **Proud Arabian Stallion** (Bay)

Aristocrat Champion Hackney — (T) **Hackney** (Bay)

Art Deco Dressage Horse — (T) **Hanoverian** (Black pinto)

Assorted Mare and Foals Stable Set — (T) **Proud Arabian Foal** (Red bay), (T) **Proud Arabian Mare** (Red bay), (T) **Stock Horse Foal** (Gray blanket appaloosa), (T) **Stock Horse Foal (Rough Coat)** (Palomino pinto)

Ayrshire Calf — (O) **Calf** (Dark red and white pinto pattern)

Ayrshire Cow — (O) **Cow** (Dark red and white pinto pattern)

Azteca — (T) **Foundation Stallion** (Dapple gray)

Azul — (C) **Terrang** (Blue roan/gray, includes neck ribbon)

Balking Mule — 1: (T) **Balking Mule** (Bay/chestnut); 2: (T) **Balking Mule** (M/SG, liver chestnut/seal brown)

Baron, Mustang — (T) **Mustang** (Gl, mahogany bay/dark chestnut)

Bay Fighting Stallion — (T) **Fighting Stallion** (Bay)

Bay Pinto — (L) **Quarter Horse Stallion** (Bay pinto)

Bay Pinto Stock Horse Foal — (T) **Action Stock Horse Foal** (Bay pinto)

Bay Quarter Horse Stock Foal — (T) **Stock Horse Foal** (Bay)

Bay Quarter Horse Stock Stallion — (T) **Stock Horse Stallion** (Bay)

Bear — 1: (O) **Bear** (Brown); 2: (O) **Bear** (Black); 3: (O) **Bear** (Medium brown)

Bear Cub — 1: (O) **Bear Cub** (Brown); 2: (O) **Bear Cub** (Black)

Bear Family — (O) **Bear** (Black), (O) **Bear Cub** (Black)

Bear Family Gift Set — (O) **Bear** (White), (O) **Bear Cub** (White)

Beat the Wind — (T) **Pacer** (Shaded gray)

Bedouin Family Gift Set — (C) **Arabian Foal** (Bay), (C) **Arabian Mare** (Black), (C) **Arabian Stallion** (Bay)

Belgian — 1: (T) **Belgian** (Chestnut/sorrel, red on yellow ribbon); 2: (T) **Belgian** (Smoke, red on yellow ribbon); 3: (T) **Belgian** (Gl, dapple gray or dapple black); 4: (T) **Belgian** (Woodgrain)

Belgian Brabant — (T) **Roy the Belgian** (Grulla)

Belle — (L) **American Saddlebred** (Bay)

Benji — (O) **Benji** (M/Sg, tan)

Benji and Tiffany Set — (O) **Benji** (Benji (tan) and Tiffany (white))

Bermese Her Majesty the Queen's Horse — (T) **Secretariat** (Black)

Best Choice, Arabian — (T) **Sham** (Mahogany bay)

Best Tango — (T) **Adios** (Light bay)

Big Ben — (T) **Big Ben** (Chestnut)

Bighorn Ram — (O) **Bighorn Ram** (Tan)

Bitsy Breyer and Arabian Stallion Beach Set — (L) **Arabian Stallion** (Bay, chestnut, or gray)

Bitsy Breyer and Morgan English Set — (L) **Morgan Stallion** (Bay, black, and chestnut)

Bitsy Breyer and Quarter Horse Western Set — (L) **Quarter Horse Stallion** (Bay, buckskin, and palomino)

Bitsy Breyer and Thoroughbred Jockey Set — (L) **Thoroughbred Stallion** (Bay, chestnut, or black models)

Bitsy Breyer Riding Academy — (L) **Morgan Stallion** (Bay)

Black Angus Bull — 1: (O) **Black Angus Bull** (Black); 2: (O) **Black Angus Bull** (Woodgrain); 3: (O) **Walking Black Angus Bull** (Gl, black)

Black Angus Calf — (O) **Calf** (Black)

Black Beauty — 1: (T) **Black Beauty** (Black); 2: (T) **Black Beauty** (Unpainted); 3: (C) **Black Beauty** (Gl, black); 4: (T) **Fury Prancer** (Gl, black (gold or silver bridle, white tipped tail)); 5: (T) **Western Horse** (Gl, black); 6: (T) **Western Pony** (Gl, black)

Black Beauty 1991 — (T) **Morganglanz** (Black)

Black Beauty Family — (C) **Black Beauty** (Black), (C) **Duchess** (Bay), (C) **Ginger** (Chestnut), (C) **Merrylegs** (Dapple gray)

Black Foundation Stallion — (T) **Foundation Stallion** (Black)

Black Gold — (T) **San Domingo** (M/Sg, black)

Black Jack — (C) **Kelso** (Black pinto)

Black Silk — (C) **Swaps** (Black)

Blanket Appaloosa — 1: (T) **San Domingo** (Dark gray blanket appaloosa); 2: (T) **Stud Spider** (Chestnut blanket appaloosa)

Bloodhound — (O) **Basset Hound** (Dark brown)

Bluegrass Foal — (T) **Running Foal** (Blue roan)

Bold — (T) **Stud Spider** (Palomino)

Bolya the Freedom Horse — (T) **Halla** (Buckskin)

Bond Snippet, Miniature Horse — (C) **Merrylegs** (Chestnut pinto)

Borodino II, Hanoverian — (T) **Hanoverian** (Matte,bay, blaze)

Bosley Blue & Trusty — (T) **Quarter Horse Yearling** (Gray roan leopard appaloosa), (T) **Lying Foal** (Gray leopard appaloosa)

Boxer — 1: (O) **Boxer** (M or Sg or Gl, tan/fawn); 2: (O) **Boxer** (Woodgrain); 3: (O) **Boxer** (Gl, white/very light shaded gray)

Brahma Bull — 1: (O) **Brahma Bull** (Sg/M, gray); 2: (O) **Brahma Bull** (Gl, gray); 3: (O) **Brahma Bull** (Woodgrain)

Brandy St. Bernard — (O) **St. Bernard** (Golden)

Breezing Dixie Famous Appaloosa Mare — (T) **Lady Phase** (Dark bay blanket appaloosa. LE)

Brenda Breyer and Harness Racing Set — (T) **Pacer** (Alabaster)

Brenda Breyer Gift Set — (T) **Appaloosa Performance Horse** (Dark chestnut blanket appaloosa)

Brenda Western Gift Set — (T) **Western Prancing Horse** (Chestnut pinto)

Breyer Classic Collector's Arabian Family Set — (C) **Arabian Foal** (Black), (C) **Arabian Mare** (Black), (C) **Arabian Stallion** (Black)

Breyer Mustang Family — (C) **Mustang Foal** (Grulla), (C) **Mustang Mare** (Bay), (C) **Mustang Stallion** (Buckskin)

Breyer Parade of Breeds — (L) **American Saddlebred** (Brown pinto), (L) **Arabian Stallion** (Alabaster), (L) **Morgan Stallion** (Bay), (L) **Quarter Horse Stallion** (Leopard appaloosa), (L) **Quarter Horse Stallion** (Gray), (L) **Thoroughbred Stallion** (Bay)

Breyer Parade of Breeds Collector's Assortment 2nd Ed. — (L) **American Saddlebred** (Dark bay), (L) **Arabian Stallion** (Black), (L) **Clydesdale** (Sorrel), (L) **Morgan Stallion** (Chestnut), (L) **Quarter Horse Stallion** (Black), (L) **Thoroughbred Stallion** (Bay)

Breyer Parade of Breeds Collector's Assortment 3rd Ed. — (L) **American Saddlebred** (Palomino pinto), (L) **Arabian Stallion** (Dapple gray), (L) **Clydesdale** (Dapple gray), (L) **Morgan Stallion** (Bay), (L) **Quarter Horse Stallion** (Black leopard appaloosa), (L) **Thoroughbred Stallion** (Rose gray)

Breyer Quarter Horse Family — (C) **Quarter Horse Foal** (Alabaster), (C) **Quarter Horse Mare** (Dark chestnut/bay), (C) **Quarter Horse Stallion** (Dark chestnut/bay)

Breyer Rider Gift Set — (T) **Adios** (Palomino, 5 made)

Breyer Three Generations Appaloosa Set — (T) **Adios** (Bay blanket appaloosa), (T) **Quarter Horse Yearling** (Bay blanket appaloosa), (T) **Stock Horse Foal (Rough Coat)** (Chestnut appaloosa)

Breyer Traditional Horse Set — (T) **Lady Phase** (Dapple gray), (T) **Quarter Horse Gelding** (Palomino), (T) **Rugged Lark** (Red chestnut)

Breyers Traditional Collector's Family Set — (T) **Stock Horse Mare** (Bay roan peppercorn appaloosa), (T) **Action Stock Horse Foal** (Bay roan peppercorn appaloosa), (T) **Stock Horse Stallion** (Bay roan peppercorn appaloosa)

Bright Socks — (T) **Stock Horse Foal (Rough Coat)** (Black pinto)

Bright Zip — (T) **San Domingo** (Chestnut appaloosa)

Brighty 1991, or Marguerite Henry's Brighty — (T) **Brighty** (Brownish-gray)

Brighty Gift Set — (T) **Brighty** (Gray)

Brown and White Pinto Stock Horse — (T) **Stock Horse Stallion** (Bay pinto)

Brown Swiss Calf — (O) *Calf* (Cocoa brown; solid)

Brown Swiss Cow — (O) *Cow* (Cocoa brown)

Buck — (C) *Terrang* (Buckskin)

Buck Deer — (O) *Buck Deer* (Tan)

Buckaroo and Skeeter — (C) *Arabian Mare* (Buckskin), (T) *Stormy* (Bay pinto)

Bucking Bronco — 1: (C) *Bucking Bronco* (Gray); 2: (C) *Bucking Bronco* (Black); 3: (C) *Bucking Bronco* (Bay); 4: (C) *Bucking Bronco* (Gray); 5: (C) *Bucking Bronco* (Red roan); 6: (C) *Bucking Bronco* (Chestnut); 7: (C) *Bucking Bronco* (Black leopard appaloosa); 8: (C) *Bucking Bronco* (Black pinto)

Buckshot Famous Spanish Barb — (T) *Buckshot* (Grulla)

Buffalo — 1: (O) *Buffalo* (M/Sg, bronze); 2: (O) *Buffalo* (Brown); 3: (O) *Buffalo* (Woodgrain)

Burnt Sienna, American Saddlebred Weanling — (T) *Saddlebred Weanling* (Red roan)

Buster and Brandi Twin Appaloosa Foal Set — (T) *Lying Foal* (Bay blanket appaloosa), (T) *Scratching Foal* (Bay appaloosa)

Butterscotch — (S) *Arabian Mare* (Roan/leopard appaloosa)

Buttons and Bows Gift Set — (T) *Grazing Foal* (Chestnut/red dun), (T) *Grazing Mare* (Chestnut/red dun)

Cactus — (T) *Balking Mule* (Red roan)

Calf — (O) *Calf* (Unpainted)

Calico Kitten — (O) *Kitten* (Orange tabby)

Calife, Arabian — (T) *Family Arabian Stallion* (Shaded gray)

Calypso — (T) *Trakehner* (Light bay)

Calypso, Quarter Horse — (T) *Quarter Horse Yearling* (Red dun)

Cantering Welsh Pony — 1: (T) *Cantering Welsh Pony* (Chestnut, red ribbons); 2: (T) *Cantering Welsh Pony* (Seal brown, blue ribbons); 3: (T) *Cantering Welsh Pony* (Bay, yellow ribbons); 4: (T) *Cantering Welsh Pony* (Chestnut, no ribbons); 5: (T) *Cantering Welsh Pony* (Unpainted)

CH Imperator — (T) *Five Gaiter* (Gl, dark chestnut, blue on red ribbons)

Chaparral — (T) *Fighting Stallion* (Buckskin pinto, LE)

Chaser Hound Dog — (O) *Basset Hound* (Brown/bi-color)

Chaval — (C) *Anadalusian Mare* (Red roan/chestnut)

Chestnut Stock Horse Foal — (T) *Action Stock Horse Foal* (Chestnut)

Cheyenne American Mustang — (T) *Indian Pony* (Roan)

Chincoteague Foal — (T) *Sea Star* (Buckskin)

Chinook — (T) *Indian Pony* (Dark dapple gray)

Chocolate and Jeannie — (L) *Quarter Horse Stallion* (dark bay)

Cinnamon Bear and Cub — (O) *Bear* (Reddish brown), (O) *Bear Cub* (Reddish brown)

Cinnamon, Appaloosa — (T) *Lady Roxanna* (Bay blanket appaloosa)

Circus Extravaganza Set — (L) *Clydesdale* (Bay), (T) *Clydesdale Stallion* (Roan/flea bit gray; red, white, and blue bobs)

Circus Set with Ringmaster — (T) *Fighting Stallion* (Fl, white)

Cisco Western Pony with Saddle — (T) *Western Pony* (Buckskin)

Citation — (S) *Citation* (Bay)

Classic Andalusian Family — 1: (C) *Andalusian Foal* (Dark chestnut), (C) *Andalusian Mare* (Dapple gray), (C) *Andalusian Stallion* (Alabaster); 2: (C) *Andalusian Foal* (Bay), (C) *Andalusian Mare* (Alabaster), (C) *Andalusian Stallion* (Dapple gray)

Classic Arabian Family — 1: (C) *Arabian Foal* (Chestnut), (C) *Arabian Mare* (Chestnut), (C) *Arabian Stallion* (Sorrel); 2: (SR 84) (C) *Arabian Foal* (Red bay), (C) *Arabian Mare* (Alabaster), (C) *Arabian Stallion* (Bay); 3: (SR 88) (C) *Arabian Foal* (Dapple gray), (C) *Arabian Mare* (Dapple gray), (C) *Arabian Stallion* (Dapple gray)

Classic Beauty Gift Set — (C) *Andalusian Foal* (Shaded light gray), (C) *Black Stallion* (Flea-bit gray)

Clayton Quarter Horse — (T) *Adios* (Dapple palomino)

Cleopatra Kitten — (O) *Kitten* (Orange tabby)

Cloud — (C) *Swaps* (Dapple gray, includes neck ribbon)

Clue II, American Quarter Horse — (T) *Fighting Stallion* (Palomino)

Clydesdale — 1: (T) *Clydesdale Mare* (Fl, bay, red ribbons); 2: (T) *Clydesdale Stallion* (Bay, gold bobs and tail ribbon); 3: (T) *Clydesdale Stallion* (Gl, bay, gold ribbons, muscle and no-muscle versions); 4: (T) *Clydesdale Stallion* (Woodgrain, no-muscle and muscle versions); 5: (T) *Clydesdale Stallion* (Gl, dapple gray, gold bobs, no-muscle and muscle versions); 6: (L) *Clydesdale* (Chestnut)

Clydesdale Family Set — (T) *Clydesdale Foal* (Bay, true bay), (T) *Clydesdale Mare* (Red bay, true bay), (T) *Clydesdale Stallion* (Bay, true bay, red bobs, stenciled stockings)

Clydesdale Foal — 1: (T) *Clydesdale Foal* (Chestnut); 2: (T) *Clydesdale Foal* (Light bay)

Clydesdale Mare — 1: (T) *Clydesdale Mare* (Chestnut); 2: (T) *Clydesdale Mare*

(Light bay); 3: (T) *Clydesdale Mare* (Unpainted)

Clydesdale Stallion — 1: (T) *Clydesdale Stallion* (Bay, alternating white and red bobs, red tail ribbon); 2: (T) *Clydesdale Stallion* (Light bay, gold and white bobs, gold tail ribbon)

Cobalt and Veronica — (L) *Thoroughbred Stallion* (Black)

Cody — (T) *Buckshot* (Dark bay pinto)

Collectible Stock Horse Family — (T) *Action Stock Horse Foal* (Buckskin, black points), (T) *Stock Horse Mare* (Buckskin), (T) *Stock Horse Stallion* (Buckskin)

Collector's Edition Appaloosa Family — (C) *Quarter Horse Foal* (Chestnut blanket appaloosa), (C) *Quarter Horse Mare* (Chestnut blanket appaloosa), (C) *Quarter Horse Stallion* (Chestnut blanket appaloosa)

Collector's Mare and Foal Set — (T) *Running Foal* (Fl, palomino), (T) *Running Mare* (Fl, palomino)

Collector's Rocking Horse — (T) *Saddlebred Weanling* (Fl, chestnut)

Colleen — (C) *Ruffian* (Chestnut)

Comanche Pony — (T) *San Domingo* (Palomino)

Corky and Bimbo — (O) *Elephant* (M/Sg, battleship gray, white tusks)

Cow Family — (O) *Calf* (Black and white pinto pattern), (O) *Cow* (Black and white pinto pattern)

Cricket Quarter Horse Foal — (T) *Action Stock Horse Foal* (Brown bay)

Crooked Horned Holstein Cow — (O) *Cow* (Black and white pinto pattern)

Dakota Bucking Bronco — (C) *Bucking Bronco* (Palomino)

Dakotah Indian Horse - "Lightning" Waykinyan — (T) *San Domingo* (Light bay/red dun pinto)

Dakotah Indian Horse - "Thunder" Waykinyan Hoton — (T) *San Domingo* (Black pinto)

Dall Sheep — (O) *Bighorn Ram* (Tan)

Dan Patch — (T) *Pacer* (M/Sg, red bay, LE)

Deer Family — (O) *Buck Deer* (Tan), (O) *Doe Deer* (Tan), (O) *Fawn Deer* (Tan with spots)

Delilah — (L) *Morgan Stallion* (Palomino)

Delivery Wagon — (C) *Keen* (Fl, chestnut)

Dempsey, Clydesdale Mare — (T) *Clydesdale Mare* (Chestnut/bay pinto)

Denver and Blaze Dutch Warmbloods — (C) *Quarter Horse Foal* (Red bay), (C) *Kelso* (Mahogany bay)

Desert Arabian Family — (C) *Arabian Foal* (Bay), (C) *Arabian Mare* (Bay), (C) *Arabian Stallion* (Red bay)

Desperado, Fall Show Horse — (T) *El Pastor* (Black pinto)

Devil Wind, Family Arabian Stallion — (T) *Family Arabian Stallion* (Seal brown/dark bay)

Diamondot Buccaneer, Appaloosa — (T) *Appaloosa Performance Horse* (Gray roan appaloosa, varnish roan)

Docs Keepin Time, Quarter Horse — (T) *Stock Horse Stallion* (Black)

Doe Deer — (O) *Doe Deer* (Tan)

Domino — (T) *Roemer* (Black pinto, with saddle)

Domino The Happy Canyon Trail Horse — (T) *San Domingo* (Black/dark gray pinto, CE)

Donkey — 1: (T) *Donkey* (Gray); 2: (T) *Donkey* (Gray, with red baskets)

Donovan Running Appaloosa Stallion — (T) *Black Beauty* (Gray blanket appaloosa chestnut spots)

Double Take — (T) *Justin Morgan* (Dark chestnut)

Dover, Trakehner — (T) *Misty's Twilight* (Bay)

Dr. Peaches, Three-Day Event Champion — (T) *Phar Lap* (Bay)

Draft Horse — 1: (S) *Draft Horse* (Dark or light sorrel/chestnut); 2: (S) *Draft Horse* (Dapple gray); 3: (S) *Draft Horse* (Bay)

Drafters Set — (T) *Belgian* (Alabaster, light blue on white tail ribbon), (T) *Roy the Belgian* (Chocolate sorrel), (T) *Shire* (Palomino; white mane and tail)

Draw Horses with Sam Savitt — (C) *Kelso* (Bay)

Dream Weaver — (T) *Black Beauty* (Sorrel, LE)

Dressage Set of Two Horses — (T) *Hanoverian* (Mahogany bay), (T) *Misty's Twilight* (Black, green braids)

Drinkers of the Wind — (C) *Arabian Foal* (Rose gray), (C) *Arabian Stallion* (Gray), (C) *Johar* (Flea bit gray)

Duroc Hog — (O) *Jasper The Market Hog* (Red and brown)

Duke, Pinto — (T) *Stock Horse Foal (Rough Coat)* (Chestnut pinto)

Dustin — (T) *Phar Lap* (Dun)

Eagle and Pow Wow — (C) *Johar* (Black pinto)

El Campeador — (T) *Legionario* (Dark dapple gray)

El Pastor Paso Fino — (T) *El Pastor* (Bay, star face)

Elephant — 1: (O) *Elephant* (M/Sg, gray, white tusks); 2: (O) *Elephant* (Gray); 3: (O) *Elephant* (Woodgrain); 4: (O) *Elephant* (Sg, pale pink); 5: (O) *Elephant* (Light gray); 6: (O) *Elephant* (Sg/M/Gl Gold); 7: (O) *Elephant* (Unpainted)

Elk — (O) **Elk** (Brown)

Embajador XI, Andalusian — (T) **Pluto** (Medium dapple gray)

English Horse Collector's Set — (T) **Black Stallion** (Sandy bay), (T) **Indian Pony** (Red dun), (T) **Justin Morgan** (Chestnut)

Equus, Arabian Racehorse — (T) **Black Stallion** (Alabaster)

Fade to Grey — (T) **Black Beauty** (Dark dappled gray)

Family Appaloosa Foal — (T) **Stock Horse Foal** (Red bay appaloosa)

Family Appaloosa Mare — (T) **Lady Phase** (Black leopard appaloosa)

Family Appaloosa Stallion — (T) **Stud Spider** (Bay blanket appaloosa)

Family Arabian Foal — 1: (T) **Family Arabian Foal** (Bay, hind socks); 2: (T) **Family Arabian Foal** (Red chestnut); 3: (T) **Family Arabian Foal** (Liver chestnut)

Family Arabian Mare — 1: (T) **Family Arabian Mare** (Woodgrain); 2: (T) **Family Arabian Mare** (Bay); 3: (T) **Family Arabian Mare** (Liver chestnut)

Family Arabian Stallion — 1: (T) **Family Arabian Stallion** (Bay, hind socks); 2: (T) **Family Arabian Stallion** (Liver chestnut)

Family Foal — 1: (T) **Family Arabian Foal** (Palomino); 2: (T) **Family Arabian Foal** (Gl, palomino)

Family Mare — 1: (T) **Family Arabian Mare** (Palomino); 2: (T) **Family Arabian Mare** (Gl, palomino)

Family Stallion — 1: (T) **Family Arabian Stallion** (Palomino); 2: (T) **Family Arabian Stallion** (Gl, palomino); 3: (T) **Family Arabian Stallion** (Woodgrain)

Family to Church on Sunday — (C) **Duchess** (Fl, bay), (C) **Jet Run** (Fl, bay)

Fanciful Mare and Pony Set — (T) **Running Foal** (Fl, white), (T) **Running Mare** (Fl, white; pink mane and tail)

Fashionably Late — (T) **Sherman Morgan** (Sorrel; cold cast porcelain)

Favory — (T) **Pluto** (Red roan)

Fawn Deer — (O) **Fawn** (Tan)

Fighting Stallion — 1: (T) **Fighting Stallion** (Bay); 2: (T) **Fighting Stallion** (Alabaster); 3: (T) **Fighting Stallion** (Gl, charcoal); 4: (T) **Fighting Stallion** (Woodgrain); 5: (T) **Fighting Stallion** (Gl, gray blanket appaloosa); 6: (T) **Fighting Stallion** (Gl, palomino); 7: (T) **Fighting Stallion** (Palomino); 8: (T) **Fighting Stallion** (Gl, alabaster); 9: (T) **Fighting Stallion** (Gl, Copenhagen); 10: (T) **Fighting Stallion** (Gl, Florentine); 11: (T) **Fighting Stallion** (Gl, Gold Charm); 12: (T) **Fighting Stallion** (Wedgewood); 13: (T) **Fighting Stallion** (Black leopard appaloosa)

Fine Horse Family — (C) **Kelso** (Roan), (C) **Mustang Foal** (Roan), (C) **Silky Sullivan** (Dark chestnut/bay)

Fine Porcelain Icelandic Horse — (T) **Fine Porcelain Icelandic Horse** (Buckskin pinto)

Fine Porcelain Premier Arabian Mare — (T) **Fine Porcelain Premier Arabian Mare** (Light gray, wearing traditional Arabian costume)

Fine Porcelain Premier Series Circus Ponies in Costume — (T) **Porcelain Circus Ponies** (Alabaster with circus costume)

Fine Porcelain Premier Series Great Horse in Armor — (T) **Porcelain Great Horse in Armor** (Black, wearing armor)

Fine Porcelain Shire — (T) **Fine Porcelain Shire** (Bay)

Fine Porcelain Spanish Barb — (T) **Fine Porcelain Spanish Barb** (Grulla)

First Competitor — (T) **Gem Twist** (Buckskin)

Five Gaiter — 1: (T) **Five Gaiter** (Sorrel, red on white braids); 2: (T) **Five Gaiter** (Gl, palomino, red on yellow ribbons); 3: (T) **Five Gaiter** (Gl, white, turquoise on yellow ribbons); 4: (T) **Five Gaiter** (Woodgrain, blue on white ribbons); 5: (T) **Five Gaiter** (Gl, Copenhagen, black on blue ribbons); 6: (T) **Five Gaiter** (Gl, Florentine, black on gold ribbons); 7: (T) **Five Gaiter** (Gl, Gold Charm, black on gold ribbons); 8: (T) **Five Gaiter** (Wedgewood, black on blue ribbons); 9: (T) **Five Gaiter** (Unpainted)

Flabbehoppen - Knabstrupper — (T) **Misty's Twilight** (Bay leopard appaloosa)

Foal's First Day — (C) **Arabian Foal** (Light bay), (C) **Johar** (Rose gray)

Foundation Stallion — (T) **Foundation Stallion** (Unpainted)

Freckle Doll — (T) **Galiceno** (Bay pinto)

Freedom, Legend of the Bloody Shoulder Arabian — (T) **Proud Arabian Stallion** (Flea-bit gray)

Friesian — (T) **Friesian** (Black)

Frisky Foals Set — (T) **Action Stock Horse Foal** (Yellow dun), (T) **Nursing Foal** (Palomino pinto), (T) **Proud Arabian Foal** (Chestnut/bay), (T) **Running Foal** (Black blanket appaloosa)

Fugir Cacador Lusitano Stallion — (T) **Foundation Stallion** (Buckskin, LE)

Full Speed, Appaloosa — (T) **Indian Pony** (Shaded palomino appaloosa)

Fury — (T) **Fury Prancer** (Gl, black, star face, black or brown bridle)

Fury Prancer — 1: (T) **Fury Prancer** (Gl, black); 2: (T) **Fury Prancer** (Gl, dark plum brown); 3: (T) **Fury Prancer** (Gl, alabaster; also with Robin Hood, William Tell, Canadian Mountie); 4: (T) **Fury Prancer** (Woodgrain); 5: (T) **Fury Prancer** (Gl, black pinto; also with Lucky Ranger, Cowboy, Indian Brave, Indian Chief); 6: (T) **Fury Prancer** (Gl, palomino; also with Lucky Ranger or Cowboy); 7: (T) **Fury Prancer** (Gl, chestnut pinto; with Lucky Ranger, Cowboy, Indian Brave, or Indian Chief); 8: (T) **Fury Prancer** (Gl, dark brown; with Davy Crockett, Kit Carson, or Canadian Mountie)

Future Champions Set — (T) **Saddlebred Weanling** (Bay pinto)

Gaited Breeds of America — (T) **Five Gaiter** (Bay Pinto), (T) **Midnight Sun** (Shaded liver chestnut), (T) **Saddlebred Yearling** (Palomino)

Galant, Lusitano — (T) **Legionario** (Shaded chestnut)

Galaxias — (T) **Sham** (Dappled gray; cold cast porcelain)

Galena, Family Arabian Mare — (T) **Family Arabian Mare** (Shaded chestnut)

Galiceno — (T) **Galiceno** (Bay)

Galloping Thoroughbred — (T) **Phar Lap** (Dark bay)

Gambler, Western Pony — (T) **Western Pony** (Palomino)

Gaucho — (C) **Terrang** (Red roan)

Gem Twist Champion Show Jumper — (T) **Gem Twist** (Alabaster)

German Olympic Set — (C) **Jet Run** (Bay), (C) **Keen** (Red bay), (C) **Might Tango** (Bay)

German Shepherd — (O) **Rin Tin Tin** (M/Sg, charcoal gray)

Geronimo and Cochise — (C) **Kelso** (Light bay appaloosa), (T) **Sea Star** (Bay blanket appaloosa)

Gifted — (T) **Hanoverian** (Bay, LE)

Giltedge — (T) **Aristocrat** (Florentine)

Glory and Plank Jump Gift Set — (C) **Ruffian** (Dun/buckskin, with jump)

Goin For Approval, Appaloosa — (T) **Stock Horse Mare** (Chestnut snowflake appaloosa)

Golden Joy, Paint — (T) **Stock Horse Foal** (Palomino pinto)

Goliath the American Cream Draft Horse — (T) **Belgian** (Light palomino, blue on red ribbon)

Grayingham Lucky Lad — (T) **Clydesdale Stallion** (Sg, black, red mane, red and white bobs and tail ribbon)

Grazing Foal — 1: (T) **Grazing Foal** (Bay); 2: (T) **Grazing Foal** (Palomino); 3: (T) **Grazing Foal** (Black); 4: (T) **Grazing Foal** (Bay blanket appaloosa)

Grazing Mare — 1: (T) **Grazing Mare** (Bay); 2: (T) **Grazing Mare** (Palomino); 3: (T) **Grazing Mare** (Black)

Greystreak Action Arabian — (T) **Black Stallion** (Gray)

Guernsey Calf — (O) **Calf** (Tan and white pinto pattern)

Guernsey Cow — 1: (O) **Cow** (Tan and white pinto pattern); 2: (O) **Cow** (Sg, brown and white)

Guinevere — (T) **Touch Of Class** (Reddish bay)

Haflinger — (T) **Haflinger** (Sorrel)

Halayi — (T) **Indian Pony** (Palomino appaloosa)

Halla, Famous Jumper — (T) **Halla** (Bay)

Hampshire Hog — (O) **Jasper The Market Hog** (Black and white)

Hanover Trakehner — (T) **Trakehner** (Liver chestnut)

Hanoverian — 1: (T) **Hanoverian** (Bay); 2: (T) **Hanoverian** (Unpainted)

Hanoverian Family — (C) **Andalusian Foal** (Bay), (C) **Ginger** (Light bay), (C) **Keen** (Black)

Hatatitla — (C) **Ginger** (Bay)

Hawk — (C) **Swaps** (Black)

Henry, Norwegian Fjord — (T) **Henry** (Dun)

Hereford Bull — 1: (O) **Hereford Bull** (M/Gl, dark brown); 2: (O) **Hereford Bull** (Woodgrain)

Hickock — (T) **Buckshot** (Blue roan pinto)

High Flyer Tennessee Walker — (T) **Midnight Sun** (Chestnut pinto, white on blue braids)

Highland Clydesdale — (T) **Clydesdale Stallion** (Bay, stenciled markings, blue and white bobs, blue tail ribbon)

Hobo — 1: (C) **Hobo** (Buckskin); 2: (T) **Phar Lap** (Buckskin)

Hobo the Mustang of Lazy Heart Ranch — (C) **Hobo** (Buckskin)

Hog — 1: (O) **Jasper The Market Hog** (Tan); 2: (O) **Jasper The Market Hog** (Black)

Holstein Calf — (O) **Calf** (Black and white pinto pattern)

Holstein Cow — 1: (O) **Cow** (Black pinto pattern); 2: (O) **Cow** (M/Sg, black and white, polled); 3: (O) Cow (Black pinto pattern w/small spots)

Honey Collie — (O) **Lassie** (Golden bi color)

Hornless Hereford — 1: (O) **Walking Black Angus Bull** (Gl, red brown and white); 2: (O) **Walking Black Angus Bull** (Gl, red brown and white, poodle cut)

Horse Salute Gift Set — (T) **Lady Phase** (Chestnut leopard appaloosa), (T) **Morganglanz** (Bay), (T) **Phar Lap** (Dark bay)

Horses Great and Small Set — (C) **Merrylegs** (Palomino), (T) **Cantering Welsh Pony** (M/Sg, black, no ribbons), (T) **Clydesdale Stallion** (Grulla/roan, yellow tail ribbon)

Hyksos the Egyptian Arabian — (T) **Black Stallion** (Sg, Ageless Bronze, CE)

Ichilay — (T) **Indian Pony** (Gray, 4 markings variations)

Iltschi — (C) **Black Beauty** (Black, Karl may set)

Indian Pony — 1: (T) **Indian Pony** (Dark bay blanket appaloosa); 2: (T) **Indian Pony** (Brown pinto); 3: (T) **Indian Pony** (Buckskin); 4: (T) **Indian Pony** (Alabaster); 5: (T) **Indian Pony** (Unpainted)

International Equestrian Collector's Set — (T) **Hanoverian** (Dark dapple gray), (T) **Halla** (Flea bit gray), (T) **Morganglanz** (Bay)

Irish Warrior — (T) **Secretariat** (Black)

Iron Metal Chief, Missouri Fox Trotter — (T) **Iron Metal Chief** (Black)

Jasper the Market Hog — (O) **Jasper The Market Hog** (White and gray)

JB Andrew, Adopt A Horse Drafter Type — (T) **Friesian** (Black, with freeze brand)

Jeremy — (C) **Kelso** (Brown)

Jersey Calf — (O) **Calf** (Tan; solid)

Jersey Cow — 1: (O) **Cow** (Dark tan); 2: (O) **Cow** (Sg, dark tan)

Jersey Cow Family Gift Set — (O) **Calf** (Tan), (O) **Cow** (Tan, polled)

Joe Patchen Sire of Dan Patch — (T) **John Henry** (Black)

Joey's Pony Cart — (C) **Merrylegs** (Fl, black pinto)

John Henry — (T) **John Henry** (Dark bay)

Jolly Cholly Basset Hound — (O) **Basset Hound** (Sg, tri color)

Julian, Family Arabian Foal — (T) **Family Arabian Foal** (Dark chestnut)

Jumping Gem Twist — (T) **Jumping Horse** (Alabaster)

Jumping Horse — (T) **Jumping Horse** (Bay)

Just Justin, Quarter Pony — (T) **Pony of the Americas** (Coffee dun)

Justin Morgan — (T) **Justin Morgan** (Red bay)

Justin Morgan Gift Set — (T) **Justin Morgan** (Red bay)

Kaleidoscope the Pinto Sporthorse — (T) **Trakehner** (Red bay pinto)

Karinthia, Buckskin Mare — (T) **Running Mare** (Light buckskin)

Karma Gypsy, Pinto Half-Arab — (T) **Proud Arabian Mare** (Bay pinto)

Kelly Reno and Little Man Gift Set — (T) **Stock Horse Stallion** (Palomino)

Kelso — (C) **Kelso** (M to Sg, dark bay/brown)

Kentuckiana Saddlebred Weanling — (T) **Saddlebred Weanling** (Dark chestnut)

Kentucky Saddlebred — (T) **Five Gaiter** (Chestnut)

Khemosabi +++ — (T) **Khemosabi** (Red bay)

King — (C) **Man O'War** (Dark chestnut)

King of Hearts, Spring Show Horse — (T) **Secretariat** (Appaloosa)

King of the Wind Set — (C) **Black Beauty** (Bay), (C) **Black Stallion** (Blood bay), (C) **Duchess** (Alabaster)

Kipper — (T) **Kipper** (Chocolate brown)

Korinth, Buckskin Foal — (T) **Running Foal** (Light buckskin)

Kris Kringle — (T) **Friesian** (Shaded dapple gray)

Laag, Standardbred — (T) **Pacer** (Gray, CE)

Laddie II, Shire — (T) **Clydesdale Stallion** (Matte or Sg, black overo)

Lady Phase — (T) **Lady Phase** (Unpainted)

Lady Roxanna — (T) **Lady Roxanna** (Alabaster)

Lakota Pony — (T) **Foundation Stallion** (Alabaster with blue markings)

Lassie — (O) **Lassie** (Sg, bi color)

Legionario — (T) **Legionario** (Unpainted)

Legionario III — (T) **Legionario** (Alabaster)

Legionario III Gift Set — (T) **Legionario** (Alabaster)

Leonardo Kitten — (O) **Kitten** (Gray tabby)

Lipizzan Stallion — 1: (C) **Lipizzan Stallion** (Alabaster); 2: (C) **Lipizzan Stallion** (Shaded alabaster)

Lippitt Pegasus — (T) **Morgan** (Red bay)

Little Andy Wind "Bo Diddley," Quarter Horse — (T) **Rugged Lark** (Chestnut)

Little Bits Horse Assortment (set) — (L) **Thoroughbred Stallion** (1 each in bay, black, and chestnut)

Little Bub — (T) **Running Foal** (Red bay)

Little Chaparral — (C) **Rearing Stallion** (Buckskin pinto)

Llanarth True Briton, Champion Welsh Cob — (T) **Llanarth True Briton** (Dark chestnut)

Lone Star — (T) **Running Stallion** (Light dapple rose gray)

Lula — (C) **Ruffian** (Bay)

Lying Down Foal — 1: (T) **Lying Foal** (Buckskin); 2: (T) **Lying Foal** (Black blanket appaloosa); 3: (T) **Lying Foal** (Red roan)

Lying Down Unicorn — (T) **Lying Foal** (Alabaster)

Lynn Anderson's Lady Phase — (T) **Lady Phase** (Chestnut)

Lynn Anderson's Lady Phase Gift Set — (T) **Lady Phase** (Chestnut)

Majestic Arabian Stallion — (T) **Black Stallion** (Black leopard appaloosa)

Majesty, Quarter Horse — (T) **Quarter Horse Gelding** (Light dapple gray)

Malibu — (T) **Hackney** (Wedgewood Blue)

Man O'War — 1: (T) **Man O'War** (Red chestnut); 2: (C) **Man O'War** (Red chestnut)

Marabella, Morgan Broodmare — (T) **Marabella** (Bay)

Mare and Foal Set — (T) **Grazing Mare** (Bay blanket appaloosa), (T) **Nursing Foal** (Chestnut leopard appaloosa)

Marguerite Henry's Stormy and Misty — (T) **Misty** (Fl, palomino pinto), (T) **Stormy** (Fl, chestnut pinto)

Marguerite Henry's Brighty — (T) **Brighty** (Gray)

Marguerite Henry's Misty — (T) **Misty** (Palomino pinto)

Marguerite Henry's Our First Pony Gift Set — (T) **Shetland Pony** (Black pinto), (C) **Arabian Foal** (Bay pinto), (C) **Mustang Foal** (Black pinto)

Marguerite Henry's Sea Star — (T) **Sea Star** (Dark chestnut)

Marguerite Henry's Sham — (T) **Sham** (Red bay, also with wheat ear)

Marguerite Henry's Stormy — (T) **Stormy** (Chestnut pinto)

Martin's Dominique Champion Miniature Horse — (C) **Merrylegs** (Sg, black)

McDuff Old Timer — (T) **Old Timer** (Gray blanket appaloosa)

Medicine Hat Mare and Foal Gift Set — (T) **Nursing Foal** (Chestnut pinto), (T) **Thoroughbred Mare** (Chestnut pinto)

Medieval Knight — (T) **Legionario** (Gray/roan)

Mego — (T) **Adios** (Palomino pinto)

Memphis Storm — (T) **Midnight Sun** (Gl, charcoal, red on white braids)

Merry Go Round Horse — (L) **Morgan Stallion** (Light purple)

Mesa — (T) **Adios** (M/Sg, very dark bay)

Mesteno, the Messenger — (C) **Mesteno** (Dark buckskin)

Midnight Sun, Tennessee Walker — (T) **Midnight Sun** (Black, red on white braids)

Midnight, Bronco — (C) **Rearing Stallion** (M/Sg, black)

Mighty Buck — (T) **Running Stallion** (Buckskin)

Mister Mister, Champion Paint — (T) **Stud Spider** (Chestnut pinto)

Misty — (T) **Misty** (Palomino pinto, cold cast porcelain)

Misty and Stormy Gift Set — (T) **Misty** (Palomino pinto), (T) **Stormy** (Chestnut pinto)

Misty Gift Set — (T) **Misty** (Palomino pinto)

Misty II, Black Mist, and Twister — (C) **Mesteno The Foal** (Alabaster), (C) **Ruffian** (Chestnut pinto), (C) **Swaps** (Black pinto)

Misty's Twilight — (T) **Misty's Twilight** (Chestnut pinto)

Modernistic Buck — (O) **Modernistic Buck** (Sg, metallic gold)

Modernistic Doe — (O) **Modernistic Doe** (Sg, metallic gold)

Montana Mountain Goat — (O) **Mountain Goat** (Alabaster)

Monte, Thoroughbred — (T) **Gem Twist** (Chestnut)

Moonglow — (L) **Quarter Horse Stallion** (Chestnut)

Moonshadows — (T) **Five Gaiter** (Blue roan, silver on blue ribbons)

Moose — 1: (O) **Moose** (Dark brown); 2: **Moose** (Light brown)

Morgan — 1: (T) **Justin Morgan** (Dark bay); 2: (T) **Morgan** (Black); 3: (T) **Morgan** (Bay); 4: (T) **Morgan** (Woodgrain); 5: (T) **Morgan** (Light bay); 6: (T) **Morgan** (Unpainted)

Morgan and Foal — (S) **Morgan Stallion** (buckskin), (S) **Lying Foal** (buckskin)

Morgan Horse Stallion — 1: (L) **Morgan Stallion** (Black); 2: (L) **Morgan Stallion** (Chestnut); 3: (L) **Morgan Stallion** (Bay)

Morgan Mare — 1: (S) **Morgan Mare** (Chestnut); 2: (S) **Morgan Mare** (Bay); 3: (S) **Morgan Mare** (Black); 4: (S) **Morgan Mare** (Palomino); 5: (S) **Morgan Mare** (Red chestnut)

Morgan Stallion — 1: (L) **Morgan Stallion** (Sorrel/palomino); 2: (S) **Morgan Stallion** (Chestnut); 3: (S) **Morgan Stallion** (Black); 4: (S) **Morgan Stallion** (Bay); 5: (S) **Morgan Stallion** (Chestnut); 6: (S) **Morgan Stallion** (Bay)

Morganglanz — 1: (T) **Morganglanz** (Chestnut); 2: (T) **Morganglanz** (Unpainted)

Mountain Pony — (T) **Haflinger** (Sorrel)

Mustang — 1: (T) **Mustang** (Buckskin); 2: (T) **Mustang** (Gl, charcoal); 3: (T) **Mustang** (Gl, alabaster); 4: (T) **Mustang** (Gl, gray blanket appaloosa); 5: (T) **Mustang** (Woodgrain); 6: (T) **Mustang** (Gl, Copenhagen); 7: (T) **Mustang** (Gl, Florentine); 8: (T) **Mustang** (Gl, Gold Charm); 9: (T) **Mustang** (Wedgewood)

Mustang Family — 1: (C) **Mustang Foal** (Chestnut), (C) **Mustang Mare** (Chestnut pinto), (C) **Mustang Stallion** (Chestnut); 2: (SR 85) (C) **Mustang Foal** (Chestnut pinto), (C) **Mustang Mare** (Bay/chestnut), (C) **Mustang Stallion** (Buckskin)

Mustang Lady, Endurance Champion — (T) **Indian Pony** (Gray)

My Companion Rocking Horse — (T) **Saddlebred Weanling** (Fl, white)

My Favorite Rocking Horse — (T) **Saddlebred Weanling** (Fl, purple)

My Prince, Thoroughbred — (T) **Man O'War** (Chestnut)

Mystique — (T) **Jumping Horse** (Gl, gray blanket appaloosa)

Native Dancer — (S) **Native Dancer** (Gray)

Native Diver Champion Thoroughbred — (T) **Phar Lap** (Black)

Nevada Star — (C) **Hobo** (Silver Dust gray)

Night Deck — (T) **Lady Phase** (Black)

Night Vision — (T) **Stock Horse Foal** (Dark bay snowflake appaloosa)

No Doubt — (T) **Family Arabian Stallion** (Red roan)

Noble Jumper — (T) **Halla** (Dapple gray)

Norita — (C) **Kelso** (Dapple gray)

Ofir — (T) **Black Stallion** (Dark bay)

Old Timer — 1: (T) **Old Timer** (Gl, dapple gray); 2: (T) **Old Timer** (Dapple gray); 3: (T) **Old Timer** (Alabaster); 4: (T) **Old Timer** (Bay); 5: (T) **Old Timer** (Red roan)

One Horse Open Sleigh — (C) **Black Beauty** (Fl, dapple gray)

Open Top Buggy — (T) **Proud Arabian Stallion** (Fl, chestnut)

Our Rocking Horse — (T) **Saddlebred Weanling** (Fl, black appaloosa)

Overo Paint — (T) **Stud Spider** (Chestnut pinto)

Overo Paint Stock Horse Mare — 1: (T) **Stock Horse Mare** (Bay pinto); 2: (T) **Stock Horse Mare** (Bay pinto (leg up))

Oxydol Rodeo Appaloosa — (T) **San Domingo** (Alabaster)

Pacer — (T) **Pacer** (M/Sg, dark bay)

Paint — (L) **Quarter Horse Stallion** (Black pinto)

Paint American Mustang — (T) **Mustang** (Bay pinto)

Paint Horse Foal — 1: (T) **Stock Horse Foal** (Dark chestnut pinto); 2: (T) **Stock Horse Foal** (Light chestnut pinto)

Paint Horse Mare — (T) **Stock Horse Mare** (Dark chestnut pinto)

Paint Horse Stallion — (T) **Stock Horse Stallion** (Liver chestnut pinto)

Palomino Horse and Foal Set — (T) **Foundation Stallion** (Palomino), (T) **Stock Horse Foal** (Palomino)

Pantomime — (T) **Pony of the Americas** (Black blanket appaloosa)

Patches — (C) **Ruffian** (Bay pinto)

Pegasus — (C) **Lipizzan Stallion** (Alabaster)

Pegasus Flying Horse — (C) **Lipizzan Stallion** (Fl, blue toned white)

Pepe — (C) **Man O'War** (Light chestnut)

Pepper and Lisa — (L) **Morgan Stallion** (Dapple gray)

Performing Misty — (T) **Performing Misty** (Gl, palomino pinto porcelain Hagen-Renaker)

Phantom Wings, Misty's Foal — (T) **Stock Horse Foal (Rough Coat)** (Palomino pinto)

Phar Lap Famous Race Horse — (T) **Phar Lap** (Red chestnut)

Pieraz (Cash) (T) **Morganglanz** (Flea-bit gray)

Pine, Shetland Pony — (T) **Shetland Pony** (Palomino)

Pine Lodge Riding School — (S) **Riding Stable Set** (Various)

Pinto American Saddlebred — (T) **Five Gaiter** (Black pinto, red on white ribbons)

Pinto Mare and Foal — (S) **Arabian Mare** (chestnut pinto), (S) **Lying Foal** (chestnut pinto)

Pinto Mare and Foal Set — (T) **Action Stock Horse Foal** (Black pinto), (T) **Stock Horse Mare** (Black pinto)

Pinto Mare and Suckling Foal — (T) **Nursing Foal** (Bay pinto), (T) **Thoroughbred Mare** (Bay pinto)

Pinto Stock Horse Foal — (T) **Stock Horse Foal** (Black pinto)

Plain Pixie — (T) **Cantering Welsh Pony** (Red roan, no ribbons)

Pluto the Lipizzaner — (T) **Pluto** (Light gray)

Poland China Hog — (O) **Jasper The Market Hog** (White with black spots)

Polled Ayrshire Cow — (O) **Cow** (Red and white pinto pattern)

Polled Brown Swiss Cow — (O) **Cow** (Cocoa brown)

Polled Guernsey Cow — (O) **Cow** (Tan and white pinto pattern)

Polled Hereford Bull — (O) **Polled Hereford Bull** (Red brown and white)

Polled Holstein Cow — (O) **Cow** (Black and white pinto pattern)

Polled Jersey Cow — (O) **Cow** (Dark tan; solid color)

Polled Shorthorn Bull — (O) **Charolais Bull** (Dark brown)

Polled Simmental Bull — (O) **Charolais Bull** (Brown and white)

Polo Pony — (C) **Polo Pony** (Bay)

Ponokah-Eemetah — (T) **Fighting Stallion** (Dark bay blanket appaloosa)

Pony of the Americas — 1: (T) **Pony of the Americas** (Bay/chestnut blanket appaloosa); 2: (T) **Pony of the Americas** (Chestnut leopard appaloosa)

Poodle — 1: (O) **Poodle** (Gl, black); 2: (O) **Poodle** (Gl, white); 3: (O) **Poodle** (Woodgrain); 4: (O) **Poodle** (Silver gray)

Prairie Flower - Equitana 93 — (T) **Lady Phase** (Bay blanket appaloosa)

Prancer — (L) **Thoroughbred Stallion** (Bay)

Prancing Arabian Mare — (T) **Lady Roxanna** (Chestnut)

Prancing Arabian Stallion — 1: (T) **Sham** (Palomino); 2: (T) **Sham** (Flea-bit gray)

Prancing Morgan — (T) **Sherman Morgan** (Black)

Precious Beauty Foal & Gift Set — (C) **Andalusian Foal** (Bay blanket appaloosa), (C) **Ginger** (Chestnut leopard appaloosa)

Precipitado Sin Par (Cips Champion Paso Fino) (T) **El Pastor** (Bay pinto, LE)

Pride and Joy — (T) **Nursing Foal** (Light chestnut), (T) **Thoroughbred Mare** (Light chestnut): JC Penney

Pride and Vanity — (T) **Sherman Morgan** (Alabaster)

Prince — (C) **Swaps** (Gray)

Princess of Arabia — 1: (T) **Black Stallion** (Light dapple gray, LE); 2: (T) **Black Stallion** (Red roan, LE)

Progeny of Leo, AQHA American Quarter Horse — (T) **Ideal American Quarter Horse** (Chestnut)

Project Universe — (T) **Five Gaiter** (Chestnut pinto, black on gold braids)

Promenade Andalusian — (T) **Legionario** (Bay)

Promises, Rearing Stallion — (C) **Rearing Stallion** (Dark bay pinto)

Pronghorn Antelope — 1: (O) **Pronghorn Antelope** (Brown and white); 2: **Pronghorn Antelope** (Chestnut and white)

Proud Arabian Foal — 1: (T) **Proud Arabian Foal** (Alabaster); 2: (T) **Proud Arabian Foal** (Dapple gray); 3: (T) **Proud Arabian Foal** (Mahogany bay); 4: (T) **Proud Arabian Foal** (Rose gray)

Proud Arabian Mare — 1: (T) **Proud Arabian Mare** (Alabaster); 2: (T) **Proud Arabian Mare** (Sg/M, dapple gray); 3: (T) **Proud Arabian Mare** (M/Sg, mahogany bay, front socks); 4: (T) **Proud Arabian Mare** (Dappled rose gray); 5: (T) **Proud Arabian Mare** (Red chestnut); 6: (T) **Proud Arabian Mare** (Unpainted)

Proud Arabian Mare Gift Set — 1: (T) **Proud Arabian Mare** (Sg/M, dapple gray); 2: (T) **Proud Arabian Mare** (M/Sg, mahogany bay); 3: (T) **Proud Arabian Mare** (Alabaster)

Proud Arabian Stallion — 1: (T) **Proud Arabian Stallion** (Alabaster); 2: (T) **Proud Arabian Stallion** (M/Sg, dapple gray); 3: (T) **Proud Arabian Stallion** (M/Sg, mahogany bay); 4: (T) **Proud Arabian Stallion** (Light dapple gray); 5: (T) **Proud Arabian Stallion** (Dapple rose gray); 6: (T) **Proud Arabian Stallion** (Unpainted)

Proud Mother and Newborn Foal — 1: (C) **Andalusian Foal** (Apricot dun), (T) **Lady Roxanna** (Dark chestnut); 2: (C) **Andalusian Foal** (Dark bay)

(T) **Lady Roxanna** (Apricot dun)

Pug Boxer — (O) **Boxer** (Chocolate brown/brindle)

Quarter Horse — 1: (T) **Quarter Horse Gelding** (Buckskin); 2: (T) **Quarter Horse Gelding** (Gl, bay); 3: (T) **Quarter Horse Gelding** (Woodgrain)

Quarter Horse Family — (C) **Quarter Horse Foal** (Light bay), (C) **Quarter Horse Mare** (Bay), (C) **Quarter Horse Stallion** (Palomino)

Quarter Horse Foal — 1: (C) **Quarter Horse Foal** (Red bay); 2: (C) **Quarter Horse Foal** (Black); 3: (C) **Quarter Horse Foal** (Palomino)

Quarter Horse Mare — 1: (C) **Quarter Horse Mare** (Chestnut pinto, socks); 2: (S) **Quarter Horse Mare** (Chestnut); 3: (S) **Quarter Horse Mare** (Palomino); 4: (S) **Quarter Horse Mare** (Buckskin)

Quarter Horse Mare and Foal Set — (T) **Lady Phase** (Buckskin, solid or bald face), (T) **Stock Horse Foal** (Buckskin, bald face)

Quarter Horse Stallion — 1: (T) **Adios** (Black roan); 2: (L) **Quarter Horse Stallion** (Bay); 3: (L) **Quarter Horse Stallion** (Buckskin); 4: (L) **Quarter Horse Stallion** (Palomino); 5: (L) **Quarter Horse Stallion** (Black leopard appaloosa); 6: (S) **Quarter Horse Stallion** (M/Sg, chestnut); 7: (S) **Quarter Horse Stallion** (Buckskin); 8: (S) **Quarter Horse Stallion** (Palomino); 9: (S) **Quarter Horse Stallion** (Bay)

Quarter Horse Yearling — 1: (T) **Quarter Horse Yearling** (Liver chestnut); 2: (T) **Quarter Horse Yearling** (Palomino); 3: (T) **Quarter Horse Yearling** (Presentation collection)

Quiet Foxhunters Set — (T) **John Henry** (Dark chestnut), (T) **Roemer** (Seal bay/brown), (T) **Rugged Lark** (Dappled gray)

Quincy, Clydesdale Foal — (T) **Clydesdale Foal** (Chestnut pinto)

Race Horse — 1: (T) **Racehorse** (Gl, chestnut); 2: (T) **Racehorse** (Woodgrain)

Race Horse Set — (T) **Man O'War** (Gl, red chestnut), (T) **Secretariat** (Gl, chestnut), (T) **Sham** (Gl, red bay)

Race Horses of America — (T) **Pacer** (Bay), (T) **Phar Lap** (Dapple gray), (T) **Stock Horse Stallion** (Dappled sorrel/chestnut)

Ram — (O) **Bighorn Ram** (Shaded brown)

Rana — (T) **Sham** (Dark gray)

Ranger Cow Pony — (T) **Western Prancing Horse** (Dun)

Rarin' To Go — (T) **Mustang** (Grulla)

Raven — (T) **Saddlebred Weanling** (Sg, plum black)

Rawhide the Wild Appaloosa Mustang — (T) **Mustang** (Dun roan appaloosa)

Realto, Arabian — (T) **Family Arabian Stallion** (Light gray)

Rearing Stallion — 1: (C) **Rearing Stallion** (Bay); 2: (C) **Rearing Stallion** (Palomino); 3: (C) **Rearing Stallion** (Alabaster); 4: (C) **Rearing Stallion** (Buckskin)

Red Angus — (O) **Black Angus Bull** (Chestnut)

Red Brahma Bull — (O) **Brahma Bull** (Orangish-red)

Reflections Mesteno — (C) **Reflections Mesteno** (Buckskin)

Remington, Pinto — (T) **Smoky** (Bay pinto)

Riddle Passing Through Time, Phase 1 — (C) **Hobo** (Bay blanket appaloosa)

Riddle Passing Through Time, Phase 2 — (C) **Hobo** (Red semi-leopard appaloosa)

Riddle Passing Through Time, Phase 3 — (C) **Hobo** (Red leopard appaloosa)

Riding Stable Set — (S) **Riding Stable Set** (Pine Lodge Riding School)

Rin Tin Tin — (O) **Rin Tin Tin** (M/Sg, brown)

Robin & Hot Tamale H.T. — (T) **Lying Foal** (Red roan leopard appaloosa), (T) **Quarter Horse Yearling** (Red roan leopard appaloosa)

Rocky, Champion Connemara Stallion — (T) **Pony of the Americas** (Dapple dun)

Roemer Dutch Warmblood — (T) **Roemer** (Dark chestnut)

Rough Diamond — (T) **Stock Horse Foal (Rough Coat)** (Dark brown pinto)

Rough n' Ready - Quarter Horse — (T) **Adios** (Dun)

Rox Dene, Show Hunter — (T) **Touch of Class** (Light dapple gray)

Roy Belgian Drafter — (T) **Roy the Belgian** (Sorrel/light chestnut)

Royal Te, Appaloosa — (T) **Western Horse** (Bay blanket appaloosa)

Ruby — (T) **Mustang** (Dappled chestnut/red roan)

Ruffian — (C) **Ruffian** (Dark bay)

Rugged Lark Champion American Quarter Horse Stallion — (T) **Rugged Lark** (Bay)

Rumbling Thunder — (T) **Running Stallion** (Sg, dark dapple gray)

Runaway, Mustang Kiger — (C) **Fighting Mesteno** (Cocoa dun)

Running Foal — 1: (T) **Running Foal** (Bay/chestnut); 2: (T) **Running Foal** (Gl, dapple gray); 3: (T) **Running Foal** (Alabaster); 4: (T) **Running Foal** (Smoke); 5: (T) **Running Foal** (Gl, Copenhagen); 6: (T) **Running Foal** (Gl, Florentine); 7: (T) **Running Foal** (Gl, Gold Charm); 8: (T) **Running Foal** (Wedgewood); 9: (T) **Running Foal** (M/Sg, woodgrain); 10: (T) **Running Foal** (Chestnut pinto)

Running Horse Family Set — (T) **Black Beauty** (Red bay), (T) **Running Foal** (Bay), (T) **Running Mare** (Bay, no socks)

Running Mare — 1: (T) **Running Mare** (M/Sg, bay/chestnut); 2: (T) **Running Mare** (Alabaster); 3: (T) **Running Mare** (Gl, dapple gray); 4: (T) **Running Mare** (Smoke/charcoal); 5: (T) **Running Mare** (Woodgrain); 6: (T) **Running Mare** (Red roan); 7: (T) **Running Mare** (Chestnut pinto); 8: (T) **Running Mare** (Gl, Copenhagen); 9: (T) **Running Mare** (Gl, Florentine); 10: (T) **Running Mare** (Gl, Gold Charm); 11: (T) **Running Mare** (Wedgewood)

Running Paint — (S) **Seabiscuit** (Chestnut pinto)

Running Stallion — 1: (T) **Running Stallion** (Bay/chestnut); 2: (T) **Running Stallion** (Black blanket appaloosa); 3: (T) **Running Stallion** (Red roan); 4: (T) **Running Stallion** (Alabaster); 5: (T) **Running Stallion** (Gl, charcoal)

Running Thoroughbred — (S) **Seabiscuit** (Black)

Rusty Diamond — (T) **Foundation Stallion** (Shaded chestnut)

Saddle Club Collection — (S) **Arabian Mare** (Dapple gray), (S) **Draft Horse** (Alabaster), (S) **Morgan Stallion** (Bay), (S) **Seabiscuit** (Chestnut), (S) **Thoroughbred Mare** (Black)

Saddle Club Stablemates — (S) **Arabian Mare** (Dark gray), (S) **Citation** (Buckskin), (S) **Native Dancer** (Red bay pinto), (S) **Silky Sullivan** (Mahogany bay), (S) **Swaps** (Red leopard appaloosa)

Saddlebred — 1: (S) **Saddlebred** (Dapple gray); 2: (S) **Saddlebred** (Bay); 3: (S) **Saddlebred** (Black)

Saddlebred Mare — (S) **Saddlebred Mare** (Sorrel)

Saddlebred Weanling — 1: (T) **Saddlebred Weanling** (Chestnut); 2: (T) **Saddlebred Weanling** (Palomino/light chestnut pinto, CE); 3: (T) **Saddlebred Weanling** (Unpainted); 4: (T) **Saddlebred Weanling** (Sorrel)

Sam I Am — (T) **Stock Horse Stallion** (Dark bay pinto)

Samsung Woodstock, Westphalian — (T) **Morganglanz** (Chestnut)

San Domingo — (T) **San Domingo** (Chestnut pinto)

Sapphire — (T) **Black Stallion** (Buckskin)

Sargent Pepper Appaloosa Pony — (T) **Haflinger** (Gray leopard appaloosa)

Sassafras — (T) **Cantering Welsh Pony** (Palomino pinto)

Satin Star — (T) **Clydesdale Foal** (Dark chestnut)

Scat Cat - Children's Pony — (T) **Haflinger** (Bay roan leopard appaloosa)

Scratching Foal — 1: (T) **Scratching Foal** (Black appaloosa); 2: (T) **Scratching Foal** (M/Sg, red roan); 3: (T) **Scratching Foal** (Liver chestnut)

Scribbles Paint Horse Foal — (T) **Sea Star** (Chestnut pinto)

Seabiscuit — (S) **Seabiscuit** (Bay)

Sebastian, Percheron — (T) **Roy the Belgian** (Gray roan)

Secretariat — 1: (T) **Secretariat** (Chestnut); 2: (T) **Secretariat** (Chestnut, cold cast porcelain)

Selle Francais — (T) **Touch of Class** (Dark chestnut)

Serenity Set — (T) **Grazing Mare** (Buckskin), (T) **Lying Foal** (Buckskin)

Set of 12 Miniatures — (S) **Arabian Mare** (Chestnut leopard appaloosa), (S) **Arabian Stallion** (Light bay), (S) **Citation** (Dun), (S) **Citation** (Liver chestnut blanket appaloosa), (S) **Morgan Mare** (Red sorrel), (S) **Morgan Stallion** (Black), (S) **Native Dancer** (Bay), (S) **Quarter Horse Stallion** (Chestnut), (S) **Silky Sullivan** (Rose gray), (S) **Silky Sullivan** (Red roan), (S) **Swaps** (Gray dun), (S) **Thoroughbred Mare** (Dark brown)

Sham the Godolphin Arabian — (T) **Sham** (Bay, '95 on inner hind leg)

Shane American Ranch Horse — (T) **Stock Horse Stallion** (Black roan)

Shenandoah, Mustang — (T) **Smoky** (Buckskin)

Sherman Morgan — (T) **Sherman Morgan** (Chestnut)

Shetland Pony — 1: (T) **Shetland Pony** (Gl/M, black pinto); 2: (T) **Shetland Pony** (Bay); 3: (T) **Shetland Pony** (Gl, light chestnut pinto); 4: (T) **Shetland Pony** (Gl/M, alabaster); 5: (T) **Shetland Pony** (Bay pinto); 6: (T) **Shetland Pony** (Chestnut); 7: (T) **Shetland Pony** (Woodgrain)

Shire — 1: (T) **Shire** (Honey sorrel); 2: (T) **Shire** (Dapple gray); 3: (L) **Clydesdale** (Black)

Shire Mare — (T) **Clydesdale Mare** (Dark chestnut/bay)

Show Horse, Cream of Tartar — (T) **Pony of the Americas** (Palomino blanket appaloosa)

Show Stance Morgan — (T) **Morgan** (Dark red chestnut)

Siamese Kitten — (O) **Kitten** (Gray or seal point)

Sierra — (T) **Fighting Stallion** (Red roan)

Silky Sullivan — 1: (C) **Silky Sullivan** (Brown); 2: (S) **Silky Sullivan** (Dark chestnut)

Silver — (T) **Quarter Horse Gelding** (Slate gray, CE)

Silver Comet — (C) **Polo Pony** (Light dapple gray)

Silverton, Welsh Cob — (T) **Llanarth True Briton** (Shaded gray)

Simmental Bull — (O) **Charolais Bull** (Chestnut pinto pattern)

Sirocco, Breyer Breakfast Tour Horse — (T) **Indian Pony** (Chestnut pinto)

Skipster's Chief, Famous Therapeutic Riding Horse — (T) **Stock Horse Stallion** (Sorrel)

Sky Blue Unicorn — (T) **Running Stallion** (Fl, turquoise blue)

Smoky the Cow Horse — (T) **Smoky** (Medium gray)

Smoky the Cow Horse Gift Set — (T) **Smoky** (Medium gray)

Smooth Copper, Quarter Horse — (T) **Stud Spider** (Shaded light bay)

Snowbound — (T) **Jumping Horse** (Dappled bay)

Socks, Kitten — (O) **Kitten** (M/Sg black and white)

Sorrel Quarter Horse Stock Mare — 1: (T) **Stock Horse Mare** (Sorrel); 2: (T) **Stock Horse Mare** (Sorrel, leg up version)

Spanish Barb — (T) **Buckshot** (Chestnut pinto)

Spanish Fighting Bull — 1: (O) **Spanish Fighting Bull** (Black); 2: (O) **Spanish Fighting Bull** (Shaded steel gray)

Spanish Norman Family — (C) **Andalusian Foal** (Gray), (C) **Andalusian Stallion** (Red roan), (C) **Ginger** (Alabaster)

Spanish Pride — (T) **Legionario** (Bay)

Spice — (C) **Silky Sullivan** (Bay blanket appaloosa)

Spirit of the East — (T) **Running Foal** (Soft gray), (T) **Running Mare** (Soft gray)

Spirit of the West Gift Set — (T) **Lady Phase** (Bay pinto), (T) **Stock Horse Foal** (Dark bay pinto)

Spirit of the Wind Set — (T) **Family Arabian Foal** (Dapple gray), (T) **Family Arabian Mare** (Dapple gray)

Spot and Kate — (L) **Quarter Horse Stallion** (Black blanket appaloosa)

Spotted Bear — (T) **San Domingo** (M/Sg, black pinto; cold cast porcelain)

Spotted Legacy Gift Set — (T) **Proud Arabian Foal** (Chestnut pinto), (T) **Proud Arabian Mare** (Chestnut pinto)

SS Morning Star, Pinto Half-Arabian — (T) **Proud Arabian Foal** (Bay pinto)

St. Bernard — (O) **St. Bernard** (Sg/M, bi color)

Stable Set — (S) **Lying Thoroughbred Foal** (Dark bay), (S) **Quarter Horse Mare** (Dark bay), (S) **Quarter Horse Stallion** (Dark bay), (S) **Standing Thoroughbred Foal** (Dark bay)

Stablemate Assortment II — (S) **Arabian Mare** (Black), (S) **Arabian Stallion** (Buckskin), (S) **Citation** (Chestnut), (S) **Draft Horse** (Black), (S) **Morgan Mare** (Chestnut), (S) **Morgan Stallion** (Dark red chestnut), (S) **Native Dancer** (Black point alabaster), (S) **Seabiscuit** (Palomino/sorrel), (S) **Silky Sullivan** (Light bay), (S) **Swaps** (Rose gray), (S) **Swaps** (Dark gray), (S) **Thoroughbred Mare** (Blood bay)

Stablemate Assortment III — (S) **Arabian Mare** (Red chestnut), (S) **Arabian Stallion** (Black), (S) **Citation** (Dark gray), (S) **Draft Horse** (Bay), (S) **Draft Horse** (Khaki dun), (S) **Morgan Mare** (Bay), (S) **Morgan Stallion** (Palomino), (S) **Native Dancer** (Palomino), (S) **Seabiscuit** (Dapple gray), (S) **Silky Sullivan** (Red bay), (S) **Swaps** (Dark bay), (S) **Thoroughbred Mare** (Alabaster)

Stablemate Assortment IV — (S) **Arabian Mare** (Medium gray), (S) **Arabian Stallion** (Chestnut), (S) **Citation** (Dapple gray), (S) **Draft Horse** (Creamy dun), (S) **Morgan Mare** (Chocolate sorrel), (S) **Morgan Stallion** (Black blanket appaloosa), (S) **Morgan Stallion** (Dark bay), (S) **Native Dancer** (Black), (S) **Quarter Horse Stallion** (Red leopard appaloosa), (S) **Seabiscuit** (Light gray), (S) **Silky Sullivan** (Grulla/dun), (S) **Swaps** (Buckskin)

Stablemate Foal Keychains — 1: (S) **Lying Thoroughbred Foal** (Amber plastic); 2: (S) **Lying Thoroughbred Foal** (Black plastic); 3: (S) **Lying Thoroughbred Foal** (Clear plastic); 4: (S) **Lying Thoroughbred Foal** (Blue plastic); 5: (S) **Standing Thoroughbred Foal** (Amber plastic); 6: (S) **Standing Thoroughbred Foal** (Black plastic); 7: (S) **Standing Thoroughbred Foal** (Clear plastic); 8: (S) **Standing Thoroughbred Foal** (Blue plastic):

Stablemate Set — (S) **Arabian Mare** (Alabaster), (S) **Arabian Stallion** (Gray), (S)

Citation (Red leopard appaloosa), (S) *Draft Horse* (Dapple gray), (S) *Morgan Mare* (Palomino), (S) *Morgan Stallion* (Light chestnut), (S) *Native Dancer* (Blood bay), (S) *Saddlebred* (Black), (S) *Seabiscuit* (Chestnut), (S) *Silky Sullivan* (Buckskin), (S) *Swaps* (Black leopard appaloosa), (S) *Thoroughbred Mare* (Dark bay)

Stallion Mare and Foal Set — (T) *Action Stock Horse Foal* (Red bay), (T) *Stock Horse Stallion* (Light gray)

Standing Quarter Horse Stallion — (T) *Adios* (Apricot dun)

Standing Thoroughbred — 1: (S) *Citation* (Bay); 2: (S) *Citation* (Alabaster)

Stardust — (T) *Legionario* (Dapple gray)

Starlight — (T) *Jumping Horse* (Dark bay, LE)

Starlight and Carole — (L) *Arabian Stallion* (Black)

Steel Dust — (T) *Proud Arabian Mare* (Gray)

Stock Horse Family — (T) *Stock Horse Foal* (Gray blanket appaloosa), (T) *Stock Horse Mare* (Gray blanket appaloosa), (T) *Stock Horse Stallion* (Gray blanket appaloosa)

Stock Horse Foal — 1: (T) *Stock Horse Foal (Rough Coat)* (Black blanket appaloosa); 2: (T) *Stock Horse Foal (Rough Coat)* (Brown blanket appaloosa)

Stud Spider — 1: (T) *Stud Spider* (Black blanket appaloosa); 2: (T) *Stud Spider* (Unpainted)

Stud Spider Gift Set — (T) *Stud Spider* (Black blanket appaloosa)

Sundown Proud Arabian Stallion — (T) *Proud Arabian Stallion* (Sorrel)

Sunny Action Foal — (T) *Action Stock Horse Foal* (Light dun, dark gray points)

Sunny Boy, Welsh Cob — (T) *Llanarth True Briton* (Palomino)

Sure Fire, Pinto — (T) *Sea Star* (Black pinto)

Swaps — 1: (C) *Swaps* (Chestnut); 2: (S) *Swaps* (Chestnut)

Swedish Warmblood — (T) *Morganglanz* (Palomino)

Sweet Confession, Hackney Pony — (T) *Aristocrat* (Dark dappled bay)

T Bone — (C) *Silky Sullivan* (Black roan)

Tara — (T) *Cantering Welsh Pony* (Dappled bay, no ribbons)

Tatanka — (O) *Buffalo* (Alabaster)

Ten Gallon — (C) *Terrang* (Dun)

Tennessee Walking Horse — 1: (T) *Midnight Sun* (Red bay, red on white braids); (T) *Midnight Sun* (Black, white on red ribbons); (T) *Midnight Sun* (Palomino)

Terrang — (C) *Terrang* (Dark brown)

Tesoro — (T) *El Pastor* (Palomino)

Texas Longhorn Bull — 1: (O) *Texas Longhorn Bull* (Light brown/tan); 2: (O) *Texas Longhorn Bull* (Woodgrain); 3: (O) *Texas Longhorn Bull* (Dark chestnut pinto pattern); 4: (O) *Texas Longhorn Bull* (Chestnut and white, speckles and patches)

The Black Stallion — (T) *Black Stallion* (Sg, black)

The Black Stallion and Alec Set — (T) *Black Stallion* (Sg, black)

The Black Stallion Returns Set — (C) *Black Stallion* (Black), (C) *Johar* (Alabaster), (C) *Sagr* (Sorrel)

The Black Stallion, Book and Poster Set — (T) *Black Stallion* (Sg, black)

The Challengers Mesteno and Sombra — (C) *Fighting Mesteno* (Dark buckskin), (C) *Sombra* (Grulla)

The Cree Indian Horse, Naytukskie-Kukatos — (T) *John Henry* (Bay)

The Dawning Mesteno and Mother — (C) *Mesteno The Foal* (Light dun), (C) *Mesteno's Mother* (Buckskin)

The Doctor's Buggy — (C) *Black Stallion* (Fl, bay)

The Progeny Gift Set Mesteno and His Yearling — (C) *Charging Mesteno* (M/Sg, dark buckskin), (C) *Rojo* (Light red dun)

Thoroughbred Lying and Standing Foals — 1: (S) *Lying Thoroughbred Foal* (Black), (S) *Standing Thoroughbred Foal* (Black); 2: (S) *Lying Thoroughbred Foal* (Bay), (S) *Standing Thoroughbred Foal* (Bay); 3: (S) *Lying Thoroughbred Foal* (Chestnut), (S) *Standing Thoroughbred Foal* (Chestnut)

Thoroughbred Mare — 1: (T) *Touch of Class* (Black); 2: (S) *Thoroughbred Mare* (Chestnut); 3: (S) *Thoroughbred Mare* (Black); 4: (S) *Thoroughbred Mare* (Bay); 5: (S) *Thoroughbred Mare* (Dark bay); 6: (S) *Thoroughbred Mare* (Red chestnut); 7: (S) *Thoroughbred Mare* (Dark gray)

Thoroughbred Mare and Foal Gift Set — (T) *Nursing Foal* (Light chestnut), (T) *Thoroughbred Mare* (Dark chestnut/bay)

Thoroughbred Racehorse — 1: (S) *Silky Sullivan* (Black); 2: (S) *Swaps* (Red chestnut)

Thoroughbred Stallion — 1: (L) *Thoroughbred Stallion* (Red bay); 2: (L) *Thoroughbred Stallion* (Chestnut); 3: (L) *Thoroughbred Stallion* (Black); 4: (L) *Thoroughbred Stallion* (Dark gray)

Three Piece Horse Set — (T) *Cantering Welsh Pony* (Sg, dappled rose gray, no ribbons), (T) *Haflinger* (Chestnut pinto), (T) *Pony of the Americas* (Black leopard appaloosa)

Thunder Bay Quarter Horse — (T) *Quarter Horse Yearling* (Dark bay)

Tic Toc — (T) *Western Horse* (Alabaster)

Titan Glory — (T) *Foundation Stallion* (Bay): Toys "R" Us

Tobe Rocky Mountain Horse — (T) *El Pastor* (Chocolate sorrel)

Tobiano Pinto Stock Horse Stallion — (T) *Stock Horse Stallion* (Black pinto)

Topside and Stevie — (L) *Thoroughbred Stallion* (Bright bay/buckskin)

Touch of Class — (T) *Touch of Class* (Bay)

Traditional Western Horse Collector Set — (T) *Adios* (Chestnut leopard appaloosa), (T) *Foundation Stallion* (Sg, charcoal/chocolate chestnut), (T) *San Domingo* (Bay, hind stockings)

Trakehner — 1: (T) *Trakehner* (Bay); 2: (T) *Trakehner* (Unpainted)

Trakehner Family — (C) *Duchess* (Light dapple gray), (C) *Jet Run* (Dark red chestnut), (C) *Mustang Foal* (Bay)

Tri-Mi Boot Scootin' Boogie — (T) *Justin Morgan* (Dark brown/black)

Triple Crown Winners Set I — (C) *Kelso* (Chestnut), (C) *Silky Sullivan* (Chestnut), (C) *Terrang* (Dark bay/chestnut)

Triple Crown Winners Set II — (C) *Man O'War* (Chestnut), (C) *Swaps* (Brown), (C) *Terrang* (Chestnut)

Tseminole Wind — (T) *Sham* (Bay pinto)

Tumbleweed — (C) *Man O'War* (Light bay/chestnut)

Turbo the Wonder Horse — (T) *Mustang* (Palomino)

Tyler and Hillary, B-Ranch Gift Set — (C) *Arabian Stallion* (Chestnut pinto)

U.S. Equestrian Team Gift Set — (C) *Jet Run* (Bay), (C) *Keen* (Chestnut), (C) *Might Tango* (Dapple gray)

U.S. Olympic Team Set — (C) *Jet Run* (Chestnut), (C) *Keen* (Gray), (C) *Might Tango* (Bay)

Unicorn — 1: (T) *Running Stallion* (Alabaster, gold striped horn); 2: (T) *Running Stallion* (Alabaster); 3: (T) *Smoky* (Fl, white); 4: (L) *Unicorn* (Alabaster)

Unicorn II — (T) *Running Stallion* (Gl, black, gold)

Unicorn III — 1: (C) *Lipizzan Stallion* (Sg, Pearly white), 2: (C) *Lipizzan Stallion* (Gl, Black)

Unicorn IV Black Pearl — (T) *Lying Foal* (Gl, black)

Unicorn IV White Pearl — (T) *Lying Foal* (Gl, white pearl)

Vandergelder - Dutch Warmblood — (T) *Roemer* (Bay)

Vanity — (C) *Kelso* (Bay pinto)

Vaulting Horse — (T) *Hanoverian* (Black)

Vermont Morgan — (T) *Morgan* (Chocolate sorrel)

Vigilante, Western Prancer — (T) *Western Prancing Horse* (M/Sg, black)

Watchful Mare and Foal — (T) *Lady Phase* (Alabaster), (T) *Stock Horse Foal* (Soft gray)

Western Horse — 1: (T) *John Henry* (Dark bay); 2: (T) *Western Horse* (Black pinto); 3: (T) *Western Horse* (Gl, black pinto); 4: (T) *Western Horse* (Palomino); 5: (T) *Western Horse* (Gl, palomino); 6: (T) *Western Horse* (Gl, white); 7: (T) *Western Horse* (Gl, palomino/chestnut pinto); 8: (T) *Western Horse* (Gl, black); 9: (T) *Western Horse* (Gl, black, gold hooves); 10: (T) *Western Horse* (Sg, chocolate brown); 11: (T) *Western Horse* (Chestnut pinto); 12: (T) *Western Horse* (Palomino, '95 next to mold mark)

Western Palomino — (T) *Western Horse* (Gl, palomino)

Western Pony — 1: (T) *Western Pony* (Gl/M, black pinto); 2: (T) *Western Pony* (Gl, alabaster, also with grooming kit); 3: (T) *Western Pony* (Gl, chestnut pinto); 4: (T) *Western Pony* (M/Gl, palomino, also with grooming kit); 5: (T) *Western Pony* (Gl, black; gold hooves and trim); 6: (T) *Western Pony* (M/Sg, woodgrain); 7: (T) *Western Pony* (Sg, plum brown)

Western Prancing Horse — 1: (T) *Western Prancing Horse* (Palomino); 2: (T) *Western Prancing Horse* (Smoke); 3: (T) *Western Prancing Horse* (Buckskin); 4: (T) *Western Prancing Horse* (Gl, leopard appaloosa); 5: (T) *Western Prancing Horse* (Bay); 6: (T) *Western Prancing Horse* (Gl, black pinto)

Whispers — (C) *Ruffian* (Gray appaloosa)

Wild American Horse — (T) *Phar Lap* (Gray dun/grulla)

Wild Diamond — (T) *Running Mare* (Bay)

Wild Horses of America Set — (T) *Fighting Stallion* (Sorrel), (T) *Foundation Stallion* (Bay blanket appaloosa), (T) *Mustang* (Sg, black)

Wildfire — (T) *San Domingo* (Chestnut pinto)

Willow and Shining Star — (C) *Rearing Stallion* (Dark bay blanket appaloosa)

Winchester — (T) *Buckshot* (Gl, charcoal)

Wing Commander — (T) *Five Gaiter* (Brown/bay, red ribbons)

Woodsprite — (T) *Stock Horse Foal (Rough Coat)* (Bay)

Yellow Mount Famous Paint — (T) *Adios* (Chestnut pinto)

Yorkshire Hog — (O) *Jasper The Market Hog* (White)

Young Equestrian Team — (L) *Arabian Stallion* (Chestnut), (L) *Quarter Horse Stallion* (Dark bay pinto), (L) *Thoroughbred Stallion* (Alabaster)

Regular Run Models by Number

This section lists the models by number. In many cases different models and even different molds were given the same number at different times in Breyer's history. This means of sorting the models should help you find a model that you know only by a number. You should use this list to locate the mold you need, then refer to the appropriate section for more information.

The following conventions apply to this list:
    1.) each number is listed only once;
    2.) mold names are shown in **_bold italics_**;
    3.) model color is given in the third column;
    4.) if one number designates multiple models with the same model number, each is separated by a number;
    5.) if one model number designated a set of models, the models are separated by commas;
    6.) when no finish is given (matte, semi-gloss, etc.), the model is assumed to have a matte finish.

The abbreviations for the following list are:

T = Traditional scale	O = Other Animal	Sg = Semi-gloss
C = Classic scale	LE = Limited Edition	Fl = Flocked
L = Little Bits scale	CE = Commemorative Edition	M = Matte
S = Stablemate scale	Gl = Glossy	

No.	Model	Mold	Color
P40	Black Beauty	(T) **_Fury Prancer_**	Gl, black, gold or silver bridle, white tipped tail
	Fury	(T) **_Fury Prancer_**	Gl, black, star face
	Fury Prancer	(T) **_Fury Prancer_**	Gl, dark plum brown
P41	Fury Prancer	(T) **_Fury Prancer_**	Gl, black pinto
P42	Fury Prancer	(T) **_Fury Prancer_**	Gl, chestnut pinto
P43	Fury Prancer	(T) **_Fury Prancer_**	Gl, palomino
P45	Fury Prancer	(T) **_Fury Prancer_**	Gl, alabaster
P145	1: Fury Prancer	(T) **_Fury Prancer_**	Gl, alabaster; with Robin Hood
	2: Fury Prancer	(T) **_Fury Prancer_**	Gl, alabaster; with William Tell
P241	Fury Prancer	(T) **_Fury Prancer_**	Gl, black pinto; with Indian Brave or Chief
P242	Fury Prancer	(T) **_Fury Prancer_**	Gl, chestnut pinto; with Indian Brave or Chief
P341	Fury Prancer	(T) **_Fury Prancer_**	Gl, black pinto; with Lucky Ranger or Cowboy
P342	Fury Prancer	(T) **_Fury Prancer_**	Gl, chestnut pinto; with Lucky Ranger or Cowboy
P343	Fury Prancer	(T) **_Fury Prancer_**	Gl, palomino; with Lucky Ranger or Cowboy
P440	Black Beauty	(T) **_Fury Prancer_**	Gl, black; with Canadian Mountie
	Fury Prancer	(T) **_Fury Prancer_**	Gl, dark brown; with Canadian Mountie
P445	Fury Prancer	(T) **_Fury Prancer_**	Gl, alabaster; with Canadian Mountie
P540	1: Fury Prancer	(T) **_Fury Prancer_**	Gl, dark brown; with Davy Crockett
	2: Fury Prancer	(T) **_Fury Prancer_**	Gl, dark brown; with Kit Carson
P945	Fury Prancer	(T) **_Fury Prancer_**	Woodgrain
??	Western Horse	(T) **_Western Horse_**	Sg, chocolate brown
??	Buffalo	(O) **_Buffalo_**	Bronze
??	Buffalo	(O) **_Buffalo_**	Woodgrain
??	Black Angus Bull	(O) **_Black Angus Bull_**	Woodgrain
4	1: Family Stallion	(T) **_Family Arabian Stallion_**	Gl, palomino
	2: Family Stallion	(T) **_Family Arabian Stallion_**	Palomino
5	1: Family Mare	(T) **_Family Arabian Mare_**	Gl, palomino
	2: Family Mare	(T) **_Family Arabian Mare_**	Palomino
6	1: Family Foal	(T) **_Family Arabian Foal_**	Gl, palomino
	2: Family Foal	(T) **_Family Arabian Foal_**	Palomino
7	1: Arabian Stallion	(T) **_Family Arabian Stallion_**	Gl, alabaster
	2: Arabian Stallion	(T) **_Family Arabian Stallion_**	Alabaster
8	1: Arabian Mare	(T) **_Family Arabian Mare_**	Gl, alabaster
	2: Arabian Mare	(T) **_Family Arabian Mare_**	Alabaster
	3: Arabian Mare	(T) **_Proud Arabian Mare_**	Gl, bay. Old mold
9	1: Arabian Foal	(T) **_Family Arabian Foal_**	Gl, alabaster
	2: Arabian Foal	(T) **_Family Arabian Foal_**	Alabaster
	3: Arabian Foal	(T) **_Proud Arabian Foal_**	Gl, alabaster
13	1: Arabian Stallion	(T) **_Family Arabian Stallion_**	Gl, bay
	2: Arabian Stallion	(T) **_Family Arabian Stallion_**	Bay
14	1: Arabian Mare	(T) **_Family Arabian Mare_**	Gl, bay
	2: Arabian Mare	(T) **_Family Arabian Mare_**	Bay
	3: Arabian Mare	(T) **_Proud Arabian Mare_**	Gl, alabaster, old mold
15	1: Arabian Foal	(T) **_Family Arabian Foal_**	Gl, bay
	2: Arabian Foal	(T) **_Family Arabian Foal_**	Bay
	3: Arabian Foal	(T) **_Proud Arabian Foal_**	Gl, bay
16	Marguerite Henry's Sea Star	(T) **_Sea Star_**	Dark chestnut
17	Stock Horse Foal	(T) **_Stock Horse Foal (Rough Coat)_**	Brown blanket appaloosa
18	Stock Horse Foal	(T) **_Stock Horse Foal (Rough Coat)_**	Black blanket appaloosa
19	Marguerite Henry's Stormy	(T) **_Stormy_**	Chestnut pinto
20	Marguerite Henry's Misty	(T) **_Misty_**	Palomino pinto
21	Shetland Pony	(T) **_Shetland Pony_**	Gl/black pinto
22	Shetland Pony	(T) **_Shetland Pony_**	Gl, light chestnut pinto
23	Shetland Pony	(T) **_Shetland Pony_**	Bay
25	Shetland Pony	(T) **_Shetland Pony_**	Gl/alabaster
27	Fury Prancer	(T) **_Fury Prancer_**	Gl, black
29	Phantom Wings, Misty's Foal	(T) **_Stock Horse Foal (Rough Coat)_**	Palomino pinto
30	1: Fighting Stallion	(T) **_Fighting Stallion_**	Gl, alabaster
	2: Fighting Stallion	(T) **_Fighting Stallion_**	Alabaster
32	Fighting Stallion	(T) **_Fighting Stallion_**	Gl, gray blanket appaloosa
33	1: Fighting Stallion	(T) **_Fighting Stallion_**	Gl, palomino
	2: Fighting Stallion	(T) **_Fighting Stallion_**	Palomino
34	Fighting Stallion	(T) **_Fighting Stallion_**	Gl, charcoal
35	Fighting Stallion	(T) **_Fighting Stallion_**	Bay

36	Race Horse	(T) *Racehorse*	Gl, chestnut
37	1: Arabian Stallion	(T) *Family Arabian Stallion*	Gl, gray blanket appaloosa
	2: Arabian Stallion	(T) *Family Arabian Stallion*	Gray blanket appaloosa
38	1: Arabian Mare	(T) *Family Arabian Mare*	Gl, gray blanket appaloosa
	2: Arabian Mare	(T) *Family Arabian Mare*	Gray blanket appaloosa
	3: Arabian Mare	(T) *Proud Arabian Mare*	Gl, gray blanket appaloosa, old mold
39	1: Arabian Foal	(T) *Family Arabian Foal*	Gl, gray blanket appaloosa
	2: Arabian Foal	(T) *Family Arabian Foal*	Gray blanket appaloosa
	3: Arabian Foal	(T) *Proud Arabian Foal*	Gl, gray blanket appaloosa
40	Black Beauty	(T) *Western Pony*	Gl, black
	Lynn Anderson's Lady Phase	(T) *Lady Phase*	Chestnut
	Western Pony	(T) *Western Pony*	Sg, plum brown
41	Western Pony	(T) *Western Pony*	Gl/black pinto
42	Western Pony	(T) *Western Pony*	Gl, chestnut pinto
43	1: Western Pony	(T) *Western Pony*	Gl, palomino
	2: Western Pony	(T) *Western Pony*	Palomino
44	Western Pony	(T) *Western Pony*	Gl, black; gold hooves and trim
45	Western Pony	(T) *Western Pony*	Gl, alabaster
46	Pacer	(T) *Pacer*	M/Sg, dark bay
47	Man O'War	(T) *Man O'War*	Red chestnut
48	Morgan	(T) *Morgan*	Black
49	Morgan	(T) *Morgan*	Bay
50	Adios Famous Standardbred	(T) *Adios*	Bay
50	Western Horse	(T) *Western Horse*	Gl, black, gold hooves
51 bons	Five Gaiter	(T) *Five Gaiter*	Gl, white, turquoise on yellow rib- yellow ribbons
	Yellow Mount Famous Paint	(T) *Adios*	Chestnut pinto
52	Five Gaiter	(T) *Five Gaiter*	Sorrel, red on white braids
53	Five Gaiter	(T) *Five Gaiter*	Gl, palomino, red on yellow ribbons
54	Trakehner	(T) *Trakehner*	Bay
55	1: Western Horse	(T) *Western Horse*	Gl, black pinto
	2: Western Horse	(T) *Western Horse*	Black pinto
56	Western Horse	(T) *Western Horse*	Gl, palomino/chestnut pinto
57	1: Western Horse	(T) *Western Horse*	Gl, palomino
	2: Western Horse	(T) *Western Horse*	Palomino
	Western Palomino	(T) *Western Horse*	Gl, palomino
58	Black Beauty	(T) *Western Horse*	Gl, black
	Hanoverian	(T) *Hanoverian*	Bay
	Western Horse	(T) *Western Horse*	Gl, black
59	Morganglanz	(T) *Morganglanz*	Chestnut
	Western Horse	(T) *Western Horse*	Gl, white
60	Midnight Sun Tennessee Walker	(T) *Midnight Sun*	Black, red on white braids
61	El Pastor Paso Fino	(T) *El Pastor*	Bay (star face)
62	Saddlebred Weanling	(T) *Saddlebred Weanling*	Chestnut
63	Halla, Famous Jumper	(T) *Halla*	Bay
64	Black Foundation Stallion	(T) *Foundation Stallion*	Black
	Rin Tin Tin	(O) *Rin Tin Tin*	M/Sg, brown
65	Justin Morgan	(T) *Justin Morgan*	Red bay
	Lassie	(O) *Lassie*	Sg, bi color
66	Stud Spider	(T) *Stud Spider*	Black blanket appaloosa
	Boxer	(O) *Boxer*	M/Sg/Gl, tan/fawn
67	San Domingo	(T) *San Domingo*	Chestnut pinto
	Poodle	(O) *Poodle*	Gl, black
68	Legionario III	(T) *Legionario*	Alabaster
	Poodle	(O) *Poodle*	Gl, white
69	Smoky the Cow Horse	(T) *Smoky*	Medium gray
	Poodle	(O) *Poodle*	Silver gray
70	1: Brahma Bull	(O) *Brahma Bull*	Sg/gray
	2: Brahma Bull	(O) *Brahma Bull*	Gl, gray
71	Hereford Bull	(O) *Hereford Bull*	M/Gl, dark brown
72	Black Angus Bull	(O) *Walking Black Angus Bull*	Gl, black, also poodle cut

73	1: Hornless Hereford	(O) *Walking Black Angus Bull*	Gl, red brown and white
	2: Hornless Hereford	(O) *Walking Black Angus Bull*	Gl, red brown and white, poodle cut
	Spanish Fighting Bull	(O) *Spanish Fighting Bull*	Black
74	Polled Hereford Bull	(O) *Polled Hereford Bull*	Red brown and white
75	Texas Longhorn Bull	(O) *Texas Longhorn Bull*	Light brown/tan
76	Buffalo	(O) *Buffalo*	Brown
77	Elk	(O) *Elk*	Brown
78	Bighorn Ram	(O) *Bighorn Ram*	Tan
79	Moose	(O) *Moose*	Dark brown
80	1: Clydesdale	(T) *Clydesdale Stallion*	Gl, bay, gold ribbons, muscle and no-muscle versions
	2: Clydesdale	(T) *Clydesdale Stallion*	Bay, gold bobs and tail ribbon
	Clydesdale Stallion	(T) *Clydesdale Stallion*	Bay, alternating white and red bobs, red tail ribbon
81	Donkey	(T) *Donkey*	Gray
82	Clydesdale	(T) *Clydesdale Stallion*	Gl, dapple gray, gold bobs, no-muscle and muscle versions
	Donkey	(T) *Donkey*	Gray, with red baskets
83	Clydesdale Mare	(T) *Clydesdale Mare*	Chestnut
84	Clydesdale Foal	(T) *Clydesdale Foal*	Chestnut
85	Azteca	(T) *Foundation Stallion*	Dapple gray
85	Mustang	(T) *Mustang*	Gl, alabaster, also with red eyes
	Dall Sheep	(O) *Bighorn Ram*	Tan
86	Mustang	(T) *Mustang*	Gl, gray blanket appaloosa
87	Mustang	(T) *Mustang*	Buckskin
88	Mustang	(T) *Mustang*	Gl, charcoal
	Overo Paint	(T) *Stud Spider*	Chestnut pinto
89	Black Beauty	(T) *Black Beauty*	Black
90	Phar Lap Famous Race Horse	(T) *Phar Lap*	Red chestnut
91	Elephant	(O) *Elephant*	Gray
92	Belgian	(T) *Belgian*	Smoke, red on yellow ribbon
	Elephant	(O) *Elephant*	Sg, pale pink
93	Belgian	(T) *Belgian*	Gl, dapple gray or dapple black
94	Belgian	(T) *Belgian*	Chestnut/sorrel, red on yellow ribbon
	Elephant	(O) *Elephant*	M/Sg, gray, white tusks
95	Shire	(T) *Shire*	Dapple gray
96	Shire	(T) *Shire*	Honey sorrel
97	Appaloosa Gelding	(T) *Quarter Horse Gelding*	Chestnut blanket appaloosa
98	Quarter Horse	(T) *Quarter Horse Gelding*	Buckskin
99	Appaloosa Performance Horse	(T) *Appaloosa Performance Horse*	Chestnut roan appaloosa
	Quarter Horse	(T) *Quarter Horse Gelding*	Gl, bay
100	Galiceno	(T) *Galiceno*	Bay
101	Quarter Horse Yearling	(T) *Quarter Horse Yearling*	Liver chestnut
	Modernistic Buck	(O) *Modernistic Buck*	Sg, metallic gold
102	Quarter Horse Yearling	(T) *Quarter Horse Yearling*	Palomino
	Modernistic Doe	(O) *Modernistic Doe*	Sg, metallic gold
103	Appaloosa Yearling	(T) *Quarter Horse Yearling*	Sandy bay blanket appaloosa
104	Cantering Welsh Pony	(T) *Cantering Welsh Pony*	Bay, yellow ribbons
105	1: Cantering Welsh Pony	(T) *Cantering Welsh Pony*	Chestnut, red ribbons
	2: Cantering Welsh Pony	(T) *Cantering Welsh Pony*	Chestnut, no ribbons
106	Cantering Welsh Pony	(T) *Cantering Welsh Pony*	Seal brown, blue ribbons
109	American Saddlebred	(T) *Five Gaiter*	Dapple gray, black on red ribbons
110	Western Prancing Horse	(T) *Western Prancing Horse*	Smoke
111	Western Prancing Horse	(T) *Western Prancing Horse*	Buckskin
112	Western Prancing Horse	(T) *Western Prancing Horse*	Palomino

No.	Name	Mold	Color
113	Western Prancing Horse	(T) *Western Prancing Horse*	Gl, black pinto
114	Western Prancing Horse	(T) *Western Prancing Horse*	Bay
115	Western Prancing	(T) *Western Prancing Horse*	Gl, leopard appaloosa
116	Precipitado Sin Par (Cips Champion Paso Fino)	(T) *El Pastor*	Bay pinto, LE
117	Project Universe	(T) *Five Gaiter*	Chestnut pinto, black on gold braids
118	American Mustang	(T) *Mustang*	Sorrel
119	Running Mare	(T) *Running Mare*	Red roan
120	Running Mare	(T) *Running Mare*	Alabaster
121	Running Mare	(T) *Running Mare*	Smoke/charcoal
123	Running Mare	(T) *Running Mare*	Gl, dapple gray
124	Running Mare	(T) *Running Mare*	M/Sg, bay/chestnut
125	Running Stallion	(T) *Running Stallion*	Alabaster
126	Running Stallion	(T) *Running Stallion*	Gl, charcoal
127	Running Stallion	(T) *Running Stallion*	Black blanket appaloosa
128	Running Stallion	(T) *Running Stallion*	Red roan
129	Running Stallion	(T) *Running Stallion*	Bay/chestnut
130	Running Foal	(T) *Running Foal*	Alabaster
131	Running Foal	(T) *Running Foal*	Smoke
133	Running Foal	(T) *Running Foal*	Gl, dapple gray
134	Running Foal	(T) *Running Foal*	Bay/chestnut
140	Wing Commander	(T) *Five Gaiter*	Brown/bay, red ribbons
141	Grazing Mare	(T) *Grazing Mare*	Bay
142	Grazing Mare	(T) *Grazing Mare*	Black
143	Grazing Mare	(T) *Grazing Mare*	Palomino
151	Grazing Foal	(T) *Grazing Foal*	Bay
152	Grazing Foal	(T) *Grazing Foal*	Black
153	Grazing Foal	(T) *Grazing Foal*	Palomino
154	Pony of the Americas	(T) *Pony of the Americas*	Bay/chestnut blanket appaloosa
155	Pony of the Americas	(T) *Pony of the Americas*	Chestnut leopard appaloosa
156	Haflinger	(T) *Haflinger*	Sorrel
165	Lying Down Foal	(T) *Lying Foal*	Black blanket appaloosa
166	Lying Down Foal	(T) *Lying Foal*	Buckskin
167	Lying Down Foal	(T) *Lying Foal*	Red roan
168	Scratching Foal	(T) *Scratching Foal*	Black appaloosa
169	Scratching Foal	(T) *Scratching Foal*	Liver chestnut
170	Scratching Foal	(T) *Scratching Foal*	M/Sg, red roan
174	Indian Pony	(T) *Indian Pony*	Dark bay blanket appaloosa
175	Indian Pony	(T) *Indian Pony*	Brown pinto
176	Indian Pony	(T) *Indian Pony*	Buckskin
177	Indian Pony	(T) *Indian Pony*	Alabaster
180	Rearing Stallion	(C) *Rearing Stallion*	Alabaster
183	Rearing Stallion	(C) *Rearing Stallion*	Palomino
185	Rearing Stallion	(C) *Rearing Stallion*	Bay
190	Bucking Bronco	(C) *Bucking Bronco*	Black
191	Bucking Bronco	(C) *Bucking Bronco*	Gray
192	Bucking Bronco	(C) *Bucking Bronco*	Bay
200	Old Timer	(T) *Old Timer*	Alabaster
201	1: Arabian Stallion	(T) *Family Arabian Stallion*	Charcoal
	2: Arabian Stallion	(T) *Family Arabian Stallion*	Gl, charcoal
202	1: Arabian Mare	(T) *Family Arabian Mare*	Gl, charcoal
	2: Arabian Mare	(T) *Family Arabian Mare*	Charcoal
203	1: Arabian Foal	(T) *Family Arabian Foal*	Gl, charcoal
	2: Arabian Foal	(T) *Family Arabian Foal*	Charcoal
205	1: Old Timer	(T) *Old Timer*	Gl, dapple gray
	2: Old Timer	(T) *Old Timer*	Dapple gray
206	Old Timer	(T) *Old Timer*	Bay
207	Balking Mule	(T) *Balking Mule*	Bay/chestnut
208	Balking Mule	(T) *Balking Mule*	M/SG, liver chestnut/seal brown
209	Pegasus	(C) *Lipizzan Stallion*	Alabaster
210	Unicorn	(T) *Running Stallion*	Alabaster; gold striped horn
211	Proud Arabian Stallion	(T) *Proud Arabian Stallion*	Alabaster
212	Proud Arabian Stallion	(T) *Proud Arabian Stallion*	M or Sg, mahogany bay
213	Proud Arabian Stallion	(T) *Proud Arabian Stallion*	M/Sg, dapple gray
215	Proud Arabian Mare	(T) *Proud Arabian Mare*	Sg/dapple gray
216	Proud Arabian Mare	(T) *Proud Arabian Mare*	M/Sg, mahogany bay, front socks
217	Proud Arabian Mare	(T) *Proud Arabian Mare*	Alabaster
218	Proud Arabian Foal	(T) *Proud Arabian Foal*	Alabaster
219	Proud Arabian Foal	(T) *Proud Arabian Foal*	Mahogany bay
220	Proud Arabian Foal	(T) *Proud Arabian Foal*	Dapple gray
221	American Buckskin Stock Horse Stallion	(T) *Stock Horse Stallion*	Buckskin
222	American Buckskin Stock Horse Mare	(T) *Stock Horse Mare*	Buckskin
224	American Buckskin Stock Horse Foal	(T) *Stock Horse Foal*	Buckskin
225	Action American Buckskin Stock Horse Foal	(T) *Action Stock Horse Foal*	Buckskin solid points
226	Bay Quarter Horse Stock Stallion	(T) *Stock Horse Stallion*	Bay
227	1: Sorrel Quarter Horse Stock Mare	(T) *Stock Horse Mare*	Sorrel (leg up version)
	2: Sorrel Quarter Horse Stock Mare	(T) *Stock Horse Mare*	Sorrel
228	Bay Quarter Horse Stock Foal	(T) *Stock Horse Foal*	Bay
229	Tobiano Pinto Stock Horse Stallion	(T) *Stock Horse Stallion*	Black pinto
230	1: Overo Paint Stock Horse	(T) *Stock Horse Mare*	Bay pinto
	2: Overo Paint Stock Horse	(T) *Stock Horse Mare*	Bay pinto (leg up)
231	Pinto Stock Horse Foal	(T) *Stock Horse Foal*	Black pinto
232	Appaloosa Stock Horse Stallion	(T) *Stock Horse Stallion*	Light bay blanket appaloosa
233	1: Appaloosa Stock Horse Mare	(T) *Stock Horse Mare*	Black appaloosa (leg up)
	2: Appaloosa Stock Horse Mare	(T) *Stock Horse Mare*	Black appaloosa
234	Appaloosa Stock Horse Foal	(T) *Stock Horse Foal*	Gray blanket appaloosa
236	Chestnut Stock Horse Foal	(T) *Action Stock Horse Foal*	Chestnut
237	Bay Pinto Stock Horse Foal	(T) *Action Stock Horse Foal*	Bay pinto
238	Appaloosa Stock Horse Foal	(T) *Action Stock Horse Foal*	Gray blanket appaloosa
245	Lying Down Unicorn	(T) *Lying Foal*	Alabaster
251	Norita	(C) *Kelso*	Dapple gray
252	Pepe	(C) *Man O'War*	Light chestnut
253	T Bone	(C) *Silky Sullivan*	Black roan
254	Hawk	(C) *Swaps*	Black
255	Gaucho	(C) *Terrang*	Red roan
256	Lula	(C) *Ruffian*	Bay
257	Jeremy	(C) *Kelso*	Brown
258	King	(C) *Man O'War*	Dark chestnut
259	Andrew	(C) *Silky Sullivan*	Gray
260	Prince	(C) *Swaps*	Gray
261	Ten Gallon	(C) *Terrang*	Dun
262	Colleen	(C) *Ruffian*	Chestnut
263	Black Jack	(C) *Kelso*	Black pinto
264	Apache	(C) *Man O'War*	Gray
265	Spice	(C) *Silky Sullivan*	Bay blanket appaloosa
266	Cloud	(C) *Swaps*	Dapple gray
267	Azul	(C) *Terrang*	Blue roan/gray
268	Patches	(C) *Ruffian*	Bay pinto

287	Vanity	(C) *Kelso*	Bay pinto
288	Tumbleweed	(C) *Man O'War*	Light bay/chestnut
289	Chaval	(C) *Andalusian Mare*	Red roan/chestnut
290	Black Silk	(C) *Swaps*	Black
291	Ambrosia	(C) *Terrang*	Palomino
292	Whispers	(C) *Ruffian*	Gray appaloosa
300	Jumping Horse	(T) *Jumping Horse*	Bay
301	Buck Deer	(O) *Buck Deer*	Tan
302	Doe Deer	(O) *Doe Deer*	Tan
303	Fawn Deer	(O) *Fawn*	Tan
306	Bear	(O) *Bear*	Black
307	Bear	(O) *Bear*	Brown
308	Bear Cub	(O) *Bear Cub*	Black
309	Bear Cub	(O) *Bear Cub*	Brown
310	Pronghorn Antelope	(O) *Pronghorn Antelope*	Brown and white
312	Montana Mountain Goat	(O) *Mountain Goat*	Alabaster
321	Brandy St. Bernard	(O) *St. Bernard*	Golden
322	Pug Boxer	(O) *Boxer*	Chocolate brown/brindle
323	Honey Collie	(O) *Lassie*	Golden bi color
324	Chaser Hound Dog	(O) *Basset Hound*	Brown/bi color
325	Bloodhound	(O) *Basset Hound*	Dark brown
326	Jolly Cholly Basset Hound	(O) *Basset Hound*	Sg, tri color
327	German Shepherd	(O) *Rin Tin Tin*	M/Sg, charcoal gray
328	St. Bernard	(O) *St. Bernard*	Sg/m, bi color
335	Siamese Kitten	(O) *Kitten*	Gray or seal point
336	Calico Kitten	(O) *Kitten*	Orange tabby
337	Cleopatra Kitten	(O) *Kitten*	Orange tabby
338	Leonardo Kitten	(O) *Kitten*	Gray tabby
341	Holstein Cow	(O) *Cow*	Black and white pinto pattern
342	Guernsey Cow	(O) *Cow*	Tan and white pinto pattern
343	Jersey Cow	(O) *Cow*	Dark tan
344	Ayrshire Cow	(O) *Cow*	Dark red and white pinto pattern
345	Brown Swiss Cow	(O) *Cow*	Cocoa brown
347	Holstein Calf	(O) *Calf*	Black and white pinto pattern
348	Guernsey Calf	(O) *Calf*	Tan and white pinto pattern
349	Jersey Calf	(O) *Calf*	Tan; solid
350	Ayrshire Calf	(O) *Calf*	Dark red and white pinto pattern
351	Brown Swiss Calf	(O) *Calf*	Cocoa brown; solid
355	Jasper the Market Hog	(O) *Jasper the Market Hog*	White and gray
360	Charolais Bull	(O) *Charolais Bull*	Alabaster
365	Black Angus Bull	(O) *Black Angus Bull*	Black
370	Texas Longhorn Bull	(O) *Texas Longhorn Bull*	Dark chestnut pinto pattern
375	Marguerite Henry's Brighty	(T) *Brighty*	Gray
376	Brighty 1991, or Marguerite Henry's Brighty	(T) *Brighty*	Brownish-gray
380	Tatanka	(O) *Buffalo*	Alabaster
381	American Bison	(O) *Buffalo*	Brown
382	Holstein Cow	(O) *Cow*	M/Sg, black and white (polled)
383	Socks, Kitten	(O) *Kitten*	M/Sg black and white
384	Texas Longhorn Bull	(O) *Texas Longhorn Bull*	Chestnut and white (speckles and patches)
385	Red Brahma Bull	(O) *Brahma Bull*	Orangish-red
386	Simmental Bull	(O) *Charolais Bull*	Chestnut pinto pattern
387	Moose	(O) *Moose*	light shaded brown
388	American Bison	(O) *Buffalo*	muddy brown
394	Pronghorn Antelope	(O) *Pronghorn Antelope*	Bright chestnut and white
390	Donkey	(T) *Donkey*	Gray
391	Elephant	(O) *Elephant*	Light gray
392	Bear	(O) *Bear*	Shaded medium brown
393	Ram	(O) *Bighorn Ram*	Medium shaded brown
394	Holstein Cow	(O) *Cow*	Black pinto pattern w/small spots
395	Spanish Fighting Bull	(O) *Spanish Fighting Bull*	Steel gray

401	The Black Stallion	(T) *Black Stallion*	Sg, black
410	Marguerite Henry's Sham	(T) *Sham*	Red bay
411	Prancing Arabian Stallion	(T) *Sham*	Flea-bit gray
415	Buckshot Famous Spanish Barb	(T) *Buckshot*	Grulla
416	Spanish Barb	(T) *Buckshot*	Chestnut pinto
420	Touch of Class	(T) *Touch of Class*	Bay
425	Lady Roxanna	(T) *Lady Roxanna*	Alabaster
426	Prancing Arabian Mare	(T) *Lady Roxanna*	Chestnut
430	Sherman Morgan	(T) *Sherman Morgan*	Chestnut
435	Secretariat	(T) *Secretariat*	Chestnut
445	John Henry	(T) *John Henry*	Dark bay
450	Rugged Lark Champion American Quarter Horse Stallion	(T) *Rugged Lark*	Bay
455	Roy Belgian Drafter	(T) *Roy the Belgian*	Sorrel/light chestnut
460	Khemosabi +++	(T) *Khemosabi*	Red bay
465	Roemer Dutch Warmblood	(T) *Roemer*	Dark chestnut
470	Misty's Twilight	(T) *Misty's Twilight*	Chestnut pinto
475	Pluto the Lipizzaner	(T) *Pluto*	Light gray
480	Mesteno, the Messenger	(C) *Mesteno*	Dark buckskin
481	Reflections Mesteno	(C) *Reflections Mesteno*	Buckskin
482	Henry, Norwegian Fjord	(T) *Henry*	Dun
483	Big Ben	(T) *Big Ben*	Chestnut
485	Friesian	(T) *Friesian*	Black
490	Bolya the Freedom Horse	(T) *Halla*	Buckskin
494	Llanarth True Briton Champion Welsh Cob	(T) *Llanarth True Briton*	Dark chestnut
495	Gem Twist Champion Show Jumper	(T) *Gem Twist*	Alabaster
496	Aristocrat Champion Hackney	(T) *Hackney*	Bay
497	1: AQHA Ideal American Quarter Horse	(T) *Ideal American Quarter Horse*	Dark red chestnut "mistake version"
	2: AQHA Ideal American Quarter Horse	(T) *Ideal American Quarter Horse*	Chestnut
498	Progeny of Leo, AQHA American Quarter Horse	(T) *Ideal American Quarter Horse*	Chestnut
499	AQHA Offspring of King P-234	(T) *Ideal American Quarter Horse*	Bay
601	Kelso	(C) *Kelso*	M/Sg, dark bay/brown
	Corky and Bimbo	(O) *Elephant*	M/Sg, battleship gray, white tusks
602	Man O'War	(C) *Man O'War*	Red chestnut
603	Silky Sullivan	(C) *Silky Sullivan*	Brown
604	Swaps	(C) *Swaps*	Chestnut
605	Terrang	(C) *Terrang*	Dark brown
606	Ruffian	(C) *Ruffian*	Dark bay
620	Lipizzan Stallion	(C) *Lipizzan Stallion*	Alabaster
625	Hobo the Mustang of Lazy Heart Ranch	(C) *Hobo*	Buckskin
626	Polo Pony	(C) *Polo Pony*	Bay
701	Collector's Rocking Horse	(T) *Saddlebred Weanling*	Fl, chestnut
702	Morgan	(T) *Morgan*	Light bay
703	Blanket Appaloosa	(T) *San Domingo*	Dark gray blanket appaloosa
704	Tennessee Walking Horse	(T) *Midnight Sun*	Red bay, red on white braids
705	Standing Quarter Horse Stallion	(T) *Adios*	Apricot dun
706	Family Arabian Stallion	(T) *Family Arabian Stallion*	Liver chestnut
707	Family Arabian Mare	(T) *Family Arabian Mare*	Liver chestnut

708	Family Arabian Foal	(T) *Family Arabian Foal*	Liver chestnut
709	Fighting Stallion	(T) *Fighting Stallion*	Black leopard appaloosa
710	American Indian Pony	(T) *Foundation Stallion*	Red roan/flea bit gray
711	Breezing Dixie Famous Appaloosa Mare	(T) *Lady Phase*	Dark bay blanket appaloosa. LE
801	Shetland Pony	(T) *Shetland Pony*	Bay pinto
802	Fade to Grey	(T) *Black Beauty*	Dark dappled gray
803	Galloping Thoroughbred	(T) *Phar Lap*	Dark bay
804	Proud Arabian Stallion	(T) *Proud Arabian Stallion*	Dapple rose gray
805	Proud Arabian Mare	(T) *Proud Arabian Mare*	Dappled rose gray
806	Proud Arabian Foal	(T) *Proud Arabian Foal*	Rose gray
807	Paint Horse Stallion	(T) *Stock Horse Stallion*	Liver chestnut pinto
808	Paint Horse Mare	(T) *Stock Horse Mare*	Dark chestnut pinto
809	Paint Horse Foal	(T) *Stock Horse Foal*	Dark chestnut pinto
810	Action Appaloosa Foal	(T) *Action Stock Horse Foal*	Chestnut leopard appaloosa
811	Majestic Arabian Stallion	(T) *Black Stallion*	Black leopard appaloosa
812	Prancing Arabian Stallion	(T) *Sham*	Palomino
813	Thoroughbred Mare	(T) *Touch of Class*	Black
814	Family Arabian Stallion	(T) *Family Arabian Stallion*	Bay, hind socks
815	Family Arabian Mare	(T) *Family Arabian Mare*	Bay
816	Family Arabian Foal	(T) *Family Arabian Foal*	Bay, hind socks
817	Abdullah Champion Trakehner	(T) *Trakehner*	Light dapple gray, LE
818	Saddlebred Weanling	(T) *Saddlebred Weanling*	Palomino/light chestnut pinto, CE
819	Dan Patch	(T) *Pacer*	M/Sg, red bay, LE
820	Noble Jumper	(T) *Halla*	Dapple gray
821	Rocky, Champion Connemara Stallion	(T) *Pony of the Americas*	Dapple dun
822	Morgan	(T) *Justin Morgan*	Dark bay
823	Blanket Appaloosa	(T) *Stud Spider*	Chestnut blanket appaloosa
824	Clydesdale Stallion	(T) *Clydesdale Stallion*	Light bay, gold and white bobs, gold tail ribbon
825	Clydesdale Mare	(T) *Clydesdale Mare*	Light bay
826	Clydesdale Foal	(T) *Clydesdale Foal*	Light bay
827	Pinto American Saddlebred	(T) *Five Gaiter*	Black pinto, red on white ribbons
828	Paint American Mustang	(T) *Mustang*	Bay pinto
829	Comanche Pony	(T) *San Domingo*	Palomino
830	Quarter Horse Stallion	(T) *Adios*	Black roan
831	Show Stance Morgan	(T) *Morgan*	Dark red chestnut
832	Hyksos the Egyptian Arabian	(T) *Black Stallion*	Sg, Ageless bronze, CE
833	Dream Weaver	(T) *Black Beauty*	Sorrel, LE
834	Old Timer	(T) *Old Timer*	Red roan
835	Prancing Morgan	(T) *Sherman Morgan*	Black
836	Joe Patchen Sire of Dan Patch	(T) *John Henry*	Black
837	Belgian Brabant	(T) *Roy the Belgian*	Grulla
838	Hobo	(T) *Phar Lap*	Buckskin
839	Proud Arabian Stallion	(T) *Proud Arabian Stallion*	Light dapple gray
840	Proud Arabian Mare	(T) *Proud Arabian Mare*	Red chestnut
841	Family Arabian Foal	(T) *Family Arabian Foal*	Red chestnut
842	Skipster's Chief Famous Therapeutic Riding Horse	(T) *Stock Horse Stallion*	Sorrel
843	Selle Francais	(T) *Touch of Class*	Dark chestnut
844	Paint Horse Foal	(T) *Stock Horse Foal*	Light chestnut pinto
845	Chincoteague Foal	(T) *Sea Star*	Buckskin
846	Rough Diamond	(T) *Stock Horse Foal (Rough Coat)*	Dark brown pinto
847	Black Beauty 1991	(T) *Morganglanz*	Black
848	Running Mare	(T) *Running Mare*	Chestnut pinto
849	Running Foal	(T) *Running Foal*	Chestnut pinto
850	Mountain Pony	(T) *Haflinger*	Sorrel, gray knees and hocks
851	Spanish Pride	(T) *Legionario*	Bay
852	Appy Mare	(T) *Stock Horse Mare*	Red roan/leopard appaloosa
853	Mesa	(T) *Adios*	M-Sg, very dark bay
854	Memphis Storm	(T) *Midnight Sun*	Gl, charcoal, red on white braids
855	Chaparral	(T) *Fighting Stallion*	Buckskin pinto. LE
856	Shire Mare	(T) *Clydesdale Mare*	Dark chestnut/bay
857	Shetland Pony	(T) *Shetland Pony*	Chestnut
858	Vermont Morgan	(T) *Morgan*	Chocolate sorrel
859	Family Appaloosa Stallion	(T) *Stud Spider*	Bay blanket appaloosa
860	Family Appaloosa Mare	(T) *Lady Phase*	Black leopard appaloosa
861	Family Appaloosa Foal	(T) *Stock Horse Foal*	Red bay appaloosa
862	Kentucky Saddlebred	(T) *Five Gaiter*	Chestnut
863	Rana	(T) *Sham*	Dark gray
864	Tic Toc	(T) *Western Horse*	Alabaster
865	Bluegrass Foal	(T) *Running Foal*	Blue roan
866	Plain Pixie	(T) *Cantering Welsh Pony*	Red roan, no ribbons
867	Tesoro	(T) *El Pastor*	Palomino
868	Highland Clydesdale	(T) *Clydesdale Stallion*	Bay, stenciled markings, blue and white bobs, blue tail ribbon
869	Lakota Pony	(T) *Foundation Stallion*	Alabaster with blue markings
870	Fugir Cacador Lusitano Stallion	(T) *Foundation Stallion*	Buckskin, LE
871	Domino The Happy Canyon Trail Horse	(T) *San Domingo*	Black/dark gray pinto, CE
872	Ara-Appaloosa Stallion	(T) *Family Arabian Stallion*	Leopard appaloosa
873	Ara-Appaloosa	(T) *Family Arabian Mare*	Leopard appaloosa
874	Ara-Appaloosa Foal	(T) *Family Arabian Foal*	Leopard appaloosa
875	Woodsprite	(T) *Stock Horse Foal (Rough Coat)*	Bay
876	Just Justin Quarter Pony	(T) *Pony of the Americas*	Coffee dun
877	Guinevere	(T) *Touch of Class*	Reddish bay
878	Double Take	(T) *Justin Morgan*	Dark chestnut
879	Rumbling Thunder	(T) *Running Stallion*	Sg, dark dapple gray
880	Medieval Knight	(T) *Legionario*	Gray/roan
881	Wild American Horse	(T) *Phar Lap*	Gray dun/grulla
882	Ichilay	(T) *Indian Pony*	Gray
883	Scat Cat — Children's Pony	(T) *Haflinger*	Bay roan leopard appaloosa
884	Pantomime	(T) *Pony of the Americas*	Black blanket appaloosa
885	Rough n' Ready — Quarter Horse	(T) *Adios*	Dun
886	Starlight	(T) *Jumping Horse*	Dark bay, LE
887	Gifted	(T) *Hanoverian*	Bay, LE
888	Freckle Doll	(T) *Galiceno*	Bay pinto
889	Ranger Cow Pony	(T) *Western Prancing Horse*	Dun
890	Promises Rearing Stallion	(C) *Rearing Stallion*	Dark bay pinto
891	Sunny Action Foal	(T) *Action Stock Horse Foal*	Light dun, dark gray points
892	Tara	(T) *Cantering Welsh Pony*	Dappled bay, no ribbons
893	Scribbles Paint Horse Foal	(T) *Sea Star*	Chestnut pinto
894	Satin Star	(T) *Clydesdale Foal*	Dark chestnut
895	Bright Socks	(T) *Stock Horse Foal (Rough Coat)*	Black pinto

#	Name		Model	Color
896	Rarin' To Go	(T)	*Mustang*	Grulla
897	Ponokah-Eemetah	(T)	*Fighting Stallion*	Dark bay blanket appaloosa
898	Martin's Dominique Champion Miniature Horse	(C)	*Merrylegs*	Sg, black
899	Greystreak Action Arabian	(T)	*Black Stallion*	Gray
900	Vandergelder Dutch Warmblood	(T)	*Roemer*	Bay
901	Lippitt Pegasus	(T)	*Morgan*	Red bay
902	Wild Diamond	(T)	*Running Mare*	Bay
903	Little Bub	(T)	*Running Foal*	Red bay
904	CH Imperator	(T)	*Five Gaiter*	Gl, dark chestnut, blue on red ribbons
905	1: Princess of Arabia	(T)	*Black Stallion*	Light dapple gray, LE
	2: Princess of Arabia	(T)	*Black Stallion*	Red roan, LE (unannounced color change)
906	Goliath the American Cream Draft Horse	(T)	*Belgian*	Light palomino, blue on red ribbon
907	Family Arabian Stallion	(T)	*Family Arabian Stallion*	Woodgrain
908	Arabian Mare	(T)	*Proud Arabian Mare*	Woodgrain, old mold
	Family Arabian Mare	(T)	*Family Arabian Mare*	Woodgrain
909	Arabian Foal	(T)	*Family Arabian Foal*	Woodgrain
910	Cisco Western Pony with Saddle	(T)	*Western Pony*	Buckskin
911	Clayton Quarter Horse	(T)	*Adios*	Dapple palomino
912	Hanover Trakehner	(T)	*Trakehner*	Liver chestnut
913	High Flyer Tennessee Walker	(T)	*Midnight Sun*	Chestnut pinto, white on blue braids
914	Tobe Rocky Mountain Horse	(T)	*El Pastor*	Chocolate sorrel
915	Kentuckiana Saddlebred Weanling	(T)	*Saddlebred Weanling*	Dark chestnut
916	Mister Mister Champion Paint	(T)	*Stud Spider*	Chestnut pinto
917	Oxydol Rodeo Appaloosa	(T)	*San Domingo*	Alabaster
918	Promenade Andalusian	(T)	*Legionario*	Bay
919	Donovan Running Appaloosa Stallion	(T)	*Black Beauty*	Gray blanket appaloosa (chestnut spots)
920	Running Mare	(T)	*Running Mare*	Woodgrain
921	Native Diver Champion Thoroughbred	(T)	*Phar Lap*	Black
922	Cody	(T)	*Buckshot*	Dark bay pinto
923	Hickock	(T)	*Buckshot*	Blue roan pinto
924	Majesty Quarter Horse	(T)	*Quarter Horse Gelding*	Light dapple gray
925	Shetland Pony	(T)	*Shetland Pony*	Woodgrain
926	Sargent Pepper Appaloosa Pony	(T)	*Haflinger*	Gray leopard appaloosa
927	Thunder Bay Quarter Horse	(T)	*Quarter Horse Yearling*	Dark bay
928	Lone Star	(T)	*Running Stallion*	Light dapple rose gray
929	Cheyenne American Mustang	(T)	*Indian Pony*	Roan
930	Running Foal	(T)	*Running Foal*	M/Sg, woodgrain
931	Fighting Stallion	(T)	*Fighting Stallion*	Woodgrain
932	Dakota Bucking Bronco	(C)	*Bucking Bronco*	Palomino
933	Sundown Proud Arabian Stallion	(T)	*Proud Arabian Stallion*	Sorrel
934	Cricket Quarter Horse Foal	(T)	*Action Stock Horse Foal*	Brown bay
935	McDuff Old Timer	(T)	*Old Timer*	Gray blanket appaloosa
936	Race Horse	(T)	*Racehorse*	Woodgrain
937	Calypso Quarter Horse	(T)	*Quarter Horse Yearling*	Red dun
938	Shane American Ranch Horse	(T)	*Stock Horse Stallion*	Black roan
939	Cinnamon, Appaloosa	(T)	*Lady Roxanna*	Bay blanket appaloosa
940	Laag, Standardbred	(T)	*Pacer*	Gray, CE
941	Robin & Hot Tamale H.T.	(T)	*Lying Foal*	Red roan leopard appaloosa
		(T)	*Quarter Horse Yearling*	Red roan leopard appaloosa
942	Bosley Blue & Trusty	(T)	*Lying Foal*	Gray leopard appaloosa
		(T)	*Quarter Horse Yearling*	Gray roan leopard appaloosa
943	JB Andrew, Adopt A Horse Drafter Type	(T)	*Friesian*	Black, with freeze brand
944	Pine, Shetland Pony	(T)	*Shetland Pony*	Palomino
945	Tri-Mi Boot Scootin' Boogie Western Pony	(T)	*Justin Morgan*	Dark brown/black
		(T)	*Western Pony*	M/Sg, woodgrain
946	Diamondot Buccaneer, Appaloosa	(T)	*Appaloosa Performance Horse*	Gray roan appaloosa (varnish roan)
947	Bond Snippet, Miniature Horse	(C)	*Merrylegs*	Chestnut pinto
948	Karma Gypsy, Pinto Half-Arab Morgan	(T)	*Proud Arabian Mare*	Bay pinto
		(T)	*Morgan*	Woodgrain
949	Clue II, American Quarter Horse	(T)	*Fighting Stallion*	Palomino
950	Dover, Trakehner	(T)	*Misty's Twilight*	Bay
951	Borodino II, Hanoverian	(T)	*Hanoverian*	M, bay, blaze
951	Five Gaiter	(T)	*Five Gaiter*	Woodgrain, blue on white ribbons
952	Rox Dene, Show Hunter	(T)	*Touch of Class*	Light dapple gray
953	Sebastian, Percheron	(T)	*Roy the Belgian*	Gray roan
954	Goin For Approval, Appaloosa	(T)	*Stock Horse Mare*	Chestnut snowflake appaloosa
955	Samsung Woodstock, Westphalian	(T)	*Morganglanz*	Chestnut
956	Embajador XI, Andalusian	(T)	*Pluto*	Medium dapple gray
957	Midnight, Bronco	(C)	*Rearing Stallion*	M/Sg, black
958	Little Andy Wind Bo Diddley Quarter Horse	(T)	*Rugged Lark*	Chestnut
959	Monte, Thoroughbred	(T)	*Gem Twist*	Chestnut
960	Royal Te, Appaloosa	(T)	*Western Horse*	Bay blanket appaloosa
961	The Cree Indian Horse, Naytukskie-Kukatos	(T)	*John Henry*	Bay
962	Laddie II, Shire	(T)	*Clydesdale Stallion*	M/Sg, black overo
963	Baron, Mustang	(T)	*Mustang*	Gl, mahogany bay/dark chestnut
964	Realto, Arabian	(T)	*Family Arabian Stallion*	Light gray
965	Calife, Arabian	(T)	*Family Arabian Stallion*	Shaded gray
966	My Prince, Thoroughbred Boxer	(T)	*Man O'War*	Chestnut
		(O)	*Boxer*	Woodgrain
967	Appaloosa Champion Poodle	(T)	*Foundation Stallion*	Red roan appaloosa
		(O)	*Poodle*	Woodgrain
968	Vigilante, Western Prancer	(T)	*Western Prancing Horse*	M/Sg, black
969	Karinthia, Buckskin Mare	(T)	*Running Mare*	Light buckskin
970	Korinth, Buckskin Foal Brahma Bull	(T)	*Running Foal*	Light buckskin
		(O)	*Brahma Bull*	Woodgrain
971	Hereford Bull Iron Metal Chief, Missouri Fox Trotter (T)	(O)	*Hereford Bull Iron Metal Chief*	Woodgrain / Black
972	Freedom, Legend of the Bloody Shoulder Arabian	(T)	*Proud Arabian Stallion*	Flea-bit gray
973	Marabella, Morgan Broodmare	(T)	*Marabella*	Bay

974	SS Morning Star, Pinto Half-Arabian	(T) *Proud Arabian Foal*	Bay pinto
975	Texas Longhorn Bull	(O) *Texas Longhorn Bull*	Woodgrain
	Best Choice, Arabian	(T) *Sham*	Mahogany bay
976	Smooth Copper, Quarter Horse	(T) *Stud Spider*	Shaded light bay
977	Galant, Lusitano	(T) *Legionario*	Shaded chestnut
978	Sweet Confession, Hackney Pony	(T) *Aristocrat*	Dark dappled bay
979	Sunny Boy, Welsh Cob	(T) *Llanarth True Briton*	Palomino
980	Clydesdale	(T) *Clydesdale Stallion*	Woodgrain, no-muscle and muscle versions
	Silverton, Welsh Cob	(T) *Llanarth True Briton*	Shaded gray
981	Best Tango	(T) *Adios*	Light bay
982	Burnt Sienna, American Saddlebred Weanling	(T) *Saddlebred Weanling*	Red roan
983	Equus, Arabian Racehorse	(T) *Black Stallion*	Alabaster
984	Duke, Pinto	(T) *Stock Horse Foal (Rough Coat)*	Chestnut pinto
985	Mustang	(T) *Mustang*	Woodgrain
	Sure Fire, Pinto	(T) *Sea Star*	Black pinto
986	Full Speed, Appaloosa	(T) *Indian Pony*	Shaded palomino appaloosa
987	Dempsey, Clydesdale Mare	(T) *Clydesdale Mare*	Chestnut/bay pinto
988	Quincy, Clydesdale Foal	(T) *Clydesdale Foal*	Chestnut pinto
989	Runaway, Mustang Kinger	(C) *Fighting Mesteno*	Cocoa dun
990	Dakotah Indian Horse — "Thunder" Waykinyan Hoton	(T) *San Domingo*	Black pinto
991	Elephant	(O) *Elephant*	Woodgrain
	Dakotah Indian Horse — "Lightning" Waykinyan	(T) *San Domingo*	Light bay/red dun pinto
992	Belgian	(T) *Belgian*	Woodgrain
	Docs Keepin Time, Quarter Horse	(T) *Stock Horse Stallion*	Black
993	Shenandoah, Mustang	(T) *Smoky*	Buckskin
994	Remington, Pinto	(T) *Smoky*	Bay pinto
995	Julian, Family Arabian Foal	(T) *Family Arabian Foal*	Dark chestnut
996	Galena, Family Arabian Mare	(T) *Family Arabian Mare*	Shaded chestnut
997	Devil Wind, Family Arabian Stallion	(T) *Family Arabian Stallion*	Seal brown/dark bay
998	Gambler, Western Pony	(T) *Western Pony*	Palomino
999	Quarter Horse	(T) *Quarter Horse Gelding*	Woodgrain
	Golden Joy, Paint	(T) *Stock Horse Foal*	Palomino pinto
1001	Bitsy Breyer and Arabian Stallion Beach Set	(L) *Arabian Stallion*	Bay, chestnut, or gray
1005	Bitsy Breyer and Morgan English Set	(L) *Morgan Stallion*	Bay, black, and chestnut
1010	Bitsy Breyer and Thoroughbred Jockey Set	(L) *Thoroughbred Stallion*	Bay, chestnut, or black models
1015	Bitsy Breyer and Quarter Horse Western Set	(L) *Quarter Horse Stallion*	Bay, buckskin, and palomino
1016	Starlight and Carole	(L) *Arabian Stallion*	Black
1017	Topside and Stevie	(L) *Thoroughbred Stallion*	Bright bay/buckskin
1018	Pepper and Lisa	(L) *Morgan Stallion*	Dapple gray
1019	Spot and Kate	(L) *Quarter Horse Stallion*	Black blanket appaloosa
1021	Belle	(L) *American Saddlebred*	Bay
1022	Prancer	(L) *Thoroughbred Stallion*	Bay

1023	Moonglow	(L) *Quarter Horse Stallion*	Chestnut
1024	Delilah	(L) *Morgan Stallion*	Palomino
1025	Cobalt and Veronica	(L) *Thoroughbred Stallion*	Black
1026	Chocolate and Jeannie	(L) *Quarter Horse Stallion*	Dark bay
1031	Fighting Stallion	(T) *Fighting Stallion*	Gl, Copenhagen
1051	Five Gaiter	(T) *Five Gaiter*	Gl, Copenhagen, black on blue ribbons
1085	Mustang	(T) *Mustang*	Gl, Copenhagen
1120	Brenda Western Gift Set	(T) *Western Prancing Horse*	Chestnut pinto
	Running Mare	(T) *Running Mare*	Gl, Copenhagen
1130	Running Foal	(T) *Running Foal*	Gl, Copenhagen
2003	Glory and Plank Jump Gift Set	(C) *Ruffian*	Dun/buckskin, with jump
2004	Buck	(C) *Terrang*	Buckskin
2005	Precious Beauty Foal & Gift Set	(C) *Andalusian Foal* (C) *Ginger*	Bay blanket appaloosa / Chestnut leopard appaloosa
2007	Tyler and Hillary	(C) *Arabian Stallion*	Chestnut pinto
2031	Fighting Stallion	(T) *Fighting Stallion*	Gl, Florentine
2051	Five Gaiter	(T) *Five Gaiter*	Gl, Florentine, black on gold ribbons
2055	Misty Gift Set	(T) *Misty*	Palomino pinto
2065	Justin Morgan Gift Set	(T) *Justin Morgan*	Red bay
2075	Brighty Gift Set	(T) *Brighty*	Gray
2085	Mustang	(T) *Mustang*	Gl, Florentine
2090	Smoky the Cow Horse Gift Set	(T) *Smoky*	Gray
2095	The Black Stallion, Book and Poster Set	(T) *Black Stallion*	Sg, black
2120	Running Mare	(T) *Running Mare*	Gl, Florentine
2130	Running Foal	(T) *Running Foal*	Gl, Florentine
2155	Proud Arabian Mare Gift Set	(T) *Proud Arabian Mare*	Sg/dapple gray; gray points/hooves
2165	Proud Arabian Mare Gift Set	(T) *Proud Arabian Mare*	M/Sg, mahogany bay, front socks
2169	Misty and Stormy Gift Set	(T) *Misty* (T) *Stormy*	Palomino pinto / Chestnut pinto
2175	Proud Arabian Mare Gift Set	(T) *Proud Arabian Mare*	Alabaster
2446	Brenda Breyer and Harness Racing Set	(T) *Pacer*	Alabaster
3000	The Black Stallion and Alec Set	(L) *Black Stallion*	Sg, black
3030	The Black Stallion Returns Set	(C) *Black Stallion* (C) *Johar* (C) *Sagr*	Black / Alabaster / Sorrel
3031	Fighting Stallion	(T) *Fighting Stallion*	Gl, Gold Charm
3035	U.S. Equestrian Team Gift Set	(C) *Jet Run* (C) *Keen* (C) *Might Tango*	Bay / Chestnut / Dapple gray
3040	Black Beauty Family	(C) *Black Beauty* (C) *Duchess* (C) *Ginger* (C) *Merrylegs*	Black / Bay / Chestnut / Dapple gray
3045	Quarter Horse Family	(C) *Quarter Horse Foal* (C) *Quarter Horse Mare* (C) *Quarter Horse Stallion*	Light bay / Bay / Palomino
3051	Five Gaiter	(T) *Five Gaiter*	Gl, Gold Charm, black on gold ribbons
3055	Classic Arabian Family	(C) *Arabian Foal* (C) *Arabian Mare* (C) *Arabian Stallion*	Chestnut / Chestnut / Sorrel
3056	Desert Arabian Family	(C) *Arabian Foal* (C) *Arabian Mare* (C) *Arabian Stallion*	Bay / Bay / Red bay
3057	Bedouin Family Gift Set	(C) *Arabian Foal* (C) *Arabian Mare* (C) *Arabian Stallion*	Bay / Black / Bay
3060	Classic Andalusian Family	(C) *Andalusian Foal* (C) *Andalusian Mare* (C) *Andalusian Stallion*	Dark chestnut / Dapple gray / Alabaster

No.	Set Name	Mold	Color
3065	Mustang Family	(C) *Mustang Foal*	Chestnut
		(C) *Mustang Mare*	Chestnut pinto
		(C) *Mustang Stallion*	Chestnut
3066	Marguerite Henry's Our First Pony Gift Set	(T) *Shetland Pony*	Black pinto
		(C) *Arabian Foal*	Bay pinto
		(C) *Mustang Foal*	Black pinto
3068	Bear Family	(O) *Bear*	Black
		(O) *Bear Cub*	Black
3069	Cinnamon Bear and Cub	(O) *Bear*	Reddish brown
		(O) *Bear Cub*	Reddish brown
3070	Legionario III Gift Set	(T) *Legionario*	Alabaster
3071	Bear Family Gift Set	(O) *Bear*	White
		(O) *Bear Cub*	White
3075	Lynn Anderson's Lady Phase Gift Set	(T) *Lady Phase*	Chestnut
3080	Stud Spider Gift Set	(T) *Stud Spider*	Black blanket appaloosa
3085	Mustang	(T) *Mustang*	Gl, Gold Charm
	Hobo	(C) *Hobo*	Buckskin
	Stable Set	(S) *Lying Thoroughbred Foal*	Dark bay
		(S) *Standing Thoroughbred Foal*	Dark bay
		(S) *Quarter Horse Mare*	Dark bay
		(S) *Quarter Horse Stallion*	Dark bay
3090	Benji and Tiffany Set	(O) *Benji*	Tan
		(O) *Tiffany*	M/Sg, white
3095	Brenda Breyer Gift Set	(T) *Appaloosa Performance Horse*	Dark chestnut blanket appaloosa
	Breyer Rider Gift Set	(T) *Adios*	Palomino
3096	Kelly Reno and Little Man Gift Set	(T) *Stock Horse Stallion*	Palomino
3097	Arabian Mare and Foal	(C) *Arabian Foal*	Dappled bay
		(C) *Arabian Mare*	Dappled bay
3120	Running Mare	(T) *Running Mare*	Gl, Gold Charm
3123	Deer Family	(O) *Deer Family*	Tan
3130	Running Foal	(T) *Running Foal*	Gl, Gold Charm
3155	Thoroughbred Mare and Foal Gift Set	(T) *Nursing Foal*	Light chestnut
		(T) *Thoroughbred Mare*	Dark chestnut/bay
3160	Proud Mother and Newborn Foal	(T) *Lady Roxanna*	Dark chestnut
		(C) *Andalusian Foal*	Apricot dun
3161	Proud Mother and Newborn Foal	(T) *Lady Roxanna*	Apricot dun
		(C) *Andalusian Foal*	Dark bay
3162	Arabian Stallion and Frisky Foal Set	(T) *Sham*	Bay
		(C) *Arabian Foal*	Gray
3163	Arabian Stallion and Frisky Foal Set	(T) *Sham*	Bay-going-gray
		(C) *Arabian Foal*	Light bay
3165	Buttons and Bows Gift Set	(T) *Grazing Foal*	Chestnut/red dun
		(T) *Grazing Mare*	Chestnut/red dun
3170	Circus Extravaganza Set	(T) *Clydesdale Stallion*	Roan/flea bit gray; red, white, and blue bobs
		(L) *Clydesdale*	Bay
3175	Action Drafters, Big and Small	(T) *Friesian*	Dark bay
		(L) *Clydesdale*	Grulla/roan
3180	Medicine Hat Mare and Foal Gift Set	(T) *Nursing Foal*	Chestnut pinto
		(T) *Thoroughbred Mare*	Chestnut pinto
3197	Amber and Ashley, Twin Morgan Foals	(T) *Amber*	Chestnut
		(T) *Ashley*	Chestnut
3234	A Pony For Keeps	(C) *Ginger*	Alabaster
		(C) *Merrylegs*	Alabaster
		(C) *Might Tango*	Light dapple gray
		(C) *Mustang Stallion*	Chestnut, gray lower legs
3345	King of the Wind Set	(C) *Black Beauty*	Bay
		(C) *Black Stallion*	Blood bay
		(C) *Duchess*	Alabaster
3346	Hanoverian Family	(C) *Andalusian Foal*	Bay
		(C) *Ginger*	Light bay
		(C) *Keen*	Black
3347	Trakehner Family	(C) *Duchess*	Light dapple gray
		(C) *Jet Run*	Dark red chestnut
		(C) *Mustang Foal*	Bay
3348	Fine Horse Family	(C) *Kelso*	Roan
		(C) *Mustang Foal*	Roan
		(C) *Silky Sullivan*	Dark chestnut/bay
3349	Appaloosa Mustang Family Gift Set	(C) *Mustang Foal*	Bay appaloosa
		(C) *Mustang Mare*	Black blanket appaloosa
		(C) *Mustang Stallion*	Dun appaloosa
3350	Misty II, Black Mist, and Twister	(C) *Mesteno The Foal*	Alabaster
		(C) *Ruffian*	Chestnut pinto
		(C) *Swaps*	Black pinto
3447	Cow Family	(O) *Cow*	Black and white pinto pattern
		(O) *Calf*	Black and white pinto pattern
3448	Jersey Cow Family Gift Set	(O) *Cow*	Tan (polled)
		(O) *Calf*	Tan
4000	1: Arabian Foal	(C) *Arabian Foal*	Alabaster
	2: Arabian Foal	(C) *Arabian Foal*	Black
	3: Arabian Foal	(C) *Arabian Foal*	Chestnut
	4: Arabian Foal	(C) *Arabian Foal*	Gray
4001	1: Quarter Horse Foal	(C) *Quarter Horse Foal*	Red bay
	2: Quarter Horse Foal	(C) *Quarter Horse Foal*	Black
	3: Quarter Horse Foal	(C) *Quarter Horse Foal*	Palomino
4031	Fighting Stallion	(T) *Fighting Stallion*	Wedgewood
4051	Five Gaiter	(T) *Five Gaiter*	Wedgewood, black on blue ribbons
4085	Mustang	(T) *Mustang*	Wedgewood
4120	Running Mare	(T) *Running Mare*	Wedgewood
4130	Running Foal	(T) *Running Foal*	Wedgewood
4810	The Dawning, Mesteno and Mother	(C) *Mesteno The Foal*	Light dun
		(C) *Mesteno's Mother*	Buckskin
4811	The Challengers, Mesteno and Sombra	(C) *Fighting Mesteno*	Dark buckskin
		(C) *Sombra*	Grulla
4812	The Progeny Gift Set, Mesteno and His Yearling	(C) *Charging Mesteno*	M/Sg, dark buckskin
		(C) *Rojo*	Light red dun
5001	Saddlebred	(S) *Saddlebred*	Dapple gray
5002	Saddlebred	(S) *Saddlebred*	Bay
5010	1: Arabian Stallion	(S) *Arabian Stallion*	Dapple gray
	2: Arabian Stallion	(S) *Morgan Stallion*	Dapple gray
5011	Arabian Mare	(S) *Arabian Mare*	Dapple gray
5013	1: Arabian Stallion	(S) *Arabian Stallion*	Bay
	2: Arabian Stallion	(S) *Morgan Stallion*	Bay
5014	Arabian Mare	(S) *Arabian Mare*	Bay
5016	1: Arabian Stallion	(S) *Arabian Stallion*	Alabaster
	2: Arabian Stallion	(S) *Morgan Stallion*	Alabaster
5017	Arabian Mare	(S) *Arabian Mare*	Alabaster
5019	Standing Thoroughbred	(S) *Citation*	Bay
5020	Citation	(S) *Citation*	Bay
5021	Swaps	(S) *Swaps*	Chestnut
5022	Silky Sullivan	(S) *Silky Sullivan*	Dark chestnut
5023	Native Dancer	(S) *Native Dancer*	Gray
5024	Seabiscuit	(S) *Seabiscuit*	Bay
5025	Running Thoroughbred	(S) *Seabiscuit*	Black
5026	Thoroughbred Mare	(S) *Thoroughbred Mare*	Chestnut
5028	Thoroughbred Mare	(S) *Thoroughbred Mare*	Black
5030	Thoroughbred Mare	(S) *Thoroughbred Mare*	Bay
5035	Morgan Stallion	(S) *Morgan Stallion*	Bay
5036	Morgan Stallion	(S) *Morgan Stallion*	Black
5037	Morgan Stallion	(S) *Morgan Stallion*	Chestnut
5038	Morgan Mare	(S) *Morgan Mare*	Bay
5039	Morgan Mare	(S) *Morgan Mare*	Black
5040	Morgan Mare	(S) *Morgan Mare*	Chestnut
5045	Quarter Horse Stallion	(S) *Quarter Horse Stallion*	Palomino
5046	Quarter Horse Stallion	(S) *Quarter Horse Stallion*	M/Sg, chestnut
5047	Quarter Horse Stallion	(S) *Quarter Horse Stallion*	Buckskin
5048	Quarter Horse Mare	(S) *Quarter Horse Mare*	Palomino
5049	Quarter Horse Mare	(S) *Quarter Horse Mare*	Chestnut
5050	Quarter Horse Mare	(S) *Quarter Horse Mare*	Buckskin
5055	Draft Horse	(S) *Draft Horse*	Dark or light sorrel/chestnut
5060	Saddlebred Mare	(S) *Saddlebred Mare*	Sorrel

5110	Saddlebred	(S) *Saddlebred*	Black
5120	Arabian Stallion	(S) *Arabian Stallion*	Dark gray
5130	Arabian Mare	(S) *Arabian Mare*	Alabaster
5140	Thoroughbred Mare	(S) *Thoroughbred Mare*	Dark bay
5141	Thoroughbred Mare	(S) *Thoroughbred Mare*	Red chestnut
5150	Morgan Stallion	(S) *Morgan Stallion*	Chestnut
5160	Morgan Mare	(S) *Morgan Mare*	Palomino
5175	Standing Thoroughbred	(S) *Citation*	Alabaster
5176	Thoroughbred Racehorse	(S) *Swaps*	Red chestnut
5177	Thoroughbred Racehorse	(S) *Silky Sullivan*	Black
5178	Appaloosa	(S) *Native Dancer*	Bay appaloosa
5179	Running Paint	(S) *Seabiscuit*	Chestnut pinto
5180	Draft Horse	(S) *Draft Horse*	Dapple gray
5181	Arabian Stallion	(S) *Arabian Stallion*	Bay
5182	Arabian Mare	(S) *Arabian Mare*	Palomino
5183	Thoroughbred Mare	(S) *Thoroughbred Mare*	Dark gray
5184	Morgan Stallion	(S) *Morgan Stallion*	Bay
5185	Morgan Mare	(S) *Morgan Mare*	Red chestnut
5186	Quarter Horse Stallion	(S) *Quarter Horse Stallion*	Bay
5187	Draft Horse	(S) *Draft Horse*	Bay
5650	Saddle Club Collection	(S) *Arabian Mare*	Dapple gray
		(S) *Draft Horse*	Alabaster
		(S) *Morgan Stallion*	Bay
		(S) *Seabiscuit*	Chestnut
		(S) *Thoroughbred Mare*	Black
	Saddle Club Stablemates	(S) *Arabian Mare*	Dark gray
		(S) *Citation*	Buckskin
		(S) *Native Dancer*	Red bay pinto
		(S) *Silky Sullivan*	Mahogany bay
		(S) *Swaps*	Red leopard appaloosa
5700	Thoroughbred Lying and Standing Foals	(S) *Lying Thoroughbred Foal*	Bay
		(S) *Standing Thoroughbred Foal*	Bay
5701	Thoroughbred Lying and Standing Foals	(S) *Lying Thoroughbred Foal*	Black
		(S) *Standing Thoroughbred Foal*	Black
5702	Thoroughbred Lying and Standing Foals	(S) *Lying Thoroughbred Foal*	Chestnut
		(S) *Standing Thoroughbred Foal*	Chestnut
7701	Benji	(O) *Benji*	M/Sg, tan
9001	Arabian Stallion	(L) *Arabian Stallion*	Bay
		(L) *Arabian Stallion*	Chestnut
		(L) *Arabian Stallion*	Gray
9005	Morgan Horse Stallion	(L) *Morgan Stallion*	Black
		(L) *Morgan Stallion*	Chestnut
		(L) *Morgan Stallion*	Bay
9010	Thoroughbred Stallion	(L) *Thoroughbred Stallion*	Red bay
		(L) *Thoroughbred Stallion*	Chestnut
		(L) *Thoroughbred Stallion*	Black
9015	Quarter Horse Stallion	(L) *Quarter Horse Stallion*	Bay
		(L) *Quarter Horse Stallion*	Buckskin

		(L) *Quarter Horse Stallion*	Palomino
9020	Unicorn	(L) *Unicorn*	Alabaster
9025	Clydesdale	(L) *Clydesdale*	Chestnut
9030	American Saddlebred	(L) *American Saddlebred*	Bay
		(L) *American Saddlebred*	Red chestnut
		(L) *American Saddlebred*	Palomino
9035	Bay Pinto	(L) *Quarter Horse Stallion*	Bay pinto
9040	Appaloosa	(L) *Quarter Horse Stallion*	Black blanket appaloosa
9045	Arabian Stallion	(L) *Arabian Stallion*	Alabaster
9050	Morgan Stallion	(L) *Morgan Stallion*	Sorrel/palomino
9055	Thoroughbred Stallion	(L) *Thoroughbred Stallion*	Dark gray
9060	Quarter Horse Stallion	(L) *Quarter Horse Stallion*	Black leopard appaloosa
9065	Shire	(L) *Clydesdale*	Black
9070	American Saddlebred	(L) *American Saddlebred*	Black pinto
9075	Paint	(L) *Quarter Horse Stallion*	Black pinto
9080	Appaloosa	(L) *Quarter Horse Stallion*	Chestnut appaloosa
9900	Riding Stable Set	(S) *Riding Stable Set*	Pine Lodge Riding School
9950	Bitsy Breyer Riding Academy	(L) *Morgan Stallion*	Bay
9960	Kipper	(T) *Kipper*	Chocolate brown
19841	Open Top Buggy	(T) *Proud Arabian Stallion*	Fl, chestnut
19842	The Doctor's Buggy	(C) *Black Stallion*	Fl, bay
19843	Family to Church on Sunday	(C) *Duchess*	Fl, bay
		(C) *Jet Run*	Fl, bay
19845	Joey's Pony Cart	(C) *Merrylegs*	Fl, black pinto
19846	Delivery Wagon	(C) *Keen*	Fl, chestnut, Miniature Collection
59971	Morgan and Foal	(S) *Morgan Stallion*	Buckskin
		(S) *Lying Foal*	Buckskin
59972	Pinto Mare and Foal	(S) *Arabian Mare*	Chestnut pinto
		(S) *Lying Foal*	Chestnut pinto
59973	Appaloosa and Foal	(S) *Quarter Horse Stallion*	Black leopard appaloosa
		(S) *Standing Foal*	Black blanket appaloosa
59974	Arabian and Foal	(S) *Arabian Stallion*	Chestnut
		(S) *Standing Foal*	Light chestnut
79192	Fine Porcelain Icelandic Horse	(T) *Porcelain Icelandic Horse*	Buckskin pinto
79193	Fine Porcelain Shire	(T) *Porcelain Shire*	Bay
79194	Fine Porcelain Spanish Barb	(T) *Porcelain Spanish Barb*	Grulla
79195	Fine Porcelain Premier Arabian Mare	(T) *Porcelain Premier Arabian Mare*	Light gray, wearing traditional Arabian costume
79196	All American Saddlebred in Parade Costume	(T) *Porcelain Saddlebred in Parade Costume*	Palomino, wearing parade costume
79296	Fine Porcelain Premier Series Circus Ponies in Costume	(T) *Porcelain Circus Ponies in Costume*	Alabaster, wearing circus costume
79197	Fine Porcelain Premier Series Great Horse in Armor	(T) *Porcelain Great Horse in Armor*	Black, wearing armor
79293	Performing Misty	(T) *Performing Misty*	Gl, palomino pinto porcelain Hagen-Renaker

163

Special Run Models by Year

This section lists the special run models by year. This should help you find a model when you know in which year it was produced. You should use this list to locate the mold you need, then refer to the appropriate section for more information. Keep in mind that, especially in Breyer's early days of producing special run models, they (or their customers) did not always name the models or sets.

The following conventions apply to this list:
    1.) mold names are shown in **bold italics**;
    2.) model color is given in parenthesis following the mold name;
    3.) when no finish is given (matte, semi-gloss, etc.), the model is assumed to have a matte finish.

The abbreviations for the following list are:

T = Traditional scale	S = Stablemate scale	Sg = Semi-gloss
C = Classic scale	O = Other Animal	Fl = Flocked
L = Little Bits scale	Gl = Glossy	M = Matte

Uncertain years
?? (T) *Sham* (Gold bay): Source unknown
??? (O) *Elephant* (Sg/Gl, gold): Source unknown
56? – 60s? (O) *Boxer* (Gl, white/very light shaded gray): Dog breeder
74? (O) *Buffalo* (Light smoke gray): Movie props

1974
Black Angus Calf (O) *Calf* (Black): Bentley Sales

1978
(T) *Adios* (Buckskin): Vales of Phoenix
(T) *Family Arabian Foal* (Black): Model Congress
(T) *Family Arabian Mare* (Black): Model Congress
(T) *Family Arabian Stallion* (M/Sg, black): Model Congress
(T) *Mustang* (Sg, black, no markings): Model Congress

1979
(T) *Clydesdale Foal* (Dapple gray, "wild dapple"): Mail-order companies
(T) *Clydesdale Mare* (Dapple gray, "wild dapple"): Mail-order companies
(T) *Running Mare* (Buckskin): JC Penney
(T) *Belgian* (Sg, dapple gray; yellow on red tail ribbon): Model Congress/mail-order companies (Riegseckers, and others); also available 1984
(T) *Clydesdale Stallion* (M/Sg, light dapple gray, gold bobs and tail ribbon): Mail-order companies; also available 1984 – 85

1980
(T) *Lady Phase* (Buckskin, bald face): Model Congress and VaLes
(T) *Adios* (Unpainted): JAH
(T) *Black Beauty* (Unpainted): JAH
(T) *Cantering Welsh Pony* (Unpainted): JAH
(T) *Clydesdale Mare* (Unpainted): JAH
(T) *Five Gaiter* (Unpainted): JAH
(T) *Foundation Stallion* (Unpainted): JAH
(T) *Hanoverian* (Unpainted): JAH
(T) *Indian Pony* (Unpainted): JAH
(T) *Lady Phase* (Unpainted): JAH
(T) *Legionario* (Unpainted): JAH
(T) *Morgan* (Unpainted): JAH
(T) *Morganglanz* (Unpainted): JAH
(T) *Proud Arabian Mare* (Unpainted): JAH
(T) *Proud Arabian Stallion* (Unpainted): JAH
(T) *Saddlebred Weanling* (Unpainted): JAH
(T) *Stud Spider* (Unpainted): JAH
(T) *Trakehner* (Unpainted): JAH
(O) *Calf* (Unpainted): Mail-order sources
(O) *Elephant* (Unpainted): Source unknown
Duroc Hog (O) *Jasper The Market Hog* (Red and brown): Hog Breeders Association
Hampshire Hog (O) *Jasper the Market Hog* (Black and white): Hog Breeders Association
Hog (O) *Jasper the Market Hog* (Tan): Hog Breeders Association
Hog (O) *Jasper the Market Hog* (Black): Hog Breeders Association
Poland China Hog (O) *Jasper the Market Hog* (White with black spots): Hog Breeders Association
Yorkshire Hog (O) *Jasper the Market Hog* (White): Hog Breeders Association

1980s (specific year unknown)
(T) *Adios* (M/Sg, black): Model Horse Congress
(T) *Cantering Welsh Pony* (Dun, no ribbons): Model Horse Congress

1981
(T) *Pacer* (Bay): Sears; also available 1982 – 85

1982
(T) *Belgian* (Sg, black; yellow on red ribbon): Montgomery Wards; also available 1983
(T) *Family Arabian Foal* (Dark chestnut): JC Penney
(T) *Family Arabian Mare* (Dark chestnut): JC Penney
(T) *Family Arabian Stallion* (Liver chestnut): JC Penney
(T) *Jumping Horse* (Seal brown): Sears; also available 1983
(T) *Pacer* (Bay): Sears; also available 1981, and 1983 – 85
(T) *Pacer* (Black): Aldens
(T) *Pacer* (Sorrel): JC Penney; also available 1983
(T) *Running Foal* (Red roan): Model Horse Congress
(T) *Running Mare* (Palomino): Montgomery Wards
(T) *Running Mare* (M/Sg, red roan): Model Horse Congress
(T) *Shire* (Sg, dapple gray): Montgomery Ward; also available 1983
Clydesdale Family Set (T) *Clydesdale Foal* (Bay, "true bay"), (T) *Clydesdale Mare* (Red bay, "true bay"), (T) *Clydesdale Stallion* (Bay, "true bay," red bobs, stenciled stockings): JC Penney; also available 1983 – 84
Pinto Mare and Suckling Foal (T) *Nursing Foal* (Bay pinto), (T) *Thoroughbred Mare* (Bay pinto): Sears; also available 1983

1983
(T) *Belgian* (Sg, black; yellow on red ribbon): Montgomery Wards; also available 1982
(T) *Family Arabian Foal* (Light chestnut): JC Penney
(T) *Family Arabian Mare* (Chestnut/sorrel): JC Penney
(T) *Family Arabian Stallion* (Chestnut/sorrel): JC Penney
(T) *Jumping Horse* (Seal brown): Sears; also available 1982
(T) *Old Timer* (Alabaster): Montgomery Wards
(T) *Pacer* (Bay): Sears; also available 1981 – 82, and 1984 – 85
(T) *Pacer* (Sorrel): JC Penney; also available 1982
(T) *Running Foal* (Buckskin): JC Penney
(T) *Running Foal* (Dapple gray): Mail-order
(T) *Running Mare* (Dapple gray, gray mane and tail): Mail-order companies
(T) *Shire* (Sg, dapple gray): Montgomery Ward; also available 1982
Arabian Stallion with English Tack Set (T) *Proud Arabian Stallion* (Bay): JC Penney; also available 1984
Assorted Mare and Foals Stable Set (T) *Proud Arabian Foal* (Red bay), (T) *Proud Arabian Mare* (Red bay), (T) *Stock Horse Foal* (Gray blanket appaloosa), (T) *Stock Horse Foal (Rough Coat)* (Palomino pinto): JC Penney
Clydesdale (T) *Clydesdale Mare* (Fl, bay, red ribbons): Sears; also available 1984
Clydesdale Family Set (T) *Clydesdale Foal* (Bay, "true bay"), (T) *Clydesdale Mare* (Red bay, "true bay"), (T) *Clydesdale Stallion* (Bay, "true bay," red bobs, stenciled stockings): JC Penney; also available 1982 and 1984
Palomino Horse and Foal Set (T) *Foundation Stallion* (Palomino), (T) *Stock Horse Foal* (Palomino): Montgomery Ward
Pinto Mare and Suckling Foal (T) *Nursing Foal* (Bay pinto), (T) *Thoroughbred Mare* (Bay pinto): Sears; also available 1982
Quarter Horse Mare and Foal Set (T) *Lady Phase* (Buckskin, solid or bald face), (T)

Stock Horse Foal (Buckskin, bald face): JC Penney; also available 1984

Stock Horse Family (T) **Stock Horse Foal** (Gray blanket appaloosa), (T) **Stock Horse Mare** (Gray blanket appaloosa), (T) **Stock Horse Stallion** (Gray blanket appaloosa): Sears

1984

(T) *Belgian* (Sg, black, white on light blue ribbon): Disney World

(T) *Belgian* (Red roan, red on white ribbon): Horses International

(T) *Belgian* (Palomino, red on yellow ribbons): Riegseckers

(T) *Belgian* (Sorrel, red on yellow ribbon): Riegseckers

(T) *Belgian* (Sg, dapple gray; yellow on red tail ribbon): Model Congress/mail-order companies (Riegseckers, and others); also available 1979

(T) *Belgian* (Dapple gray; gold tail ribbon): Dick Eighmey's Wagon Shop; also available 1985 – 86

(T) *Clydesdale Stallion* (M/Sg, light dapple gray, gold bobs and tail ribbon): Mail-order companies; also available 1979

(T) *Foundation Stallion* (Alabaster): Mail-order companies

(T) *Haflinger* (Sorrel): Horses International; also available 1985

(T) *Legionario* (Chestnut): Model Congress and mail-order companies

(T) *Midnight Sun* (Sorrel, black on red ribbons): Model Horse Congress

(T) *Old Timer* (M/Sg, dapple gray): Liquor company

(T) *Pacer* (Bay): Sears; also available 1981 – 83, and 1985

(T) *Pacer* (Light chestnut/sorrel): Reigseckers

(T) *Pacer* (M-Sg, dapple gray): Reigseckers

(T) *Pacer* (Palomino): Reigseckers

(T) *Proud Arabian Stallion* (Fl, bay): Montgomery Ward

(T) *Quarter Horse Gelding* (M (or fl), bay): Mail-order companies

(T) *Shetland Pony* (Black pinto): Sears; also available 1985

Arabian Stallion with English Tack Set (T) **Proud Arabian Stallion** (Bay): JC Penney; also available 1983

Clydesdale (T) **Clydesdale Mare** (Fl, bay, red ribbons): Sears; also available 1983

Quarter Horse Mare and Foal Set (T) **Lady Phase** (Buckskin, solid or bald face), (T) **Stock Horse Foal** (Buckskin, bald face): JC Penney; also available 1983

Appaloosa Family (C) **Quarter Horse Foal** (Black blanket appaloosa), (C) **Quarter Horse Mare** (Black blanket appaloosa), (C) **Quarter Horse Stallion** (Black blanket appaloosa): Montgomery Ward

Appaloosa Stallion (T) **Appaloosa Performance Horse** (Gray blanket appaloosa): JC Penney

Brown and White Pinto Stock Horse (T) **Stock Horse Stallion** (Bay pinto): JC Penney

Classic Andalusian Family (C) **Andalusian Foal** (Bay), (C) **Andalusian Mare** (Alabaster), (C) **Andalusian Stallion** (Dapple gray): Sears

Classic Arabian Family (C) **Arabian Foal** (Red bay), (C) **Arabian Mare** (Alabaster), (C) **Arabian Stallion** (Bay): Sears; also available 1985

Clydesdale Family Set (T) **Clydesdale Foal** (Bay, "true bay"), (T) **Clydesdale Mare** (Red bay, "true bay"), (T) **Clydesdale Stallion** (Bay, "true bay," red bobs, stenciled stockings): JC Penney; also available 1982 – 83

Collectible Stock Horse Family (T) **Action Stock Horse Foal** (Buckskin, black points), (T) **Stock Horse Mare** (Buckskin), (T) **Stock Horse Stallion** (Buckskin): Sears

Collector's Mare and Foal Set (T) **Running Foal** (Fl, palomino), (T) **Running Mare** (Fl, palomino): JC Penney

Guernsey Cow (O) **Cow** (Sg, brown and white): Mail-order sources

Jersey Cow (O) **Cow** (Sg, dark tan): Mail-order sources

Marguerite Henry's Stormy and Misty (T) **Misty** (Fl, palomino pinto), (T) **Stormy** (Fl, chestnut pinto): Sears

One Horse Open Sleigh (C) **Black Beauty** (Fl, dapple gray): JC Penney

Pinto Mare and Foal Set (T) **Stock Horse Mare** (Black pinto), (T) **Action Stock Horse Foal** (Black pinto): JC Penney; also available 1985

Red Angus (O) **Black Angus Bull** (Chestnut): Red Angus Association

Running Horse Family Set (T) **Black Beauty** (Red bay), (T) **Running Foal** (Bay), (T) **Running Mare** (Bay, no socks): Sears

Saddlebred Weanling (T) **Saddlebred Weanling** (Sorrel): JAH

Sam I Am (T) **Stock Horse Stallion** (Dark bay pinto): Breeder, JAH, retail stores

Stallion Mare and Foal Set (T) **Action Stock Horse Foal** (Red bay), (T) **Stock Horse Stallion** (Light gray): JC Penney

Unicorn (T) **Smoky** (Fl, white): JC Penney

1985

(L) *American Saddlebred* (Sorrel): Reeves/Breyer, and Breakfast events; also available in 1990

(T) *Belgian* (Dapple gray; gold tail ribbon): Dick Eighmey's Wagon Shop; also available 1984 and 1986

(S) *Draft Horse* (Gray): Riegseckers

(S) *Draft Horse* (Black): Riegseckers

(S) *Draft Horse* (Palomino): Riegseckers

(S) *Draft Horse* (Chestnut): Riegseckers

(S) *Draft Horse* (Red sorrel): Riegseckers

(S) *Draft Horse* (Red roan): Riegseckers

(S) *Draft Horse* (Unpainted): Riegseckers

(T) *Haflinger* (Sorrel): Horses International; also available 1984

(T) *Legionario* (Fl, white): JC Penney

(T) *Pacer* (Bay): Sears; also available 1981 – 84

(T) *Proud Arabian Mare* (Light chestnut): Model Horse Congress

(T) *Shetland Pony* (Black pinto): Sears; also available 1984

(T) *Shire* (Bay): Riegseckers

(T) *Shire* (Black): Riegseckers

(T) *Shire* (Gray): Riegseckers

(T) *Shire* (Palomino, same color mane and tail): Riegseckers

(L) *Unicorn* (White, blue accents): Montgomery Wards

Black Gold (T) **San Domingo** (M/Sg, black): Montgomery Ward

Circus Set with Ringmaster (T) **Fighting Stallion** (Fl, white): JC Penney

Fanciful Mare and Pony Set (T) **Running Foal** (Fl, white), (T) **Running Mare** (Fl, white; pink mane and tail): JC Penney

Merry Go Round Horse (L) **Morgan Stallion** (Light purple): JC Penney

Mustang Family (C) **Mustang Foal** (Chestnut pinto), (C) **Mustang Mare** (Bay/chestnut), (C) **Mustang Stallion** (Buckskin): Sears

My Companion Rocking Horse (T) **Saddlebred Weanling** (Fl, white): JC Penney

My Favorite Rocking Horse (T) **Saddlebred Weanling** (Fl, purple): JC Penney

Our Rocking Horse (T) **Saddlebred Weanling** (Fl, black appaloosa): JC Penney

Pegasus Flying Horse (C) **Lipizzan Stallion** (Fl, blue toned white): JC Penney

Pinto Mare and Foal Set (T) **Stock Horse Mare** (Black pinto), (T) **Action Stock Horse Foal** (Black pinto): JC Penney; also available 1984

Polled Shorthorn Bull (O) **Charolais Bull** (Dark brown): Shorthorn Breeders Association

Polled Simmental Bull (O) **Charolais Bull** (Brown and white): Simmental breeders Association

Sky Blue Unicorn (T) **Running Stallion** (Fl, turquoise blue): JC Penney

Classic Arabian Family (C) **Arabian Foal** (Red bay), (C) **Arabian Mare** (Alabaster), (C) **Arabian Stallion** (Bay): Sears; also available 1984

1986

(T) *Adios* (Shaded chestnut): Longhorn-Potts

(T) *Belgian* (Dapple gray; gold tail ribbon): Dick Eighmey's Wagon Shop; also available 1984 – 85

(T) *Belgian* (Dapple gray; red on yellow tail ribbon): Your Horse Source and other mail-order companies; also available 1987 and 1988

(T) *Cantering Welsh Pony* (Dapple gray, red ribbons): JAH

(T) *Hanoverian* (Dapple gray): Horses International

(T) *Proud Arabian Mare* (Black): horse shows

(T) *Stud Spider* (Bay/chestnut): Your Horse Source

Breyers Traditional Collector's Family Set (T) **Stock Horse Mare** (Bay roan peppercorn appaloosa), (T) **Action Stock Horse Foal** (Bay roan peppercorn appaloosa), (T) **Stock Horse Stallion** (Bay roan peppercorn appaloosa): JC Penney

Collector's Edition Appaloosa Family (C) **Quarter Horse Foal** (Chestnut blanket appaloosa), (C) **Quarter Horse Mare** (Chestnut blanket appaloosa), (C) **Quarter Horse Stallion** (Chestnut blanket appaloosa): Sears

Little Bits Horse Assortment (L) **Thoroughbred Stallion** (1 each in bay, black, and chestnut): JC Penney

1987

(T) *Adios* (Dapple gray): Black Horse Ranch and other mail-order companies

(T) *Adios* (Palomino; same color mane and tail): Black Horse Ranch and other mail-order companies

(T) *Belgian* (Sg, black, red on white ribbons): Mail-order

(T) *Belgian* (Bay, red on yellow tail ribbon): Mail-order companies

(T) *Belgian* (Sorrel): Mail-order companies

(T) *Belgian* (Blue roan blanket appaloosa, yellow on red tail ribbon): Mail-order companies

(T) *Belgian* (Dapple gray; red on yellow tail ribbon): Your Horse Source and other mail-order companies; also available 1986 and 1988

(T) *Cantering Welsh Pony* (Red bay, alternating red and yellow ribbons): Officially unreleased

(T) *Cantering Welsh Pony* (Dapple gray, gold ribbons): Small World

(T) *Clydesdale Mare* (Light dapple gray): Mail-order companies

(T) *Clydesdale Stallion* (Dapple gray, red and white bobs, red tail ribbon): Mail-order companies

(T) *El Pastor* (Bay, solid face): horse owner

(T) *Hanoverian* (Alabaster): Your Horse Source

(T) *Hanoverian* (Medium bay): Your Horse Source

(T) *Hanoverian* (Red chestnut): Your Horse Source

(T) *Hanoverian* (Black): Your Horse Source

(T) *Indian Pony* (Gray leopard appaloosa): Black Horse Ranch

(T) *Indian Pony* (Bay): Black Horse Ranch

(T) *Indian Pony* (Black leopard appaloosa): Black Horse Ranch

(T) *Indian Pony* (Dapple gray): Black Horse Ranch

(T) *Proud Arabian Stallion* (Red bay): Black Horse Ranch

(T) *Proud Arabian Stallion* (Black): Black Horse Ranch

(T) **Proud Arabian Stallion** (Sorrel): Black Horse Ranch

(T) **Quarter Horse Gelding** (Chestnut): Mail-order companies

(T) **Running Foal** (Dapple gray, white mane and tail): Sears

(T) **Running Mare** (Light dapple gray; white mane and tail): Sears

(T) **Trakehner** (Chestnut): JAH special

(T) **Trakehner** (Bay): Small World

Traditional Western Horse Collector Set (T) **Adios** (Chestnut leopard appaloosa), (T) **Foundation Stallion** (Sg, charcoal/chocolate chestnut), (T) **San Domingo** (Bay, hind stockings): JC Penney

Triple Crown Winners Set I (C) **Kelso** (Chestnut), (C) **Silky Sullivan** (Chestnut), (C) **Terrang** (Dark bay/chestnut): Hobby Center Toys

U.S. Olympic Team Set (C) **Jet Run** (Chestnut), (C) **Keen** (Gray), (C) **Might Tango** (Bay): Sears

1988

(T) **Belgian** (Dapple gray; red on yellow tail ribbon): Your Horse Source and other mail-order companies; also available 1986 – 87

(T) **Cantering Welsh Pony** (Red roan, yellow ribbons): Small World

(T) **Cantering Welsh Pony** (Red dun, metallic blue ribbons): Small World

(T) **Cantering Welsh Pony** (Liver chestnut, green ribbons): Small World

(T) **Cantering Welsh Pony** (Flea bit gray, red ribbons): Small World

(T) **Clydesdale Foal** (Black): Horses International

(T) **Clydesdale Foal** (Dapple gray): Horses International

(T) **Clydesdale Foal** (Gray): Horses International

(T) **Family Arabian Foal** (Gl, alabaster): Enchanted Doll

(T) **Family Arabian Mare** (Gl, alabaster): Enchanted Doll

(T) **Family Arabian Stallion** (Gl, alabaster): Enchanted Doll

(T) **Mustang** (Alabaster): Black Horse Ranch

(T) **Mustang** (Bay blanket appaloosa): Black Horse Ranch

(T) **Mustang** (Black leopard appaloosa): Black Horse Ranch

(T) **Mustang** (Palomino): Black Horse Ranch

(T) **Mustang** (Flea-bit gray): Black Horse Ranch

(T) **Mustang** (Red dun): Black Horse Ranch

(T) **Phar Lap** (Red bay): Your Horse Source

(T) **Phar Lap** (Dark chestnut): Your Horse Source

(T) **Phar Lap** (Dark dapple gray): Your Horse Source

(T) **Phar Lap** (Sorrel): Your Horse Source

(T) **Running Stallion** (Sorrel): JAH

Arabian Mare and Foal Set (T) **Proud Arabian Foal** (Red bay pinto), (T) **Proud Arabian Mare** (Red bay pinto): Sears

Breyer Parade of Breeds (L) **American Saddlebred** (Brown pinto), (L) **Arabian Stallion** (Alabaster), (L) **Morgan Stallion** (Bay), (L) **Quarter Horse Stallion** (Leopard appaloosa), (L) **Quarter Horse Stallion** (Gray), (L) **Thoroughbred Stallion** (Bay): JC Penney

(C) **Bucking Bronco** (Gray): Bentley Sales Company

(C) **Bucking Bronco** (Red roan): Bentley Sales Company

(C) **Bucking Bronco** (Chestnut): Bentley Sales Company

(C) **Bucking Bronco** (Black leopard appaloosa): Bentley Sales Company

Breyer Classic Collector's Arabian Family Set (C) **Arabian Foal** (Black), (C) **Arabian Mare** (Black), (C) **Arabian Stallion** (Black): JC Penney; also available 1990

Classic Arabian Family (C) **Arabian Foal** (Dapple gray), (C) **Arabian Mare** (Dapple gray), (C) **Arabian Stallion** (Dapple gray): Export (200 – 250)

Crooked Horned Holstein Cow (O) **Cow** (Black and white pinto pattern): Mail-order sources (Black Horse Ranch, Small World)

English Horse Collector's Set (T) **Black Stallion** (Sandy bay), (T) **Indian Pony** (Red dun), (T) **Justin Morgan** (Chestnut):

Foal's First Day (C) **Arabian Foal** (Light bay), (C) **Johar** (Rose gray): Breyer Signing Party, Enchanted Doll House

Polled Ayrshire Cow (O) **Cow** (Red and white pinto pattern): Mail-order sources; also available 1993

Polled Brown Swiss Cow (O) **Cow** (Cocoa brown): Mail-order sources; also available 1993

Polled Guernsey Cow (O) **Cow** (Tan and white pinto pattern): Mail-order sources; also available 1993

Polled Holstein Cow (O) **Cow** (Black and white pinto pattern): Mail-order sources; also available 1993

Polled Jersey Cow (O) **Cow** (Dark tan, solid): Mail-order sources; also available 1993

Ruby (T) **Mustang** (Dappled chestnut/red roan): Model Horse Collector's Supply Co.

Triple Crown Winners Set II (C) **Man O'War** (Chestnut), (C) **Swaps** (Brown), (C) **Terrang** (Chestnut): Hobby Center Toys

Wildfire (T) **San Domingo** (Chestnut pinto): Model Horse Collector's Supply Co.

1989

(T) **Appaloosa Performance Horse** (Alabaster): Horses International

(T) **Appaloosa Performance Horse** (Sorrel): Horses International

(T) **Appaloosa Performance Horse** (Black leopard appaloosa): Horses International

(T) **Appaloosa Performance Horse** (Red roan): Horses International

(L) **Clydesdale** (Sg, dapple gray): Hobby Center Toys

(T) **Lady Phase** (Red roan/flea bit gray): Breyer Signing Party Model

(T) **Quarter Horse Yearling** (Black roan): JAH

(T) **Running Stallion** (Bay/chestnut): Black Horse Ranch

(C) **Quarter Horse Stallion** (Black blanket appaloosa): Montgomery Ward

Breyer Parade of Breeds Collector's Assortment 2nd Ed. (L) **American Saddlebred** (Dark bay;), (L) **Clydesdale** (Sorrel), (L) **Morgan Stallion** (Chestnut), (L) **Quarter Horse Stallion** (Black), (L) **Thoroughbred Stallion** (Bay), (L) **Arabian Stallion** (Black): JC Penney

German Olympic Set (C) **Jet Run** (Bay), (C) **Keen** (Red bay), (C) **Might Tango** (Bay): Sears

International Equestrian Collector's Set (T) **Hanoverian** (Dark dapple gray), (T) **Halla** (Flea bit gray), (T) **Morganglanz** (Bay): JC Penney

Mare and Foal Set (T) **Grazing Mare** (Bay blanket appaloosa), (T) **Nursing Foal** (Chestnut leopard appaloosa): Sears; also available 1990

Quarter Horse Mare (C) **Quarter Horse Mare** (Chestnut pinto): Export, and various mail-order companies

Silver (T) **Quarter Horse Gelding** (Slate gray; CE):

Stablemate Set (S) **Arabian Mare** (Alabaster), (S) **Arabian Stallion** (Gray), (S) **Citation** (Red leopard appaloosa), (S) **Draft Horse** (Dapple gray), (S) **Morgan Mare** (Palomino), (S) **Morgan Stallion** (Light chestnut), (S) **Native Dancer** (Blood bay), (S) **Saddlebred** (Black), (S) **Seabiscuit** (Chestnut), (S) **Silky Sullivan** (Buckskin), (S) **Swaps** (Black leopard appaloosa), (S) **Thoroughbred Mare** (Dark bay): Sears

1990

(L) **American Saddlebred** (Sorrel): Reeves/Breyer, and Breakfast events; also available 1985

(T) **Misty** (Gl, Florentine): Breyerfest '90 Raffle Model

(T) **Secretariat** (Gl, Gold Charm): Breyer Signing Party model

Appaloosa American Classic Set (T) **Appaloosa Performance Horse** (Black blanket appaloosa), (T) **Running Stallion** (Palomino blanket appaloosa), (T) **Stud Spider** (Blue roan leopard appaloosa): Sears

Bermese Her Majesty the Queen's Horse (T) **Secretariat** (Black): German Export

Breyer Classic Collector's Arabian Family Set (C) **Arabian Foal** (Black), (C) **Arabian Mare** (Black), (C) **Arabian Stallion** (Black): JC Penney; also available 1988

Breyer Parade of Breeds Collector's Assortment 3rd Edition (L) **American Saddlebred** (Palomino pinto), (L) **Clydesdale** (Dapple gray), (L) **Morgan Stallion** (Bay), (L) **Quarter Horse Stallion** (Black leopard appaloosa), (L) **Thoroughbred Stallion** (Rose gray), (L) **Arabian Stallion** (Dapple gray): JC Penney

Breyer Traditional Horse Set (T) **Lady Phase** (Dapple gray), (T) **Quarter Horse Gelding** (Palomino), (T) **Rugged Lark** (Red chestnut): JC Penney

Dr. Peaches, Three-Day Event Champion (T) **Phar Lap** (Bay): Breyerfest '90 Dinner Model

German Olympic Set (C) **Jet Run** (Bay), (C) **Keen** (Red bay), (C) **Might Tango** (Bay): Export

Mare and Foal Set (T) **Grazing Mare** (Bay blanket appaloosa), (T) **Nursing Foal** (Chestnut leopard appaloosa): Sears; also available 1989

Hatatitla, bay, (C) **Ginger** (Bay): Export

Iltschi (C) **Black Beauty** (Black): Export

Race Horse Set (T) **Man O'War** (Gl, red chestnut), (T) **Secretariat** (Gl, chestnut), (T) **Sham** (Gl, red bay): Sears

Stablemate Assortment II (S) **Arabian Mare** (Black), (S) **Arabian Stallion** (Buckskin), (S) **Citation** (Chestnut), (S) **Draft Horse** (Black), (S) **Morgan Mare** (Chestnut), (S) **Morgan Stallion** (Dark red chestnut), (S) **Native Dancer** (Black point alabaster), (S) **Seabiscuit** (Palomino/sorrel), (S) **Silky Sullivan** (Light bay), (S) **Swaps** (Rose gray). (S) **Swaps** (Dark gray), (S) **Thoroughbred Mare** (Blood bay): Sears

Three Piece Horse Set (T) **Cantering Welsh Pony** (Sg, dappled rose gray, no ribbons), (T) **Pony of the Americas** (Black leopard appaloosa), (T) **Haflinger** (Chestnut pinto): Country Store; also available 1991

Vaulting Horse (T) **Hanoverian** (Black): German Export

Western Horse (T) **Western Horse** (Chestnut pinto): JAH

1991

(T) **Jumping Horse** (Black): JAH

(T) **Legionario** (Gl, Florentine): Breyerfest '91 Raffle Model

(T) **Man O'War** (Gl, Gold Charm): Breyerfest '91 Raffle Model

(T) **San Domingo** (Gl, Copenhagen): Breyerfest '91 Raffle Model

(T) **Sham** (Wedgewood): Breyerfest '91 Raffle Model

Adorable Horse Foal Set (T) **Grazing Foal** (Bay blanket appaloosa), (T) **Lying Foal** (Sorrel), (T) **Running Foal** (Rose gray), (T) **Scratching Foal** (Alabaster): JC Penney

Breyer Quarter Horse Family (C) **Quarter Horse Foal** (Alabaster), (C) **Quarter Horse Mare** (Dark chestnut/bay), (C) **Quarter Horse Stallion** (Dark chestnut/bay): JC Penney

Galaxias (T) **Sham** (Dappled gray; cold cast porcelain): JC Penney

Mustang Lady, Endurance Champion (T) **Indian Pony** (Gray): Breyerfest '91 Dinner Model

Raven (T) **Saddlebred Weanling** (Sg, plum black): Breyer Signing Party Model

Spirit of the Wind Set (T) **Family Arabian Foal** (Dapple gray), (T) **Family Arabian**

Mare (Dapple gray): Sears

Spotted Bear (T) *San Domingo* (M/Sg, black pinto; cold cast porcelain): Sears

Stablemate Assortment III (S) *Arabian Mare* (Red chestnut), (S) *Arabian Stallion* (Black), (S) *Citation* (Dark gray), (S) *Draft Horse* (Bay), (S) *Draft Horse* (Khaki dun), (S) *Morgan Mare* (Bay), (S) *Morgan Stallion* (Palomino), (S) *Native Dancer* (Palomino), (S) *Seabiscuit* (Dapple gray),(S) *Silky Sullivan* (Red bay), (S) *Swaps* (Dark bay), (S) *Thoroughbred Mare* (Alabaster): Sears

Three Piece Horse Set (T) *Cantering Welsh Pony* (Sg, dappled rose gray, no ribbons), (T) *Pony of the Americas* (Black leopard appaloosa), (T) *Haflinger* (Chestnut pinto): Country Store; also available 1990

Arabian Horses of the World Set (T) *Family Arabian Stallion* (Black point alabaster), (T) *Proud Arabian Mare* (Flea bit gray), (T) *Proud Arabian Stallion* (Bay, blaze): Sears; also available 1992

1992

(T) *Quarter Horse Yearling* (Buckskin): Breyerfest Raffle Model

Breyer Mustang Family (C) *Mustang Foal* (Grulla), (C) *Mustang Mare* (Bay), (C) *Mustang Stallion* (Buckskin): JC Penney

Bucking Bronco (C) *Bucking Bronco* (Black pinto): Breyer Show Special

Drafters Set (T) *Belgian* (Alabaster, light blue on white tail ribbon), (T) *Roy the Belgian* (Chocolate sorrel), (T) *Shire* (Palomino; white mane and tail): Sears

Draw Horses with Sam Savitt (C) *Kelso* (Bay): Sears

Fashionably Late (T) *Sherman Morgan* (Sorrel; cold cast porcelain): Sears

Frisky Foals Set (T) *Action Stock Horse Foal* (Yellow dun), (T) *Nursing Foal* (Palomino pinto), (T) *Proud Arabian Foal* (Chestnut/bay), (T) *Running Foal* (Black blanket appaloosa): JC Penney

Future Champions Set (T) *Saddlebred Weanling* (Bay pinto): Sears

Horses Great and Small Set (C) *Merrylegs* (Palomino), (T) *Cantering Welsh Pony* (M-Sg, black, no ribbons), (T) *Clydesdale Stallion* (Grulla/roan, yellow tail ribbon, right stockings): Sears

Misty (T) *Misty* (Palomino pinto, cold cast porcelain): JC Penney

Night Deck (T) *Lady Phase* (Black): Black Horse Ranch

Night Vision (T) *Stock Horse Foal* (Dark bay snowflake appaloosa): Black Horse Ranch

Pride and Vanity (T) *Sherman Morgan* (Alabaster): JAH

Quiet Foxhunters Set (T) *John Henry* (Dark chestnut), (T) *Roemer* (Seal bay/brown), (T) *Rugged Lark* (Dappled gray): Sears

Secretariat (T) *Secretariat* (Chestnut, cold cast porcelain): Sears

Spirit of the West Gift Set (T) *Lady Phase* (Bay pinto), (T) *Stock Horse Foal* (Dark bay pinto): Sears

Turbo The Wonder Horse (T) *Mustang* (Palomino): Breyerfest '92 Dinner Model

1993

(T) *Balking Mule* (Alabaster): Black Horse Ranch

(T) *Balking Mule* (Buckskin): Black Horse Ranch

(T) *Balking Mule* (Chestnut): Black Horse Ranch

(T) *Balking Mule* (Black blanket appaloosa): Black Horse Ranch

(T) *Balking Mule* (Black leopard appaloosa): Black Horse Ranch

(T) *Balking Mule* (Dun): Black Horse Ranch

(L) *Morgan Stallion* (Light bay/buckskin): Breakfast with Peter Stone

(T) *Pluto* (Very light dapple gray): Spiegel

(T) *Proud Arabian Mare* (Gl, Silver Filigree): Breyerfest '93 Judges/Host Model

Appaloosa Sport Horse (T) *Morganglanz* (Leopard appaloosa): mid-season release

Bay Fighting Stallion (T) *Fighting Stallion* (Bay): Toys "R" Us

Breyer Three Generations Appaloosa Set (T) *Adios* (Bay blanket appaloosa), (T) *Quarter Horse Yearling* (Bay blanket appaloosa), (T) *Stock Horse Foal (Rough Coat)* (Chestnut appaloosa): JC Penney

Denver and Blaze Dutch Warmbloods (C) *Quarter Horse Foal* (Red bay), (C) *Kelso* (Mahogany bay): Aristoplay, and other retailers

Dressage Set of Two Horses (T) *Hanoverian* (Mahogany bay), (T) *Misty's Twilight* (Black, green braids): Spiegel

Drinkers of the Wind (C) *Arabian Foal* (Rose gray), (C) *Arabian Stallion* (Gray), (C) *Johar* (Flea bit gray): Toys "R" Us

Grayingham Lucky Lad (T) *Clydesdale Stallion* (Sg, black, red mane, red and white bobs and tail ribbon): Breyerfest '93 Dinner Model (less than 1500)

Little Chaparral (C) *Rearing Stallion* (Buckskin pinto): Breyer Show Special

Lipizzan Stallion (C) *Lipizzan Stallion* (Shaded alabaster): World of Horses

Nevada Star (C) *Hobo* (Silver Dust gray, slightly metallic): Breyerfest '93 Raffle model

Polled Ayrshire Cow (O) *Cow* (Red and white pinto pattern): Mail-order sources; also available 1988

Polled Brown Swiss Cow (O) *Cow* (Cocoa brown): Mail-order sources; also available 1988

Polled Guernsey Cow (O) *Cow* (Tan and white pinto pattern): Mail-order sources; also available 1988

Polled Holstein Cow (O) *Cow* (Black and white pinto pattern): Mail-order sources; also available 1988

Polled Jersey Cow (O) *Cow* (Dark tan (solid)): Mail-order sources; also available 1988

Prairie Flower - Equitana 93 (T) *Lady Phase* (Bay blanket appaloosa): Equitana 93 (German Export)

(C) *Rearing Stallion* (Buckskin): West Coast Model Horse Collector's Jamboree

Stablemate Assortment IV (S) *Arabian Mare* (Medium gray), (S) *Arabian Stallion* (Chestnut), (S) *Citation* (Dapple gray), (S) *Draft Horse* (Creamy dun), (S) *Morgan Mare* (Chocolate sorrel), (S) *Morgan Stallion* (Black blanket appaloosa), (S) *Morgan Stallion* (Dark bay), (S) *Native Dancer* (Black), (S) *Quarter Horse Stallion* (Red leopard appaloosa), (S) *Seabiscuit* (Light gray), (S) *Silky Sullivan* (Grulla/dun), (S) *Swaps* (Buckskin): Sears

Watchful Mare and Foal Set (T) *Lady Phase* (Alabaster), (T) *Stock Horse Foal* (Soft gray): Toys "R" Us

Wild Horses of America Set (T) *Fighting Stallion* (Sorrel), (T) *Foundation Stallion* (Bay blanket appaloosa), (T) *Mustang* (Sg, black): JC Penney

1994

(T) *Indian Pony* (Red roan): Breyerfest '94 Judges/Host Model

(T) *Sham* (Chocolate sorrel): West Coast Model Horse Collectors Jamboree

12 Piece Stablemates Set (S) *Arabian Mare* (Medium gray), (S) *Arabian Stallion* (Chestnut), (S) *Citation* (Dapple gray), (S) *Draft Horse* (Creamy dun), (S) *Morgan Mare* (Chocolate sorrel), (S) *Morgan Stallion* (Black blanket appaloosa), (S) *Morgan Stallion* (Dark bay), (S) *Native Dancer* (Black), (S) *Quarter Horse Stallion* (Red leopard appaloosa), (S) *Seabiscuit* (Light gray), (S) *Silky Sullivan* (Grulla/dun), (S) *Swaps* (Buckskin): JC Penney

(C) *Black Beauty* (Gl, black): Mid-season release

Bright Zip (T) *San Domingo* (Chestnut appaloosa): Breyerfest '94 Dinner Model

Chinook (T) *Indian Pony* (Dark dapple gray): Export

Domino (T) *Roemer* (Black pinto): Mid-Year release

Horse Salute Gift Set (T) *Lady Phase* (Chestnut leopard appaloosa), (T) *Morganglanz* (Bay), (T) *Phar Lap* (Dark bay): JC Penney

Moonshadows (T) *Five Gaiter* (Blue roan, silver on blue ribbons): JAH

Ofir (T) *Black Stallion* (Dark bay): Breyer Tour/Signing Party model

Silver Comet (C) *Polo Pony* (Light dapple gray): Breyer Show Special

Spanish Norman Family (C) *Andalusian Foal* (Gray), (C) *Andalusian Stallion* (Red roan), (C) *Ginger* (Alabaster): Toys "R" Us

Spirit of the East (T) *Running Foal* (Soft gray), (T) *Running Mare* (Soft gray): JC Penney

Stablemate Foal Key Chains 1: (S) *Lying Thoroughbred Foal* (Amber plastic); 2: (S) *Lying Thoroughbred Foal* (Black plastic); 3: (S) *Standing Thoroughbred Foal* (Amber plastic); 4: (S) *Standing Thoroughbred Foal* (Black plastic): (all) Breyerfest '94 Special

Steel Dust (T) *Proud Arabian Mare* (Gray): JAH

The Challengers Mesteno and Sombra (C) *Fighting Mesteno* (Dark buckskin), (C) *Sombra* (Grulla): JC Penney

Unicorn (T) *Running Stallion* (Alabaster, silver horn): Toys "R" Us

Western Horse (T) *John Henry* (Dark bay): JC Penney

Winchester (T) *Buckshot* (Gl, charcoal): Breyerfest Raffle Model

1995

(T) *Lady Phase* (Palomino): BreyerFest '95 Judges/Host Model

(T) *Cantering Welsh Pony* (Red roan): QVC

(T) *Proud Arabian Mare* (Bay): QVC

(T) *Saddlebred Weanling* (Alabaster): QVC

Art Deco Dressage Horse (T) *Hanoverian* (Black pinto): JC Penney

Race Horses of America (T) *Pacer* (Bay), (T) *Phar Lap* (Dapple gray), (T) *Stock Horse Stallion* (Dappled sorrel/chestnut): JC Penney

Buckaroo and Skeeter (C) *Arabian Mare* (Buckskin), (T) *Stormy* (Bay pinto): Toys "R" Us

Buster and Brandi Twin Appaloosa Foal Set (T) *Lying Foal* (Bay blanket appaloosa), (T) *Scratching Foal* (Bay appaloosa): JAH subscriber special

Dustin (T) *Phar Lap* (Dun): Toys "R" Us

Eagle and Pow Wow (C) *Johar* (Black pinto): mid-season release

El Campeador (T) *Legionario* (Dark dapple gray): West Coast Model Horse Collector's Jamboree

Favory (T) *Pluto* (Red roan): Export

Geronimo and Cochise (C) *Kelso* (Light bay appaloosa), (T) *Sea Star* (Bay blanket appaloosa): Toys "R" Us

Jumping Gem Twist (T) *Jumping Horse* (Alabaster): QVC

Kaleidoscope the Pinto Sporthorse (T) *Trakehner* (Red bay pinto): Breyer Tour Model

Mego (T) *Adios* (Palomino pinto): Breyerfest '95 Dinner Model

Mystique (T) *Jumping Horse* (Gl, gray blanket appaloosa): Breyerfest '95 Raffle Model

Pieraz (Cash) (T) *Morganglanz* (Flea-bit gray): USET Festival of champions

Rawhide the Wild Appaloosa Mustang (T) *Mustang* (Dun roan appaloosa): Breyer Tour Model

Riddle Passing Through Time, Phase 1 (C) *Hobo* (Bay blanket appaloosa): Mid-season release

Riddle Passing Through Time, Phase 2 (C) *Hobo* (Red semi-leopard appaloosa): Mid-season release

Riddle Passing Through Time, Phase 3 (C) *Hobo* (Red leopard appaloosa): Mid-season release

Serenity Set (T) *Grazing Mare* (Buckskin), (T) *Lying Foal* (Buckskin): JC Penney

Set of 12 Miniatures (S) *Arabian Mare* (Chestnut leopard appaloosa), (S) *Arabian Stallion* (Light bay, no black on legs), (S) *Citation* (Dun), (S) *Citation* (Liver chestnut blanket appaloosa), (S) *Morgan Mare* (Red sorrel), (S) *Morgan Stallion* (Black, gray & white mane and tail), (S) *Native Dancer* (Bay), (S) *Quarter Horse Stallion* (Chestnut), (S) *Silky Sullivan* (Rose gray), (S) *Silky Sullivan* (Red roan), (S) *Swaps* (Gray dun), (S) *Thoroughbred Mare* (Dark brown): JC Penney

Sham the Godolphin Arabian (T) *Sham* (Bay): QVC

Special Delivery (T) *Running Mare* (Dark bay): State Line Tack

Unicorn II (T) *Running Stallion* (Gl, black, gold trim): Toys "R" Us

(T) *Western Horse* (Palomino): QVC

Willow and Shining Star (C) *Rearing Stallion* (Dark bay blanket appaloosa): JAH special offer

1996:

(T) *Mustang* (Dark dapple gray/dapple black): Breyerfest '96 Judges/Host Model

(T) *Proud Arabian Mare* (Dark rose gray): Model Horse Congress

(T) *Secretariat* (Black): State Line Tack

(S) *Swaps* (Bay): Inroads Interactive (with CD ROM)

12-Piece Stablemate Set (S) *Arabian Mare* (Gray roan), (S) *Arabian Stallion* (Dark rose gray), (S) *Citation* (Bay appaloosa), (S) *Draft Horse* (Black pinto), (S) *Morgan Mare* (Light red dun), (S) *Morgan Stallion* (Alabaster), (S) *Native Dancer* (Red dun), (S) *Quarter Horse Stallion* (Buckskin), (S) *Saddlebred* (Dapple gray), (S) *Seabiscuit* (Medium red bay), (S) *Silky Sullivan* (Black leopard appaloosa), (S) *Swaps* (Bay): JC Penney

Amerigo (T) *Mustang* (Palomino pinto): Equitana USA

Appaloosa Performance Champion (T) *Haflinger* (Palomino appaloosa): Sears Wish Book

Butterscotch (S) *Arabian Mare* (Roan/leopard appaloosa): Gotz

Calypso (T) *Trakehner* (Light bay): USET

Classic Beauty Gift Set (C) *Andalusian Foal* (Shaded light gray), (C) *Black Stallion* (Flea-bit gray): Sears Wish Book

Fine Porcelain Premier Series Circus Ponies in Costume (T) *Porcelain Circus Ponies* (Alabaster with circus costume): Mid-year release

First Competitor (T) *Gem Twist* (Buckskin): Mid-year release

Flabbehoppen – Knabstrupper (T) *Misty's Twilight* (Bay leopard appaloosa): West Coast Model Horse Collectors Jamboree

Gaited Breeds of America (T) *Five Gaiter* (Bay Pinto), (T) *Midnight Sun* (Shaded liver chestnut), (T) *Saddlebred Yearling* (Palomino): JC Penney

Giltedge (T) *Aristocrat* (Florentine): Just About Horses Special Offer

Halayi (T) *Indian Pony* (Palomino appaloosa): PetSmart

Irish Warrior (T) *Secretariat* (Black): State Line Tack

Malibu (T) *Hackney* (Wedgewood Blue): BreyerFest '96 Raffle

Mighty Buck (T) *Running Stallion* (Buckskin): 1996 Tour Model

Pride and Joy (T) *Nursing Foal* (Light chestnut), (T) *Thoroughbred Mare* (Light chestnut): JC Penney

Rusty Diamond (T) *Foundation Stallion* (Shaded chestnut): Mid-States Distributing

Sapphire (T) *Black Stallion* (Buckskin): Toys "R" Us

Sassafras (T) *Cantering Welsh Pony* (Palomino pinto): Just About Horses Subscriber Special

Show Horse, Cream of Tartar (T) *Pony of the Americas* (Palomino blanket appaloosa): Show Special

Sierra (T) *Fighting Stallion* (Red roan): JAH

Snowbound (T) *Jumping Horse* (Dappled bay): USET/USOC/Miller's Harness Co.

Spotted Legacy Gift Set (T) *Proud Arabian Foal* (Chestnut pinto), (T) *Proud Arabian Mare* (Chestnut pinto): Sears Wish Book

Stablemate Foal Key Chains 1: (S) *Lying Thoroughbred Foal* (Clear plastic); 2: (S) *Lying Thoroughbred Foal* (Blue plastic); 3: (S) *Standing Thoroughbred Foal* (Clear plastic); 4: (S) *Standing Thoroughbred Foal* (Blue plastic): (all) Breyerfest '96 Special

Swedish Warmblood (T) *Morganglanz* (Palomino): JC Penney

Tennessee Walking Horse (T) *Midnight Sun* (Black, white on red ribbons): WCHE

Titan Glory (T) *Foundation Stallion* (Bay): Toys "R" Us

Tseminole Wind (T) *Sham* (Bay pinto): Breyerfest '96 Dinner Model

Unicorn 1: (C) *Lipizzan Stallion* (Sg, pearly white), 2: (C) *Lipizzan Stallion* (G, black): Toys "R" Us

Young Equestrian Team (L) *Arabian Stallion* (Chestnut), (L) *Quarter Horse Stallion* (Dark bay pinto), (L) *Thoroughbred Stallion* (Alabaster): JC Penney

1997:

(S) *Morgan Stallion* (Red roan): Götz

(T) *Misty's Twilight* (Palomino): State Line Tack

1997 Pinto Family (temp. name) (C) *Arabian Foal* (Black pinto), (C) *Black Beauty* (Bay pinto), (C) *Ginger* (Black pinto): State Line Tack

Beat the Wind — (T) *Pacer* (Shaded gray): Toys "R" Us and others

Bold — (T) *Stud Spider* (Palomino): BreyerFest '97 Dinner Model

Cactus — (T) *Balking Mule* (Red roan): BreyerFest '97 Raffle Model

Desperado, Fall Show Horse (T) *El Pastor* (Black pinto): Breyer Show Sponsors

King of Hearts, Spring Show Horse (T) *Secretariat* (Appaloosa): Breyer Show Sponsors

Kris Kringle (T) *Friesian* (Shaded dapple gray): West Coast Model Horse Collector's Jamboree

No Doubt — (T) *Family Arabian Stallion* (Red roan): Toys "R" Us

Sirocco, Breyer Breakfast Tour Horse (T) *Indian Pony* (Chestnut pinto): Breyer Breakfast Tour Stops

Stardust — (T) *Legionario* (Dapple gray): Toys "R" Us

Tennessee Walking Horse (T) *Midnight Sun* (Palomino): WCHE

Unicorn IV Black Pearl — (T) *Lying Foal* (Gl, black): Toys "R" Us

Unicorn IV White Pearl — (T) *Lying Foal* (Gl, white pearl): Toys "R" Us

Other SR models introduced in 1997 and 1998:

_____

_____

_____

_____

_____

_____

_____

_____

_____

_____

_____

_____

_____

_____

_____

_____

_____

_____

_____

_____

_____

_____

_____

_____

_____

Mold Numbers

These two lists are quick references giving you the numbers used by Breyer to designate the mold bodies. The first list is divided into the classifications (Traditional to Other Animals) and is alphabetical by mold name within each division. The second list is strictly numerical.

Mold Name	Scale/ Series	Mold Number	Year Introduced
Traditional Horse Molds			
Action Stock Horse Foal	T	236	1984
Adios	T	50	1969
Amber	T	488	1997
Appaloosa Performance Horse	T	99	1974
Aristocrat	T	496	1995
Ashley	T	489	1997
Balking Mule	T	207	1968
Belgian	T	92	1964
Big Ben	T	483	1996
Black Beauty	T	89	1979
Black Stallion	T	401	1981
Brighty	T	375	1974
Brown Sunshine	T	484	1996
Buckshot	T	415	1985
Cantering Welsh Pony	T	104	1971
Clydesdale Foal	T	84	1969
Clydesdale Mare	T	83	1969
Clydesdale Stallion	T	80	1958
Donkey	T	81	1957/1958
El Pastor	T	61	1974
Family Arabian Foal	T	9	1961
Family Arabian Mare	T	8	1961
Family Arabian Stallion	T	7	1959
Fighting Stallion	T	31	1961
Five Gaiter	T	52	1962
Foundation Stallion	T	64	1977
Friesian	T	485	1992
Fury Prancer	T	P40	1954
Galiceno	T	100	1978
Gem Twist	T	495	1993
Grazing Foal	T	151	1964
Grazing Mare	T	141	1961
Haflinger	T	156	1979
Halla	T	63	1977
Hanoverian	T	58	1980
Henry, Norwegian Fjord	T	482	1996
Ideal American Quarter Horse	T	497	1995
Indian Pony	T	175	1970
John Henry	T	445	1988
Jumping Horse	T	300	1965
Justin Morgan	T	65	1973
Khemosabi	T	460	1990
Kipper	T	9960	1986
Lady Phase	T	40	1976
Lady Roxana	T	425	1986
Legionario	T	68	1979
Llanarth True Briton	T	494	1994
Lying Down Foal	T	245	1969
Man O'War	T	47	1969
Marabella, Morgan Broodmare	T	487	1997
Midnight Sun, Tennessee Walker	T	60	1972
Misty's Twilight	T	470	1991
Misty	T	20	1972
Morgan	T	49	1965
Morganglanz	T	59	1980
Mustang	T	87	1961
Nursing Foal	T	3155FO	1973
Old Timer	T	200	1966
Pacer	T	46	1967
Phar Lap	T	90	1985
Pluto	T	475	1991
Pony of the Americas	T	155	1976
Porcelain Arabian Mare in Costume	T	79195	1995
Porcelain Circus Ponies	T	79296	1996
Porcelain Great Horse in Armor	T	79197	1997
Porcelain Icelandic Horse	T	79192	1992
Porcelain Saddlebred in Parade Tack	T	79196	1996
Porcelain Shire	T	79193	1993

Mold Name	Scale/ Series	Mold Number	Year Introduced
Porcelain Spanish Barb	T	79194	1994
Proud Arabian Foal	T	218	1956
Proud Arabian Mare	T	215	1956/1971
Proud Arabian Stallion	T	212	1971
Quarter Horse Gelding	T	98	1959
Quarter Horse Yearling	T	101	1970
Race Horse	T	36	1954
Roemer	T	465	1990
Iron Metal Chief, Missouri Fox Trotter	T	486	1997
Roy the Belgian	T	455	1989
Rugged Lark	T	450	1989
Running Foal	T	130	1963
Running Mare	T	120	1961
Running Stallion	T	210	1968
Saddlebred Weanling	T	62	1973
San Domingo	T	67	1978
Scratching Foal	T	169	1970
Sea Star	T	16	1980
Secretariat	T	435	1987
Sham	T	410	1984
Sherman Morgan	T	430	1987
Shetland Pony	T	25	1960
Shire	T	95	1972
Smoky	T	69	1981
Stock Horse Foal (Rough Coat)	T	18	1978
Stock Horse Foal	T	228	1983
Stock Horse Mare	T	227	1982
Stock Horse Stallion	T	226	1981
Stormy	T	19	1977
Stud Spider	T	66	1978
Thoroughbred Mare	T	3155MA	1973
Touch of Class	T	420	1986
Trakehner	T	54	1979
Western Horse	T	57	1950
Western Pony	T	45	early '50s
Western Prancing Horse	T	110	1961
Classic Molds			
Andalusian Foal	C	3060FO	1979
Andalusian Mare	C	3060MA	1979
Andalusian Stallion	C	3060ST	1979
Arabian Foal	C	3055FO	1973
Arabian Mare	C	3055MA	1973
Arabian Stallion	C	3055ST	1973
Black Beauty	C	3040BB	1980
Black Stallion	C	3030BS	1983
Bucking Bronco	C	190	1961
Charging Mesteno	C	4812ME	1995
Duchess	C	3040DU	1980
Fighting Mesteno	C	4811ME	1994
Ginger	C	3040GI	1980
Hobo	C	625	1975
Jet Run	C	3035JR	1980
Johar	C	3030JO	1983
Keen	C	3035KE	1980
Kelso	C	601	1975
Lipizzan Stallion	C	620	1975
Man O'War	C	602	1975
Merrylegs	C	3040ML	1980
Mesteno	C	480	1992
Mesteno's Mother	C	4810MO	1993
Mesteno the Foal	C	4810FO	1992
Might Tango	C	3035MT	1980
Mustang Foal	C	3065FO	1976
Mustang Mare	C	3065MA	1976
Mustang Stallion	C	3065ST	1976
Polo Pony	C	626	1976
Quarter Horse Foal	C	3045FO	1974
Quarter Horse Mare	C	3045MA	1974
Quarter Horse Stallion	C	3045ST	1974

Mold Name	Scale/ Series	Mold Number	Year Introduced
Rearing Stallion	C	180	1965
Reflections Mesteno	C	481	1996
Rojo	C	4812RO	1995
Ruffian	C	606	1977
Sagr	C	3030SA	1983
Silky Sullivan	C	603	1975
Sombra	C	4811SO	1994
Swaps	C	604	1975
Terrang	C	605	1975

Little Bits Molds

Mold Name	Scale/ Series	Mold Number	Year Introduced
American Saddlebred	L	9030	1985
Arabian Stallion	L	1001	1984
Clydesdale	L	1025	1984
Morgan Stallion	L	1005	1984
Quarter Horse Stallion	L	1015	1984
Thoroughbred Stallion	L	1010	1984
Unicorn	L	1020	1984

Stablemate Molds

Mold Name	Scale/ Series	Mold Number	Year Introduced
Arabian Mare	S	5011	1975
Arabian Stallion	S	5010	1975
Citation	S	5020	1975
Draft Horse	S	5055	1976
Lying Foal	S	5700LF	1975
Morgan Mare	S	5038	1976
Morgan Stallion	S	5035	1975
Native Dancer	S	5023	1976
Quarter Horse Mare	S	5048	1976
Quarter Horse Stallion	S	5045	1976
Riding Stable Set	S	n/a	1986
Saddlebred	S	5001	1975
Saddlebred Mare	S	TBA	TBA
Seabiscuit	S	5024	1976
Silky Sullivan	S	5022	1976
Standing Foal	S	5700SF	1975
Swaps	S	5021	1976

Mold Name	Scale/ Series	Mold Number	Year Introduced
Thoroughbred Mare	S	5026	1975

Other Animal Molds

Mold Name	Scale/ Series	Mold Number	Year Introduced
Basset Hound	O	325	1966
Bear	O	306	1967
Bear Cub	O	308	1967
Benji	O	3090B	1977
Bighorn Ram	O	78	1969
Black Angus Bull	O	365	1978
Boxer	O	66	1958
Buffalo	O	76	1965
Calf	O	347	1972
Charolais Bull	O	360	1975
Cow	O	341	1972
Deer Buck	O	301	1974
Deer Doe	O	302	1974
Deer Fawn	O	303	1974
Elephant	O	91	1958
Elk	O	77	1968
Jasper the Market Hog	O	355	1974
Kitten	O	335	1966
Lassie	O	65	1958
Modernistic Buck	O	101	1961
Modernistic Doe	O	102	1961
Moose	O	79	1966
Mountain Goat	O	312	1973
Polled Hereford Bull	O	74	1968
Poodle	O	67	1958
Pronghorn Antelope	O	310	1971
Rin Tin Tin	O	64	1958
Spanish Fighting Bull	O	73	1970
St. Bernard	O	328	1972
Texas Longhorn Bull	O	75	1961
Tiffany	O	3090T	1977
Walking Black Angus Bull	O	72	1960
Walking Hereford Bull	O	71	1958

This is a numerical list of the molds. A few numbers are repeated (from early in Breyer history for Other Animals and Traditional Scale horses).

Mold Number	Scale/ Series	Mold Name	Year Introduced
P40	T	Fury Prancer	1954
7	T	Family Arabian Stallion	1959
8	T	Family Arabian Mare	1961
9	T	Family Arabian Foal	1961
16	T	Sea Star	1980
18	T	Stock Horse Foal (Rough Coat)	1978
19	T	Stormy	1977
20	T	Misty	1972
25	T	Shetland Pony	1960
31	T	Fighting Stallion	1961
36	T	Race Horse	1954
40	T	Lady Phase	1976
45	T	Western Pony	early '50s
46	T	Pacer	1967
47	T	Man O'War	1969
49	T	Morgan	1965
50	T	Adios	1969
52	T	Five Gaiter	1962
54	T	Trakehner	1979
57	T	Western Horse	1950
58	T	Hanoverian	1980
59	T	Morganglanz	1980
60	T	Midnight Sun, Tennessee Walker	1972
61	T	El Pastor	1974
62	T	Saddlebred Weanling	1973
63	T	Halla	1977
64	T	Foundation Stallion	1977
64	O	Rin Tin Tin	1958
65	T	Justin Morgan	1973
65	O	Lassie	1958
66	T	Stud Spider	1978
66	O	Boxer	1958
67	T	San Domingo	1978
67	O	Poodle	1958
68	T	Legionario	1979
69	T	Smoky	1981
71	O	Walking Hereford Bull	1958
72	O	Walking Black Angus Bull	1960
73	O	Spanish Fighting Bull	1970
74	O	Polled Hereford Bull	1968
75	O	Texas Longhorn Bull	1961
76	O	Buffalo	1965
77	O	Elk	1968
78	O	Bighorn Ram	1969
79	O	Moose	1966
80	T	Clydesdale Stallion	1958
81	T	Donkey	1957/1958
83	T	Clydesdale Mare	1969
84	T	Clydesdale Foal	1969
87	T	Mustang	1961
89	T	Black Beauty	1979
90	T	Phar Lap	1985
91	O	Elephant	1958
92	T	Belgian	1964
95	T	Shire	1972
98	T	Quarter Horse Gelding	1959
99	T	Appaloosa Performance Horse	1974
100	T	Galiceno	1978
101	T	Quarter Horse Yearling	1970
101	O	Modernistic Buck	1961
102	O	Modernistic Doe	1961
104	T	Cantering Welsh Pony	1971
110	T	Western Prancing Horse	1961
120	T	Running Mare	1961

Mold Number	Scale/ Series	Mold Name	Year Introduced
130	T	Running Foal	1963
141	T	Grazing Mare	1961
151	T	Grazing Foal	1964
155	T	Pony of the Americas	1976
156	T	Haflinger	1979
169	T	Scratching Foal	1970
175	T	Indian Pony	1970
180	C	Rearing Stallion	1965
190	C	Bucking Bronco	1961
200	T	Old Timer	1966
207	T	Balking Mule	1968
210	T	Running Stallion	1968
212	T	Proud Arabian Stallion	1971
215	T	Proud Arabian Mare	1956/1971
218	T	Proud Arabian Foal	1956
226	T	Stock Horse Stallion	1981
227	T	Stock Horse Mare	1982
228	T	Stock Horse Foal	1983
236	T	Action Stock Horse Foal	1984
245	T	Lying Down Foal	1969
300	T	Jumping Horse	1965
301	O	Deer Buck	1974
302	O	Deer Doe	1974
303	O	Deer Fawn	1974
306	O	Bear	1967
308	O	Bear Cub	1967
310	O	Pronghorn Antelope	1971
312	O	Mountain Goat	1973
325	O	Basset Hound	1966
328	O	St. Bernard	1972
335	O	Kitten	1966
341	O	Cow	1972
347	O	Calf	1972
355	O	Jasper the Market Hog	1974
360	O	Charolais Bull	1975
365	O	Black Angus Bull	1978
375	T	Brighty	1974
401	T	Black Stallion	1981
410	T	Sham	1984
415	T	Buckshot	1985
420	T	Touch of Class	1986
425	T	Lady Roxana	1986
430	T	Sherman Morgan	1987
435	T	Secretariat	1987
445	T	John Henry	1988
450	T	Rugged Lark	1989
455	T	Roy the Belgian	1989
460	T	Khemosabi	1990
465	T	Roemer	1990
470	T	Misty's Twilight	1991
475	T	Pluto	1991
480	C	Mesteno	1992
481	C	Reflections Mesteno	1996
482	T	Henry, Norwegian Fjord	1996
483	T	Big Ben	1996
484	T	Brown Sunshine	1996
485	T	Friesian	1992
486	T	Iron Metal Chief, Missouri Fox Trotter	1997
487	T	Marabella, Morgan Broodmare	1997
488	T	Amber	1997
489	T	Ashley	1997
494	T	Llanarth True Briton	1994
495	T	Gem Twist	1993
496	T	Aristocrat	1995
497	T	Ideal American Quarter Horse	1995
601	C	Kelso	1975
602	C	Man O'War	1975
603	C	Silky Sullivan	1975
604	C	Swaps	1975

Mold Number	Scale/ Series	Mold Name	Year Introduced
605	C	Terrang	1975
606	C	Ruffian	1977
620	C	Lipizzan Stallion	1975
625	C	Hobo	1975
626	C	Polo Pony	1976
1001	L	Arabian Stallion	1984
1005	L	Morgan Stallion	1984
1010	L	Thoroughbred Stallion	1984
1015	L	Quarter Horse Stallion	1984
1020	L	Unicorn	1984
1025	L	Clydesdale	1984
3030BS	C	Black Stallion	1983
3030JO	C	Johar	1983
3030SA	C	Sagr	1983
3035JR	C	Jet Run	1980
3035KE	C	Keen	1980
3035MT	C	Might Tango	1980
3040BB	C	Black Beauty	1980
3040DU	C	Duchess	1980
3040GI	C	Ginger	1980
3040ML	C	Merrylegs	1980
3045FO	C	Quarter Horse Foal	1974
3045MA	C	Quarter Horse Mare	1974
3045ST	C	Quarter Horse Stallion	1974
3055FO	C	Arabian Foal	1973
3055MA	C	Arabian Mare	1973
3055ST	C	Arabian Stallion	1973
3060FO	C	Andalusian Foal	1979
3060MA	C	Andalusian Mare	1979
3060ST	C	Andalusian Stallion	1979
3065FO	C	Mustang Foal	1976
3065MA	C	Mustang Mare	1976
3065ST	C	Mustang Stallion	1976
3090B	O	Benji	1977
3090T	O	Tiffany	1977
3155FO	O	Nursing Foal	1973
3155MA	T	Thoroughbred Mare	1973
4810MO	C	Mesteno's Mother	1993
4810FO	C	Mesteno the Foal	1992
4811ME	C	Fighting Mesteno	1994
4811SO	C	Sombra	1994
4812ME	C	Charging Mesteno	1995
4812RO	C	Rojo	1995
5001	S	Saddlebred	1975
5010	S	Arabian Stallion	1975
5011	S	Arabian Mare	1975
5020	S	Citation	1975
5021	S	Swaps	1976
5022	S	Silky Sullivan	1976
5023	S	Native Dancer	1976
5024	S	Seabiscuit	1976
5026	S	Thoroughbred Mare	1975
5035	S	Morgan Stallion	1975
5038	S	Morgan Mare	1976
5045	S	Quarter Horse Stallion	1976
5048	S	Quarter Horse Mare	1976
5055	S	Draft Horse	1976
5700LF	S	Lying Foal	1975
5700SF	S	Standing Foal	1975
9030	L	American Saddlebred	1985
9960	T	Kipper	1986
79192	T	Porcelain Icelandic Horse	1992
79193	T	Porcelain Shire	1993
79194	T	Porcelain Spanish Barb	1994
79195	T	Porcelain Arabian Mare in Costume	1995
79196	T	Porcelain Saddlebred in Parade Tack	1996
79197	T	Porcelain Great Horse in Armor	1997
79296	T	Porcelain Circus Ponies	1996

✎ Appendix B — Suggested Reading ✎

This section gives you several sources for more information on model horses as well as real horses. The contact information is current as of January 1997. None of the lists here are all-encompassing, so keep your eyes open for new and different materials.

Newsletters and Magazines

Many of these newsletters are very well done. They contain a variety of articles on collectible model horses, techniques for showing, remaking, photography, and more. Also, they have advertising (some are mostly ads) for models, special runs, shows, and other events. Always send a business sized self-addressed stamped envelope (SASE) when requesting more information.

Just About Horses is Breyer's magazine, and often gives good, detailed information about old models, upcoming models, how the models are made and remade, and future events. New subscriptions: $12 per year (6 issues). c/o Reeves International, 14 Industrial Road, Pequannock, NJ 07440

The Hobby Horse News, $20 ($30 first class) per year; sample issue $3.50 ($5.00 first class). Paula Hecker, Editor, 2053 Dyrehaven Drive, Tallahassee, FL 32311

TRR Pony Express. Paula Beard, 71 Aloha Circle, North Little Rock, AR 72120-1670

The Model Horse Trader, $24 per year, make checks payable to "Horse-Power Graphics." 143 Mercer Way, Upland, CA 91786

Model Horse Trading Post. Lynn Luther, 314 N. Redbud Trail, Buchanan, MI 49107

Patroonews. P.M.H.O.A, Linda Sturhann, RR 1 Box B7, Mount Upton, NY 13809

Horsing Around. $36 per year (Air Mail), make checks payable to "Miss V Fairs" in US funds or in sterling. Miss V. Fairs, P.O. Box 61, Evesham, Worcestershire WR11 5WY England

Catalogs

You might find the following commercial catalogs helpful for both finding books on horses and tack, and for illustrations (for examples of tack and harness fit, etc.) to help you show your models more successfully.

Breakthrough Publications, Books on Horses, phone 1-800-824-5000 (books and videos)

The Book Stable, phone 1-800-274-2665 (horse books, magazines, and videos)

State Line Tack, Inc., Route 121, P.O. Box 1217, Plaistow, NH 03865-1217, phone 1-800-228-9208 (tack and equipment, videos, books, Breyer models, etc.)

World Champion Horse Equipment, phone 1-800-251-3490 (tack and equipment, models)

Insurance Guides

Values from insurance guides should not be used to price models for sale (the prices are high to account for replacement costs in the event of an insured loss). Look for ads in the model horse magazines for ordering information. These guides contain lists of models and their insurance values. In general, insurance companies seem to require photographic evidence of the contents of your collection, and at least three estimates on the values of the models.

Model Trading Post Insurance Guide, current edition. Lynn Luther (see above address for Model Horse Trading Post)

Breyer Model Insurance Guide, current edition. Paula DeFeyter.

Market Price Guides

The following books give estimated market values for the models. These values may differ from those provided in this book.

The Breyer Model Quick Reference, by Felicia Browell; for order form, write to Other Stuff, 123 Hooks Lane, Canonsburg, PA 15317-1835

Breyer Model Collector's Value Guide, Kimberly Gackowski; for more information, write the author at 23046 Bagpipe Ct., Hawthorn Woods, IL 60047

✐ Glossary ✐

The following terms and abbreviations are found in this book and in many articles and sales lists in the various model horse magazines listed in Appendix B.

alab — alabaster
app — appaloosa
appy — appaloosa
ASHF — Action Stock Horse Foal
ASB — American Saddlebred
bald — white faced (no paint)
blk — black
BO — best offer
brn — brown
buck — buckskin
CA — Classic Arabian
CAF/CAM/CAS — Classic Arabian Foal/Mare/ Stallion
catalog run — same as regular run
CE — Commemorative Edition (produced for one year only)
chalky — models with chalky plastic or white base coat
chest — chestnut
CL/Clas — Classic series
CLArab — Classic Arabian
CM — Customized Model (same as RRH)
CWP — Cantering Welsh Pony
dap — dapple gray, or dappled
disc — discontinued
ex/exc — excellent condition
FAF/FAM/FAS — Family Arabian Foal/Mare/Stallion
fin — finish (matte, glossy, etc.)
FL — flocked finish
fr — fair condition

gd — good condition
glossy — high gloss finish
haired — models with faux hair or string manes and tails
JAH — Just About Horses
LB — Little Bits Series
LE — Limited Edition (limited quantity made)
LP — Lady Phase
LSASE — large, self-addressed stamped envelope (business size)
LSQ — Live Show Quality
MIB — Mint in Box
model — the animal made from a certain mold
mold — the body of an animal (from which models are made)
NIB — New in Box
OBO — Or Best Offer
OS — original sculpture
overdappling — a method of dappling/roaning using layers of spattered paint until model is covered
PAF/PAM/PAS — Proud Arabian Foal/Mare/Stallion
pal — palomino
pearly — a pearlescent finish on a model
POA — Pony of the Americas
points — the mane, tail, and lower legs on a horse; sometimes also the muzzle and edge of the ears.
PPD — Postage Paid
PSQ — Photo Show Quality

QH — Quarter Horse
regular run — model listed in annual dealer/consumer catalogs
Rep — repainted model
resist dappling — a dappling method using a resistant substance to leave lighter or white spots
RR — repainted and remade model (same as CM)
RRH — repainted, remade, and haired model (same as CM with hairing)
S/H — Shipping and Handling
SASE — self-addressed stamped envelope (generally means business size)
SBW — Saddlebred Weanling
SHF/SHM/SHS — Stock Horse Foal/Mare/Stallion
SM — Stablemat
socks — white legs to mid-canon bone
special run — model produced for specific dealers/events/sources; not listed in annual catalogs
SR — Special Run
SSHF — Standing Stock Horse Foal
stockings — white legs up to knee
TB — Thoroughbred
Test/TC — Test color model
Trad — Traditional Series
TWH — Tennessee Walking Horse
VG — very good condition
Woodie — Woodgrain model

✐ Bibliography ✐

This book is a revised edition of *The Breyer Animal Identification Guide* (ISBN 0-9647865-3-2), 1995, by Felicia Browell. The following sources were used to collect or verify data for the first edition, and/or this new guide.

The Breyer Model Hunter's Price Guide, Second Edition, by Felicia Browell.

Just About Horses: All available issues from 1979 to present.

Breyer Dealer Catalogs: All those available from 1956 to present.

Breyer Consumer Catalogs: All those available from 1970 to present.

Sears, JC Penney, Your Horse Source, Montgomery Wards, and Spiegel catalog pages: All those available from 1982 to present.

Model Trading Post Insurance Guide, 1994 Edition. Lynn Luther.

Know Your Breyers, 1994 edition. Judith Miller.

Breyer Molds and Models, Third Edition. Nancy Atkinson Young. 1993.

≋ Index ≋

Action Stock Horse Foal . . .11, 12, 59, 65, 73, 86, 88, 89, 146
Adios 6, 12, 13, 36, 70, 79, 84
Ageless Bronze (color) 7, 19
Amber .14, 15, 122
Andalusian
  Foal 50, 98, 99, 101, 103, 105
  Mare 98, 99
  Stallion 98, 99, 103
Appaloosa Performance Horse . . .14, 77, 90
Arabian
  Foal
    Classic 81, 99, 173
    Family 27, 28, 141
    Proud 12, 59, 64–66, 73
  Mare
    Classic 89, 100
    Family 27–29, 143
    Proud 7, 22, 31, 65–68, 78, 84, 143
    Stablemate 118, 122
  Stallion
    Classic 100, 109
    Family 30
    Little Bits 114, 115
    Proud 31, 66–68, 145
    Stablemate 119, 122
Aristocrat, Champion Hackney 15
Ashley 15
Basset Hound .128
Bear
  Cub 136
  Sow 136
Belgian 16, 17, 71, 83, 84, 141
Benji 130
Bighorn Ram .138
Black Beauty
  Classic .98, 101
  Traditional 18, 19, 73, 76
Black Stallion
  Classic 102, 105, 112
  Traditional 7, 19
Bows, ribbons, and braids 8
Boxer 129
Brahma Bull 132
Braids, ribbons, and bows 8
Brands or symbols 8
Breyer Animal Creations . .5, 8, 11, 20, 71, 139
Brighty 20
Broken models
  effect on value 9
Bronze 7
Brown Sunshine 20
Bucking Bronco 20, 98, 102, 103
Buckshot 20
Buffalo 7, 135, 142
Bull
  Black Angus 133
  Brahma 132
  Charolais 133
  Hereford 133, 134
  Spanish Fighting 134
  Texas Longhorn 128, 134, 135
Calf 131
Cantering Welsh Pony . .21, 40, 64, 66, 78, 107
Catalogs 6
Chalkies 8

Challengers — see Mesteno and Sombra
Charolais Bull .133
Citation .106, 120
Clocks 73, 139
Clydesdale
  Foal 23, 24
  Little Bits 115
  Mare 23, 24, 145
  Stallion (Traditional) 24, 115
Collie 130
Colors
  dappling 8
  decorator 7
  names of 6
  other 7
  roaning 8
  variations in 6
  woodgrain .7
Condition of models 9
Consumer catalogs 6
Copenhagen (color) 7
Cow 131
Dawning — see Mesteno the Foal,
  and Mesteno's Mother
Dealer catalogs 6, 23, 55, 87, 90, 107, 113
Decorator color descriptions 7
Deer
  Family 137
  Modernistic 137
Description conventions 10
Descriptions 11
Donkey 11, 26
Draft Horse 16, 120
Duchess 101, 103, 107, 108
El Pastor, Paso Fino 26
Elephant 7, 139
Elk 137
Eye whites 5, 7, 82, 128, 134
Family Arabian
  Foal .27, 28, 141
  Mare 27–29, 143
  Stallion 30, 31, 66, 68
Fighting Stallion 32, 33, 59, 141
Finish 8
Five Gaiter 34, 35, 53, 78
Flocked models 8
Florentine (color) . . .7, 15, 32, 34, 51, 54, 57, 72, 75
Foundation Stallion 13, 33, 35, 59, 79, 85
Fury Prancer 37, 140, 141, 143
Galiceno .38, 145
Gem Twist .39, 46
German Shepherd 130
Ginger 98, 99, 101, 103, 109
Gold Charm (color) 7, 32, 34, 52, 57, 72, 75, 80
Grazing
  Foal 39, 40, 52, 73, 80
  Mare 39, 40, 52, 59
Haflinger 22, 40, 64
Halla 6, 41, 56
Hanoverian 6, 41, 54, 56, 98, 103, 105, 145, 146
Height variations 6
Henry, Norwegian Fjord 42
Hobo 42, 62, 98, 104

Ideal American Quarter Horse 43
Indian Pony 19, 35, 43
Insuring models 172
Iron Metal Chief, Missouri Fox Trotter . . .45
Jasper 135
Jet Run 103–105, 108
Johar 99, 101, 102, 104, 105, 112
John Henry 45, 71, 72
Jolly Cholly (Basset Hound) 128
Jumping Horse 46, 47
Just About Horses 10, 19, 21, 23, 24, 33, 35, 36, 41, 44, 46, 49, 51, 52, 55, 66, 68, 70, 77, 78, 80, 82, 88, 90, 91, 93
Justin Morgan 19, 44, 47
Keen 98, 103, 105, 108
Kelso 80, 105, 108, 110, 112, 113
Khemosabi 48
Kipper 48
Kitten 130, 131
Lady
  Phase 48, 49, 56, 62, 69, 72, 85, 144
  Roxana 50, 98, 103
Lassie 130
Lamps 7, 65, 74, 129, 134, 135, 139
Legionario 50, 51, 146
Lipizzan Stallion 106
Little Bits Series 114
Live model showing 10
Llanarth True Briton 51
Lying Down Foal (Traditional) 52
Lying Foal (Stablemate) 119, 121, 124
Man O'War
  Classic 106, 107
  Traditional .52
Marabella, Morgan Broodmare 53
Market values for models 172
Markings
Merrylegs 22, 25, 101, 103, 107, 108
Mesteno
  -'s Mother .107
  and Sombra 107
  Charging .107
  Reflections 107, 108
  Rojo 107
  the Foal 107, 112, 113
  the Messenger 107
Midnight Sun, Tennessee Walker 53
Might Tango 104, 105, 107–109
Misty 7, 15, 53, 80, 84, 89, 107, 112, 113
Misty's Twilight 42, 54
Model
  dates on 9
  markings 7
Model colors 6
Model value
  breaks 9
  broken models 11
  common models 10
  identifying models 11
  in this guide 11
  model age .11
  rubs/scratches 9
  yellowing 9
Models
  definition 6
  finishes 8

insuring 172
listing by name 147
listing by number 155
live shows .10
numbered 9
photo shows 10
producing .5
regular run 6
scale 5
showing 10
signed 9
special runs 6
stickers 8
Modernistic Buck and Doe 137
Mold
definition .6
size variations 6
variations .6
Mold marks 9
Molds
numbers .169
numerical list 170
Moose 137
Morgan 55
Justin 19, 44, 47
Mare (Stablemate) 123
Sherman 5, 82
Stallion 115, 116, 122–124
Morgan Stallion 115
Morganglanz 42, 49, 55, 62
Mountain Goat 138
Mule
Balking 15
Brown Sunshine 20
Music boxes .139
Mustang
Foal 83, 99, 103–105, 108, 109, 112
Mare 108, 109
Stallion (Classic) 109
Traditional (Semi-rearing) 56
Names of models 147
Native Dancer 124
Night lights 17, 18, 65, 59, 137, 139
Numbered editions 9
Numerical list of models 155
Nursing Foal 12, 40, 59, 65, 73, 90
Old Timer 60
Pacer 61, 89
Pearlies 8
Performing Misty 53
Phantom Wings 65, 66
Phar Lap 49, 56, 62, 63, 89
Photo showing 10
Pig 135
Pluto the Lipizzaner 63
Polled Hereford Bull 133
Polo Pony 64, 98, 109
Pony of the Americas 22, 40, 64, 145
Poodle .129, 134

Porcelain
Arabian Mare in Costume 97
Circus Ponies in Costume 97
Icelandic Horse 96
Saddlebred in Parade Tack 97
Shire 96
Spanish Barb 96
Prancing Morgan — see Sherman Morgan
Progeny — see Mesteno, Charging, and Rojo
Pronghorn Antelope 138
Proud Arabian
Foal 12, 59, 64–66, 73
Mare 7, 22, 31, 65–68, 78, 84, 143
Stallion 31, 66–68, 145
Quarter Horse
Foal 12, 85, 106, 109, 110
Gelding 49, 69, 72, 143
Ideal American 43
Mare
Classic 110, 111
Stablemate 124
Stallion
Classic .110
Little Bits 116, 117
Stablemate 122, 125
Yearling 13, 52, 70, 84
Race Horse 52, 62, 63, 71, 80, 81, 89, 98
Reading the descriptions 11
Rearing Stallion 71, 98, 111, 141
Reflections — see Mesteno, Reflections
Regular runs
definition .6
Ribbons, braids, and bows 8
Riding Stable Set 118, 125
Rin Tin Tin .130
Roemer, Dutch Warmblood 71
Rojo 107
Roy, Belgian Drafter 71
Rubs and scratches 9
Ruffian 107, 111–113
Rugged Lark 45, 49, 69, 71, 72
Running
Foal .12, 49, 52, 59, 65, 72–76, 80, 141, 142
Mare 19, 73–76, 142
Stallion 6, 14, 76, 77, 90
Saddlebred
American (Little Bits) 114
Mare 118, 126
Stablemate 125
Weanling (Traditional) 77
Sagr .102, 112
San Domingo 9, 13, 36, 79, 146
Scale of models 5
Scratching Foal 80
Sea Star 80
Seabiscuit 126
Secretariat 80
Semi-rearing Mustang — see Mustang
Sham 81

Sherman Morgan 5, 82
Shetland Pony 82
Shire 83
Show Stance Morgan
see Morgan 55
Showing models 10
Signatures on models 9
Silky Sullivan
Classic 112, 113
Stablemate 126, 127
Silver Filigree (color) 7
Size variations 6
Smoky 84
Sombra 107
Spanish Fighting Bull 134
Special run models 10
Special runs
definition .6
listed by year 164
St. Bernard .130
Standing Foal (Stablemate) . . .119, 122, 125
Standing Stock Horse Foal 85
Stickers on models 8
Stock Horse
Foal
Action .11
Rough Coat 65, 66, 70, 84
Standing 85
Mare 85
Stallion 87
Stormy 89
Stretch Morgan (Morgan)
Stud Spider .90
Suckling Foal (Nursing Foal) 59
Swaps
Classic 113
Stablemate 127
Terrang 113
Texas Longhorn Bull 134
Thoroughbred
Mare
Stablemate 128
Traditional 90
Stallion .117
Tiffany 130
Touch of Class 91
Traditional Scale 11
Trakehner 91
Unicorn 52, 77, 84, 106, 114, 118
Using this guide 10
Variations .6, 7
Walking Bull 134
Wedgewood (color) 7
Western
Horse 92
Pony 93
Prancing Horse 94
Woodgrain (color) 7
Yellowing on models 9